Off Ramp

Off Ramp

Adventures

and Heartache

in the

American

Elsewhere

HANK STUEVER

HENRY HOLT AND COMPANY ▪ NEW YORK

Henry Holt and Company, LLC
Publishers since 1866
115 West 18th Street
New York, New York 10011

Henry Holt® is a registered trademark
of Henry Holt and Company, LLC.

Library of Congress Cataloging-in-Publication Data

Stuever, Hank.
    Off ramp : adventures and heartache in the American elsewhere /
Hank Stuever.—1st ed.
      p.   cm.
    ISBN 0-8050-7573-9
      1. United States—Description and travel.   2. United States—Social life
and customs—1971–   3. United States—Biography.   4. Stuever, Hank—Travel—
United States.   5. Journalists—United States—Biography.   I. Title.

E169.04S74   2004
973.92—dc22

                                                        2003067715

Henry Holt books are available for special promotions and
premiums. For details contact: Director, Special Markets.
First Edition 2004
Designed by Victoria Hartman

Printed in the United States of America
10 9 8 7 6 5 4 3 2 1

For
Laura Trujillo

Contents

Off Ramps

Could It Happen Here

Elsewhere, Next Exit
A Preface

Our country is sometimes a *kountry*, spelled with a k, built entirely upon particleboard. It has kastles, kampgrounds, komfort. I used to sit in my car in strip-mall parking lots, seeking some solitary komfort, thinking it all through. When the stories I was reporting and writing for one newspaper or another didn't seem to be going well (there were edits to my turns of phrase and tangential information deleted), I found some reasons to go on living by driving around the access roads, bypassing the turnpikes, and taking all the off ramps to a place I came to regard as the Elsewhere.

Gradually, the Elsewhere became my beat, my source, my writerly home: the big-box stores, the municipal arenas, the empty lots surrounded by fences. The optimistically named suburbs that were already fading, the drive-thrus, the multiplexes, the strip, the drag, the freeway spans under construction, the futon places, the yogurt places, the ten-minute lube places, the Slurpees, the billboards offering open-sided MRI scans. I took on that which was contained, as in the Container Store, and also that which was un-contained, which felt loose, wild, krazy.

I liked "plazas" that weren't actually plazas, and favored strip centers with words like "garden" and "glen" and "meadows" in their names, especially when nothing about them featured anything natural, conventionally pretty, or nationally blessed. I found strange relief in extended-stay corporate suite motels filled with temporary, transient souls; I liked the people who travel by RV from one outlet mall to the next, searching for special bargains; I liked self-storage facilities that held the secret, unwanted narrative of divorces, business failures, or broken Ping-Pong tables.

I also happened and still happen to love almost-dead shopping malls. Shepherd Mall, in Oklahoma City, where I worked as a teenager at a greeting card store in the 1980s, was built in the late 1950s. It was the kind of place where high school students, in search of cosmopolitan élan, held their proms. Its ceilings were high, and acres of faux mosaic tile shimmered on the walkways. Deep within the mall was an ice cream place with a French café theme. When I was very little, and my grandmother would take me there, I thought this actually was France.

But as the century neared an end, the place became more desolate. Only a Furr's Cafeteria—frequented mainly on Sunday afternoons by cheerful ladies from African-American churches wearing their biggest hats—kept its vitality. Perhaps I was alone in seeing this regress as progress, although I also felt melancholy when the department stores were shuttered, followed by the smaller shops, one by one. (You know it's bad, in Elsewhere, when even the Radio Shack loses faith, and departs.) The lonesome quality of vacant spaces—I like to think they whisper, lovingly, about our itinerant lives as consumers.

Shepherd Mall would be completely gone now, I am sure, if not for the American terrorist Timothy McVeigh. After his bombing of the Alfred P. Murrah Federal Building in downtown Oklahoma City in 1995, the federal government needed a large place to put Social Security, other branch offices, a federal-employee credit union, and, should anyone have the heart for it, a day-care center. Here was an afterlife for my favorite forgotten mall, a couple miles northwest of where the bomb killed all those people. (A few months after the Murrah bombing, my grandmother died after a long stay in a nursing home. My grandfather had to close the file on her benefits by riding an escalator in what used to be a department store to get to the makeshift Social Security office.) The government has since moved on to a new federal building, and most of the mall is now leased out as drab cubicle farms—customer-service call centers, telemarketing firms, or regional divisions for the official association of something, nothing, nowhere, Elsewhere.

This is the kind of world where I look for ideas, for joy and loss and the marginal things, the funny quirks of what is bland and true. This is the America I grew up in, and the one I try to write about. The movie theater where I saw *Star Wars* as a boy, the NorthPark Cinema 4, survives as a dollar theater, in a shopping mall that at one time housed the only Chanel store in Oklahoma. The dollar theater is there with a few other remaining tenants. The tile fountains have no water in them. There is an absence here that isn't exactly quantifiable, or considerable to people who don't feel it. It's one thing to talk about the death of the mid-century American drive-in movie theater—people understand that as a clearly defined loss of something iconic, the kind of thing you would preserve and pay homage to in a museum about postwar lifestyles. It's another thing to try to tell a story of the former glory of a '70s fourplex, for which there is less sentimentality or understanding.

But the great American noplace makes the most sense to me as a journalist preoccupied with how life feels, and what it's been like to live in millennial times. Elsewhere offers what I consider to be true mystery and has taken me to places and events where I could draw connections, and arrive at certain meanings among the discarded fads and treasures: Guitars that were bought but never played, or warpy cassette-tape collections left out with the trash. Defunct swimming pools filled with leaves. The Sirloin Stockade that became a tattoo parlor that became a mattress discounter. If I was looking, I could find the Lord, death, porn, destruction, tanning booths, and teriyaki chicken bowls. It was enough to write about.

■ ■ ■

My first job was on the city desk at the evening newspaper in Albuquerque, New Mexico, in 1990, when that newspaper had, at best, a circulation of 40,000 and falling fast, compared to the morning newspaper's circulation of 100,000.

I was twenty-two years old, and had been hired as a "general assignment" reporter, who would, in theory, be on hand to cover whatever story wasn't being covered by any of the dozen or so other full-time news reporters, most of whom had been assigned beats: There was the crime reporter, the schools reporter, the social issues/medical reporter, the "drunk Indians" reporter, the science reporter, the environment reporter, two state politics reporters, two city hall reporters, the city columnist, and one reporter with two central obsessions: the iffy finances of the public utilities company, and her unrelated hunch that the U.S. government had experimentally injected unwitting Americans with plutonium in the 1940s, which, it turned out, was true. My job was to write about everything and anything else, which could and would include news of murders and fires (usually occurring in strip malls), or university regent meetings, or various protests, or events like the hot-and-spicy chile festival at the convention center.

"This is going to be a hard job," the editor of the *Albuquerque Tribune*, Tim Gallagher, assured me: "You're going to be writing one story and have to stop and write another on deadline. Then you'll have to write a third. When you're almost done with the third, you'll remember that you forgot about the first." He compared it to housework: You'll be doing a sink of dishes when somebody tells you to stop and vacuum. You'll be vacuuming when suddenly there's a story requiring an instant round of furniture dusting. You'll be dusting when you realize you never finished the dishes.

It was Tim Gallagher who also told me that any day in which you hear a song on the radio by the Rolling Stones is going to be a good day.

■   ■   ■

Journalism is one of those gigs where everyone professes to know how to do it better than everyone else, and yet so many of us wind up feeling as if we're doing it wrong. Editors instruct their writers on a litany of personal dictums, rules of thumb, and other absolutes. Not all of these hold up, and so I can tell you, after some years of experience, that in fact any day you hear a song by the Cars on the radio is going to be a good day. And here is another rule: You have to hear the Cars on the radio *while driving in your car*. (And a corollary, also from evidence: Any day you hear *two* songs by the Cars, in a row, in your car, means you have a very good chance of getting laid. This bodes well for Twofer Tuesdays.) Newspapers have all kinds of stylebooks, word taboos, forbidden verb tenses, formats, traditions. Many of them can be broken, from time to time, by the right writer, at the right paper, for the right story, under the right editor.

The most helpful tip I ever heard from another journalist—the only surefire method I really still follow—came from a columnist in Detroit named Susan Ager: Always ask, at some point, to use the bathroom when you're interviewing somebody. Ask this in their home, especially, but also in their office or workplace, whether you need to use the bathroom or not. If you're in the subject's home, it's just another way further in—down the hall, on your right, past all these fascinating pictures of the children when they were in high school, including the one your subject didn't yet mention, the child who drowned in 1973. The little pearly soaps in the dish by the sink, the potpourri Glade, the old issue of *Cosmopolitan* opened to the horoscope. I can't tell you why—or if—these things belong in your notebook, but more than once, while writing a story, I have been relieved to see them in mine.

■ ■ ■

Going over the pieces considered for the chapters of this book, I am for some reason drawn to an afternoon in July 1994, when I was writing a story about what kind of people camp (and in lesser circumstances, live) at the Kampgrounds of America franchise, or KOA, off Interstate 40 and Tramway Boulevard at the foothills of Albuquerque's mountains. This kampground is not far from the leftovers of Route 66, and just downhill from the hidden nuke silos above a national science laboratory. The area around the KOA had seen, in Action 7 News parlance, *a recent upsurge in crime*. So I camped there for a few days.

Or, rather, I *kamped*.

Among the RV grannies and itinerant motorcyclists staying at the KOA were a group of European college students traveling slowly toward Los Angeles. At the small, overchlorinated KOA swimming pool, one of them walked over to the newspaper photographer and me and said, in a Euro-accent:

"We are from the Netherlands, and we are for two days wonderink who it is you are, and why you are all the time with cameras and writing down things?"

I have not since heard a more lovely or correct string of words that could so perfectly capture what I believed I was trying to do in newsprint, writing stories that contained almost no important news, no investigative scoops, no Pulitzer-worthy moments of triumph or inspiration, and would be on the recycling stack with the trash in a matter of hours.

Who it is you are.

All the time with cameras and writing down things.

We are wonderink.

As exact and accurate as I tried to get the facts and quotes about the proposed fiscal budget numbers, to get correct titles of spokespersons, to have the right spelling of names and exact ages of the dead little girls—sisters—pulled from the crumpled automobile on Christmas Eve, I was always going over one distinct boundary in newspapers, and it has to do with the first part of the question, *Who It Is You Are*:

I was the narrator.

I was the one calling the shots, the reporter who'd long stopped trying to solve the maddening riddles of "objectivity" and just tell a story about what happened. The context was me, mine. I chose the quotes, made notes in the margins, decided whether it goes from the events at the hospital to the living room, or straight to the funeral home and skip all the rest. I was a voice that crept into the paragraphs; sometimes I was even more directly in there, as the dreaded vertical pronoun: *I*.

I intruded on the writing, but I intruded on the reporting, too. I asked dumb questions, often twice. I tripped on people's stairs. I got lost a lot. I was too tall or too big to be invisible, and I was not terribly cool. I didn't help rock bands lift equipment into their Econoline vans once the show was over. I didn't dance at wedding receptions, or dance at the reunion party of the elderly alumni of the high school that no longer existed, or dance at Lollapalooza. I watched hungrily, pathetically.

■ ■ ■

I am unassigned, mostly. I was a child born and raised and now living in a permanent Elsewhere, and because I didn't have a beat, I gave myself one. It started out as a private list I taped next to my computer, in my newsroom cubicle, for several years: I put "false cities" on my beat, which meant airports, the Best Buy, bland buildings. I put "things kept in shoeboxes in spare closets" on my beat. I claimed "teenagers who don't help out the community" for my own. Also:

People Who Are Loathed.

Spare Freezers Kept in the Garage.

People Who Move Heavy Things; Rock Bands Who Have Not Yet Figured Out That They're Not Going to Be Famous; Stories Where People Voluntarily Get Out Their Old Yearbooks. Also I wanted exclusive rights to stories about embalming, algebra, bedrooms, breakfast cereal, and pieces of furniture that cost under $500. This was just part of my template for ideas.

I left Albuquerque after almost six years writing for the *Tribune*. By then the daily circulation of the newspaper had fallen another 13,000 copies, on average. Tim Gallagher had left for another newspaper, and was now listening to Rolling Stones songs in Southern California. I went to Texas with my car radio set to "seek/scan," and a broken air conditioner, still thrillingly lost. Now I live in Washington, D.C., and I usually have to get on a plane, or drive aimlessly for

an hour or two up or down Route 1, in order to find and write about
the Elsewhere, since the inner city and Capitol Hill are both entirely too newsy, too somewhere, too surreally real, for me to accu-
rately and efficiently describe. I do better lurking on the edges of
the Miss America pageant, or the Olympics, or the California recall
vote for governor—events that transpire under some glitter and narrative urgency and yet, two steps back, occur just off freeways, inside prefab hotels, in front of false backdrops, attended to by
souvenir sales booths. I find America loosely united around all this:
the exurbs, the bridal fairs, the monster truck rallies, the
megachurches, the water parks, the turnpike rest areas. I drive
rental Dodge Neons and check into various Hampton Inns. (Or the
ExecuStay, or the La Quinta, which one of my colleagues jokes is
Spanish for "across from Applebee's.") A good day of reporting begins with the stupid, stale bagel at the complimentary continental
breakfast in the lobby. This is where, one February morning, I heard
the FEMA guys talking quietly to one another, enumerating the
body parts recovered thus far from the space shuttle debris in the
woods near Hemphill, Texas.

   One afternoon in 2002, in Indianapolis, I was working on a story
for the *Washington Post* about several hundred men (and a few
women) who all like to dress, in their spare time, as Imperial
stormtroopers from *Star Wars*. They were in town for a sci-fi convention. A few minutes after I met up with them and began taking
notes, they were marching in formation in their identical, white
plastic armor through one of the city's biggest shopping malls. I
sensed a kind of postmodern, ritualistic American folk dance here:
Darth Vader goes to the mall. (The only thing that ruins it, a participant confessed, is when two Darth Vaders show up to the same
event, somehow negating the evil.) After that, the stormtroopers
piled into passenger vans and went to a hospital for terminally ill
children. The cancer kids, even the smallest ones, were thrilled to
see masked, armed men from outer space.

   To most readers, I suppose, this story seems like nothing more
than a wacky newspaper feature, dressed up with a measure of

cheeky flair by the funny homosexual guy in the Style section. But these stories and moments were always something more for me, something a shade darker and more intimate.

This particular story assignment, I felt, was really about the storm trooper club president, whose name is Albin Johnson. Here was a man who had lost his leg in a car accident in the mid-nineties, and found that dressing up as a storm trooper and hanging out at his local multiplex had given him a reason to get out of the house, to get on with his life. The vaccu-form polyresin storm-trooper suit cost him $3,000, and, in addition to looking exactly like the costume seen in the movies, it hid Albin's prosthetic leg. He got the idea to seek out people like himself and start a club, "the Fighting 501st," each member of which had also bought his or her own suit of stormtrooper armor. (Because one stormtrooper marching alone past a Limited Express store in a midwestern shopping mall doesn't feel quite right. You need dozens, hundreds even, for the right vibe.)

Albin and I are the same age. He grew up in the Ozark mountains in a family of fundamentalist Christians, a far more rural and strict existence than my boyhood of felt appliqué, folksy Catholicism, and *The Bionic Woman* on Wednesday nights. But he went to see *Star Wars* the same summer I did—the same summer we all did—on a rare trip to the city, in a fourplex that no longer exists. His family had gone to see *The Late Great Planet Earth* and wound up in *Star Wars* instead. We'd both understood the components here of loss and pleasure and accidental living, stopping to make inane connections between the two.

He became part of my episodic outer-space saga, my adventures and heartache in the American Elsewhere, hanging around in a mall and watching a bunch of guys emulate a fascistic fiction as a national pastime, exulting in low culture. Later that weekend, 'a costumed stormtrooper from Phoenix proposed to his girlfriend (she was an Imperial officer in an olive green uniform) on the steps of the massively banal Indianapolis convention center, in front of all the other storm troopers, several Boba Fetts, and a few hundred onlookers. There were two Darth Vaders (one short, one tall), who clasped their gloved fists in sinister joy. This was a moment at once touching and absurd, and it was just one of the reasons why I am *all the time with writing down things,* looking for a glimmer of *who it is you are.*

(2004)

Traded
Spaces

The Couch That Warped Space-Time

Washington, D.C.

First the love story, a love-in-Washington story, a love-in-Washington story that is also about space and matter and furniture. For a while they loved each other, then didn't, then did, and still do. Sometime after the period when they first fell for each other, she would drag him into those "commitment" discussions. There was the background music and the way that Sunday afternoons can collapse on themselves. There was a period of puppy shopping, and there were the hockey games and the long, sometimes weird phone calls, all of it, all of it.

Into this came two sleeper sofas:

1. The Jennifer Convertible.
2. The Hecht's Department Store Special.

But right now let us turn our attention to the size of the universe. Theoretical physicists would like very much for the cosmos to fit nicely into the mathematical space they've calculated for it, only, of course, it doesn't. There is an indescribable longing to know what we're dealing with here, and in how many dimensions—a tidy "final theory" explaining both the subatomic and the celestial. You could go mad trying. Einstein died without resolving the scale issue, and so the universe goes on not quite fitting. Some physicists have deemed it larger than previously thought; others see it as smaller. One day it is older than they ever estimated; the next day, younger.

This does not mean that occasionally someone won't come along with another TOE, which stands for "theory of everything"—a superstring theory, for example—to explain away the heavens above and the atoms within. Everyone grabs a corner of the universe and lifts. Papers are presented at Los Alamos.

▪ ▪ ▪

By now you may have figured out the problem. Neither sofa—the Jennifer Convertible nor the Hecht's Special—will fit up the stairs of the couple's three-story row house in Mount Pleasant in Northwest Washington, which was built about 120 years ago, shortly after the supposed Big Bang, when things were small.

"Of course, we've tried," says Sanford "Sandy" Ring, thirty-eight, husband of Jamie, thirty-three, when asked if he's tried—*oh, the ways he has tried*—to get either of the couches up the stairs. He's a lawyer who works in international trade, and he will be the first to tell you how much he doesn't know about furniture, or physics, or the exact science of heavy lifting. Jamie will tell you of Sandy's misadventure the other day during the simple act of hanging a mirror. He has his side of the story about this, but both versions end up the same, with four significant holes in the wall. Oh, how she laughs at him. Oh, how he laughs at himself, laughs and laughs. Sigh. But the sofas: That would be funny, too, if it were funny anymore. For five years it has bugged them, like a low hum off in the distance. The sofas are not where they belong. What is chaos, after all, if not the sum total of a trillion slight disorders, of things not having happened as much as those that are happening? Is the most complicated concept in fact terribly simple? Is there a man who can make a couch fit up the stairs? (Yes. And we shall know him by his DeWalt power tools.) Is there a secret to everything? (Absolutely. But you have to take it on faith, and just start believing in all those equations scrawled across all those chalk-boards.) Stars colliding. Sofas in wide orbits.

■   ■   ■

Our first exhibit, *the Jennifer Convertible*. She remembers that they were dating when she helped him pick it out for his apartment, but she thinks they had broken up by the time it was delivered. In any case, she is sure they were together again by the time the dog had messed it up, because by then they were married. He now looks at this sofa and remembers feeling a little taken in, not only by the gravity of life's unfolding but by advertising: "You know, the big Jennifer Convertible ad on the side of the bus? The ad that says, 'This Sleeper Sofa: Only $499,' but then you get there and there's the basic foam mattress that no one would really be able to sleep on. . . . So, okay, let's get the better mattress, so right there it's $599. And not in this upholstery design in the picture, but this one, this one is nicer, so now we're up to, what, $699? And oh, do you really want to protect the fabric? Pretty soon that's added on, and then delivery. . . . Before you know it, it's an $800 sofa."

She looks at the Jennifer Convertible now as if it is a refugee object from some other time: "Well, look at it. You can tell exactly when it was popular, and that's when we were dating or, actually, when we were in one of our 'off' periods," she says, and she is at least right about this phenomenon, that every sofa has its time, its story. This one has light blue stripes on white, and big cushions. There was a name for this style, then: "Mattress Ticking." Let us say 1989.

■   ■   ■

Next we have *the Hecht's Department Store Special*. This other sofa was hers. It was hers because she had all these cosmopolitan ideas. She imagined people were going to be visiting her and needing not only a place to sit, but also a place to sleep. She lived in one of those cozy apartments on California Street Northwest, the kind in which you want to put potted ferns and funky shower curtains, and then wait for life to catch on like a sparkler. (Theory: The universe is simply your own little sitcom.) This apartment was passed around among her law-school girlfriends, who each lived there until they met the man of their dreams, moved out, and got married. The previous occupant would toss the lease like a bouquet—what luck to catch it. In the time she was living there, single, sometimes loving him and sometimes not loving him, she went to the Hecht's department store and picked out her sleeper sofa. She did it fast and sure. Also, she seems to remember, it cost around $700—"which was, like, such a big deal at the time, right? This major, major purchase, real furniture that you don't assemble." The Hecht's Special is cream-colored and modular and ultimately unremarkable. No one, her husband claims, ever spent a night on its foldout mattress, not ever. The Hecht's Special sits in the basement under a pile of boxes, old baby clothes, hockey pads, picture frames, next to the punching bag that Sandy had hung from the rafters and punched a few times until it seemed that by doing this the ceiling might collapse on top of him, so he unhooked it from the rafters and did not punch it again.

The Jennifer Convertible is in the front sitting room on the first floor, where Jamie thinks it looks fine but not quite right. When they looked at the house, they were impressed by the size of the rooms. So much space—three floors and a basement! They gave no thought to the stairwell, which at its hairpins has about two or three feet of maximum leeway. (Let the stairs equal x; let y equal the facts previously overlooked.) "First the movers tried, and it just wouldn't budge," Sandy remembers, "and I suppose they tried everything, although I pretty much accepted it without really challenging them on it—I just took it as a fact that they couldn't do it." A couple of friends tried to help Sandy move the couches up the stairs, which quickly led to defeat, and beers. Over the years there were other delivery men—strong men, sometimes not speaking English—bringing various new purchases into the Ring household, and Sandy would tempt them, with cash and certain subtly flattering indications, that maybe they were smart enough, strong enough to get the couch up the stairs. And they would try, perhaps out of a sense of pride. They'd look at the stairwell, look at the couch, give it a go: "They'd get up to that first turn," Sandy says, "then couldn't get any farther."

What is it the Rings want, exactly?

"The sofa in the basement needs to be on the third floor," Jamie says.

And that is because?

"The baby is due May 4."

Of course. Later, in confidence, Sandy says it's all about his mother-in-law. Yes, the sofa has always needed to be on the third floor, but now time is a factor. Not just space, not just matter, but time. The mother-in-law is coming when the baby—Sandy and Jamie's second child—is born. (Pushing sofas through narrow stairwells! Birth metaphors!) They don't want to put the mother-in-law on the Jennifer Convertible in the living room because that's not good enough. There is a perfect third bedroom on the top floor, with its own bathroom, and this is where Sandy Ring would like to put his mother-in-law, at last, after five years: "Unless she sleeps in the basement, which I like to joke about," he says, and then backtracking a bit, lowering his voice, wondering if I can strike that last comment from the record, which, I assure him, I cannot.

Of the couch, people said: You could hoist it up outside and through the windows.

People said this because they were drunk. "What did people do one hundred years ago?" is what Jamie wants to know. "Didn't they have furniture?"

A hundred years ago people sat on tiny striped Victorian settees and waited to succumb to fevers. In another incarnation, the Rings' place had been leased as a group house, shared by members of the futon generation who probably did not own any furniture that could not be squeezed through the window of a Volkswagen—a disassembled tribe of disassemblable things, living in and out of various dimensional realities.

■　■　■

Fact: 99.9 percent of a single atom is just empty space.

Problem: Tell it to anyone who ever moved a chifforobe, a sectional, a refrigerator, a pool table.

. . .

On a Sunday afternoon last month, Sandy gets up from the football game he was watching and walks down to the basement to again confront the sleeper-sofa problem.

"What are you doing?" Jamie asks.

"Looking at the couch," he says, disappearing down to the darkness, flicking on the light in the cold concrete hole, pulling some of the benign, piled excess of their lives off the Hecht's Special, revealing it in its dingy cream-coloredness, and then pulling slightly at the fabric on the back. Pulling, until it rips loose a little with a tearing sound, and he can see that up inside there, a couch isn't much at all. He continues ripping the upholstery seam away several inches, until he realizes that to go any further than this point will mean setting down his beer.

. . .

It should be said that there is yet another couch in Sandy and Jamie Ring's lives, a more perfect third couch, a recent purchase. It's expensive: a caramel-color leather couch, a behemoth, not a sleeper, and Jamie is happy about its arrival. Perhaps, you're thinking, the other two couches now don't belong in the house at all.

Jamie disagrees. True, the leather sofa represents the kind of thing a lawyer and his wife and their darling daughter and imminently darling infant could and should have in the house. But maybe they are not ready to say good-bye to the other sofas. Maybe they will fit in other rooms of the future house they've not yet moved into.

. . .

Fact: Astronomers, peering into the farthest reaches of the known universe, have discovered a halogen floor lamp that belonged to your ex-girlfriend.

■ ■ ■

Somewhere in this, there is mythic talk of a sofa surgeon. Sandy hears about these miracle workers who come to your house, cut the sofa apart, put it where you want it, and then put it back together. This blows his mind. Here, all along, after five years of living with this problem, is a solution. He turns to his neighbors, to furniture store owners, to the Internet. Jamie calls the furniture store in Rockville where a "sofa knockdown specialist" is alleged to some-times work on special cases. She is told that she can leave her num-ber. For days nothing happens. "And why does it have to be so clandestine?" Jamie wonders. Sandy tries his luck at getting a mes-sage through to the sofa surgeon via the furniture store, and this time emerges with at least a name: John Errico.

One hopes against hope that the sofa surgeon would look exactly like Sigmund Freud. (Or Einstein.) He doesn't.

He comes by Volkswagen Jetta through the deep snow on a Jan-uary night. He is thirty-three, burly, goateed, with his long, wild hair held back in a ponytail. He has a kind smile. "I'm John," he says, and the Rings' half-husky, half–Great Pyrenees, Max, sniffs at him and approves. Their darling two-and-a-half-year-old daughter, Molly, leaps up and down excitedly upon the perfect leather sofa. "Let me get my tools," the sofa surgeon says. He does not look at the stairs. He does not look at the couch. He does no math, no siz-ing, no fretting.

■ ■ ■

What is the universe if not the random chitchat between chaos and order? Sandy plays it cool in the presence of the sofa surgeon. Sandy wears a gray sweater and snow boots with his jeans rolled up ("Is this your macho guy outfit?" Jamie asks him) and he watches reverently as the sofa surgeon drills the bed frame out of the Hecht's Special and then gently tears off the upholstery on the backside. Jamie laughs at the absurdity of it, a bit dejected by the sight of her sofa peeled open: "You pay all that money and it's made of card-board inside?"

There is brief fascination with the power tools. There is good noise, productive sawing noises and hammering noises and the sound of something being taken apart, and wipings of the brow. A parade of sofa parts makes its way to the third floor, along with much clomping up and down the stairs. The sofa surgeon breaks into a heavy sweat. There, on the third floor, the Hecht's Special is reassembled, the frame screwed together, and slowly, the Herculon upholstery stapled back into place. All the while, the sofa surgeon tells his tale: Thirteen years of moving couches through space, and only once has he ever been defeated, by a two-piece sectional and an impossible doorway. One time he peeled all the leather off a sofa and put it back on. Sometimes the customers cannot bear to watch. "The initial reaction is that they don't want to see it, they don't believe it can be done," Errico says. "They think sofas are constructed like tanks. Most people are quite astounded when it's all over. Like you turned water into wine."

■ ■ ■

"And what of the ultimate fate of the universe?" asks Wendy L. Freedman in "The Expansion Rate and Size of the Universe" in the March 1999 issue of *Scientific American* (which you no doubt missed, or left in the wicker basket by the toilet): "If the average density of matter in the universe is low, as current observations indicate, the standard cosmological model predicts that the universe will expand forever."

Of course, and how comforting. Also, Jamie will go on loving Sandy, and there will be more furniture, more dense matter, but no more than a universe could conceivably hold. The Hecht's Special is now where it was cosmically meant to be. (The Jennifer Convertible is but one slipcover from transformation into a new sort of matter.) At least in this universe, though, wherever this love goes, one sofa will not be moved again. (Unless by cataclysm. Which is always possible.)

The sofa surgeon drinks two glasses of water and chats politely, then packs his tools and leaves with his check for $125, the smell of his sweat lingering, the darling daughter up way past her bedtime, the dog lying low. His Jetta climbs the icy asphalt hills of Mount Pleasant and disappears in the night, a night so uncharacteristically dotted with the available stars that one is compelled to hesitate for a minute, on the walk home, and wonder.

(2000)

Panic Rooms

Plano, Texas

Every day, and more frequently on weekends, Dorito chips suspended midway between bags and mouths, some 5 million people watch *Trading Spaces,* a hit cable television home-improvement show. It's the one where friendly neighbors swap houses and redecorate a room in two days, each with a $1,000 budget and the gently dictatorial help of a professional interior designer, usually one from New York. The neighbors reveal the results to one another at the show's climax, with reactions of shock, glee, weeping, or the clenched and polite grimaces of barely suppressed disgust.

Not very deep down, *Trading Spaces* is about human insecurity. The idea here is that your house might not look as good as someone else's—which is to say your life, your marriage, your everything else might be inferior, too. Even early man lamented the conditions of his surroundings, wanting badly to have etchings like the etchings in Dak's cave. Trudging back from the Ikea of his day, he slipped on the cusp of a glacier and turned up five millennia later, frozen solid, looking depressed. *Trading Spaces* is about that longing within. Comparison, envy, the conflicts around matters of taste. The show, in attempting to assist us in simple room makeovers, transmits covert information on the real biggies: friendship, fidelity, change, window treatments. Its producers hope that it is a show that will teach people things they didn't know about paint or power saws. But it can also be seen with whatever vicarious urges feed the amateur porn and vice-cop ride-along genres. *Trading Spaces* is an ongoing attempt to salvage the American dream, and brighten up the dreamers. It shows what happens if you let someone else decorate your world. It shows that sometimes people have to take a stand on who they really are, whoever that is.

Like these two nice women, both of whom are named Angie.

One of the Angies will soon go down in the footnotes of cable TV history as the woman who refused to let Hildi Santo-Tomas—a strong-willed, Prada-sandaled designer from Atlanta—dye the other Angie's beige bedroom carpet a bright, highway-cone shade of orange. "This is Plano, Texas," she will plead, while the camera rolls in the kitchen and Santo-Tomas begins mixing the dye. It is a narrative arc so striking that the producer asks to film it twice, an apparent technique of making reality television. "People here are conservative," Angie notes. "We cannot dye her carpet orange. No."

Across the street, the other Angie, meanwhile, is being just as careful a friend:

"Her house is not *country*," she objects to Douglas Wilson, a New York–based interior designer with leading-man blue eyes. Wilson has just laid out his plans to turn the absent Angie's game room into something that looks like the inside of what he hopes will evoke thoughts of a pretty, moss green barn.

"Look around," Wilson tells this Angie. "You tell me this house isn't country."

"It isn't country," Angie says.

Angie lives across the street from Angie. One Angie and her husband moved in about a year after the other Angie and her husband did. The couples were some of the first homeowners on Shady Valley Road, set in a sea of houses and subdivisions stretching to the horizon, in a county north of Dallas where the average home size is 3,787 square feet, and the population has quadrupled since 1980 to a half-million people. There is neither shade nor a valley associated with Shady Valley Road. Angie and Angie get the joke about that: They make gentle cracks about "Plano princesses," the gossipy housewives tooling around in their sport-utes. They see the wry symbolism in the pitiful little trees tethered to their lawns, trying to grow. Once in a while, an Angie admits, there is the occasional flash of awareness that the exteriors of life here are governed by certain conventions (every yard has a tree, or should; these drapes go with these pillows), and the interiors are mostly secret. "It's weird here. You want to tell people to get over themselves sometimes," she says. "But it's nice, too."

The Angies became good friends. They are both blond, and both have their hair cut short, and fringy on the very ends, the way women do it here, and, in fact, the agreed-upon hairstyle of much of the rest of Mrs. America, if subsequent viewings of *Trading Spaces* reruns are any measure. They helped decorate one another's houses, adhering to a postcountry country, upper-middle-class style. Their vaulted, tiled entryways are painted in similarly warm tones. (This style, the "lawyer foyer," is Plano's dominant architectural feature.) They both bought the thick furniture and overstuffed sofas you see in popular catalogues. They both added big candles, and "tried some different things," such as plastic fruit and ivy stuck to the distressed-patina mirror frames. Shabby chic called them to a vocation, and they answered. They did all the kids' rooms in themes—in one, they spelled out the lyrics to "Deep in the Heart of Texas" in cursive lariat rope along the walls.

Still, a faint dissatisfaction lingered. The second Angie has had her husband repaint their master bedroom three times in four years. They have spent $5,000 on bedroom furniture and boast sumptuous white linens on a new king-size bed. But . . . Angie just doesn't know, something's "blah" about it. Even the sage green paint seems "a little too much of the same, like everybody else's house," she says. The first Angie, meanwhile, is unhappy with her family's game room, which is cluttered with toys, an old futon couch, two worn-out chairs, an ottoman, an entertainment stand.

The Angies and their husbands were deemed, by a *Trading Spaces* scout who flew to Plano and interviewed them, to be good candidates for the show. He took Polaroids, made exact measurements, and seemed pleased that the couples live in a recognizably untrendy, commonly well-off universe. There was room on Shady Valley Road to park the *Trading Spaces* trucks, and a clean, wide alley running behind the garages. It would be very possible here for the *Trading Spaces* crew to come and preach the gospel of the bargain makeover, the steady steamrolling of higher design onto the misguided innocence of the rest of us, with easy-in and easy-out. Most important, the Angies are willing: willing to let the world look inside their houses, pass judgment, and decide not only whether the rooms (before and after) are pretty and functional but also whether the people are.

This is how television came for a couple days to Shady Valley Road, where one Angie is married to a man named John, and the other Angie is married to a man named Jeff.

Angie and John Doyen. (Three kids under six, plus a twelve-year-old son from John's first marriage.) John works in database sales.

Angie and Jeff Rexford. (Twin boys, age four, plus a new baby.) Jeff works in medical-supply sales.

Sometimes the Angies, both stay-at-home moms, leave the kids with the husbands and go see a weekend matinee. Some nights the Angies and their husbands go over to a neighbor's house, long after the rest of the world has gone to bed, and . . .

"It'll sound kind of odd," John says.

And what? Go ahead and tell me. What do you do at the neighbor's house?

"It's really fun," he hesitates.

Tell me your secret.

"We play Risk."

■ ■ ■

Trading Spaces airs on TLC, which formerly called itself The Learning Channel, but realized, in the shadow of its sister network, The Discovery Channel, that there was less learning to be done about the animal kingdom, and more science to plumb in mainstream human behavior. Now TLC specializes in real-life shows that follow first dates, weddings, emergency-room traumas. The network has ditched or rescheduled most of its science shows, billing itself now as "Life Unscripted." Even though there are two programs about childbirth, forceps and all, it is the home improvement show that gives the purest glimpse into the private world of suburban married life, and rescued TLC from the slagheap at the far end of the cable yard. "I keep waiting for *Trading Spouses*," one camera guy jokes, noting the deeply subtextual, entirely symbolic metaphor of the show. *Trading Spaces* is a peek over the marital fence, suggesting that, if all else fails, let's switch. *Trading Spaces* confirms that real estate is the new sex. It is Bob and Carol and Ted and Alice and Medium-Density Fiberboard.

Like many devotees, the Angies have spent hours deconstructing each episode of *Trading Spaces*—the painting over of heirloom furniture, the gluing of hay to the walls, the sawing of legs off coffee tables. There was the time Genevieve Gorder (one of the six rotating designers) used real moss. There was Hildi Santo-Tomas's gridded "orthogonal" navy and white paint job in a basement. And the chocolate-colored walls and white fireplace wainscoting by Douglas Wilson that made a woman named Pam cry.

"Oh, she is *not* happy," her worried husband remarked, in that now-legendary episode taped in 2001 in Puyallup, Washington, a Tacoma suburb. The wife excused herself to go wail in another room. Her microphone was still on, however, and America will not soon forget the exact pitch of her sobs. (Even now, Pam doesn't see herself the way television saw her. Months later, in an e-mail, she told me that she cried so much because she believed the wainscoting had violated local building codes.) It is generally accepted that the Puyallup episode perfectly sums up all the ecstasy and dread of *Trading Spaces*. Pam—amply sized, happily outdated, stubbornly unadventurous—mourns the loss of her saggy floral sofas and the dull brick of her fireplace. Her husband—doing as he's told, generally clueless—looks like he wants to flee. What made them recoil in horror seemed to be this: The room strongly suggested a New York kind of modernism. Clean, elegant, dark. Here you had a familiar and delicious culture clash on the deepest level, like the 2000 election map showing a divided, red and blue America. Sophistication versus lowbrow. (Fat versus thin? Gayness versus straightness? City versus suburb?) "This is going to have to come down," Pam's husband pronounced.

Having seen all this and more, the Angies braced themselves. "We knew," says Angie Rexford, "that if we were going to do *Trading Spaces* we couldn't do it halfway and get all freaked out at new ideas. We couldn't tell them what not to do. We agreed to let them come in here and do it. Because let's face it: If we knew what to do with these rooms, we would have done it already."

The designers who rotate starring roles on *Trading Spaces* all come from an aesthetic doctrine that deplores the clutter of everyday life. (One exception is the more folksy, artsy-craftsy Frank Bielec—an effete grandfatherly type who leans toward bright colors and painting animals on the wall.) *Trading Spaces* is a slow, steady assault on faux-country, gingham-and-basket charm. It's also the end of glass-and-chrome dining sets; the show's professional designers seem to have a particular allergy to mass-produced furniture. There is an ongoing purge of poorly assembled entertainment centers and computer desks. In the "before" shots, we see bonnet-wearing ducks and bric-a-brac arranged on Victorian dining-room hutches; we see ceiling fans whirring lopsidedly like boozy drunks. (Ceiling fans are almost always the first thing to go in a *Trading Spaces* makeover, as if they were pestilence.) We see grimy Formica countertops that, we are told, must go; we see favorite La-Z-Boys doomed for Goodwill; we see bedrooms occupied by sagging TV armoires and ignored Exercycles. We see ourselves.

■   ■   ■

On a chilly Thursday afternoon in late March, the *Trading Spaces* truck parks in the alley behind Shady Valley Road and the crew starts unloading for a two-day shoot of Episode 41, where the Rexfords will redo the Doyens' game room with Douglas Wilson and the Doyens will redo the Rexfords' master bedroom with Hildi Santo-Tomas. Paige Davis, an actress who serves as the show's hyperkinetically gamine host, will flit between houses, prodding the homeowners to meet deadline and stay under the $1,000 budget.

The show's other mainstay—and in many ways most popular character—is Ty Pennington, an Atlanta-based carpenter who looks like he's just finished skateboarding a half-pipe. (Pennington alternates episodes with Amy Wynn Pastor, who in contrast to his fumble-fingered antics lends her episodes a Habitat for Humanity air, a table-saw Zen.) Pennington sets up shop under a tent in the driveway, and to viewers it appears he is solely responsible for bringing the designer's furnishing visions to reality. He builds headboards and beds, end tables, countertops, sectional sofas, fireplace mantels.

Off-camera, however, it's soon clear that the homeowners, designers, and carpenter cannot, by themselves, pull off a redecorating project in just two days. Coming to their aid is Eddie Barnard, the show's quiet and unassuming prop manager. Known as "Fast Eddie" and never seen on-camera, he quickly pounds together medium-density fiberboard—or MDF to everyone on the set—into armoires and shelves. (*Trading Spaces* could be an ode to the cheap and durable glory of MDF; thus Lowe's Home Improvement Warehouse is a key sponsor.) Another secret weapon sets up shop across the street, in the other homeowners' garage, plugging in irons and two sewing machines. Although the crew will film the designers and homeowners doing some of the sewing, it is Daniel Hawks—a chain-smoking Knoxville seamster with chrome-colored polish on his manicured nails and a CD player blasting techno—who stitches together a flurry of drapes, slipcovers, and pillows.

A *Trading Spaces* shoot requires a crew of fifteen, with an operating budget of about $30,000 per episode. No one escapes the work of redecorating: From production assistants to producers, everyone helps paint (and sand, stain, saw, staple, move furniture, hold ladders), none of which is shown on television. "It's just the reality of the reality," executive producer Denise Cramsey explains, having just sanded and primed a child's table and chairs that will go in the Doyens' game room. "Because of the time and energy we

spend getting the different shots ready, it's basically an acknowledg-
ment that this is the only way we can make up the lost time. We're
helping the homeowners because we're always in their way." There
is an absurdity to it: a husband and wife in their neighbor's empty
bedroom, painting, in a moment of supposed privacy, performing a
terribly intimate and secret act of transformation, under three
bright studio lights, with a camera guy, a sound guy, a grip, two production assistants, a producer, the executive producer, a publicist,
and a reporter all in the same room, watching, just out of the frame
of reality.

■ ■ ■

The show's designers, accustomed to working for picky clients with
much larger personal home decor budgets (who, says Santo-Tomas,
"will spend a thousand dollars just on a lampshade"), have to think
of low-cost approaches to innovation. The trade-off for them,
Santo-Tomas says, is the chance to show the audience "that there is
no need to fear something new. You can do these designs. You,
yourself, in your home." She admits she'd rather not work entirely
with MDF, or the vases she unearths at Cost Plus, or the pillows
sewn from the sale bins at Jo-Ann Fabrics. (And, no matter how un-
charted an American exurb that *Trading Spaces* flings her to, she
can always find the strip mall that has the Cost Plus and the Jo-Ann
Fabrics, like an animal tracks a scent.)

But she enjoys the power of suggestion in a $1,000 budget, laid
out here on the everyday turf of the great masses. In Seattle, she
spray painted two old love seats hot pink, "and it would have worked,
too," she emphasizes, if the crew and homeowners hadn't left the
couches outdoors in the rain. Santo-Tomas declared victory anyway:
Spray painting sofas is now thought by countless viewers to be within
the realm of the possible. ("They were ugly already," she says.)

At the time of the taping of the Plano episode, Santo-Tomas is
forty-one years old. She refused to tell me her age, even after I told
her that I must know, because viewers couldn't decide if she was in
her forties or somewhat younger: Her stern insistence on her own

sophistication, and her skill level, suggested years of experience, but her low-rise Gucci pants and stiletto Manolos stepping around drop cloths suggested something else. Finally I had to do the despicable thing and look it up, by running her identity through motor-vehicle and credit bureau databases. She was about to be married to a very rich older man, and move to Paris, while still managing her decorating business in Atlanta and taping her share of *Trading Spaces* episodes—eighteen per season.

In present tense, she is driving her rented Jaguar around Plano on the evening before the house swapping, slamming on the brakes when she sees a Pier 1 in a strip mall. Wilson is following in his rented minivan. The two have already blown into an enormous Lowe's Home Improvement Warehouse with the vague panic of people looking to prepare for a hurricane, announcing to the paint lady the exact colors they'll need. (The paint lady seems unaware of the celebrities in her midst.) They then coast over to the lumber department, where they bicker with Ty Pennington about measurements and costs.

Now they are back on the rush-hour suburban boulevards, looking for, in no particular order, a fabric store, a Bed Bath & Beyond, a T.J. Maxx, and some decent sushi. Customers in stores recognize them and whisper. A cashier in Target pleads: "Will y'all come do my house? It needs somethin'." It's as if they've been here a hundred times. There is an intuitive landscape to what urban planners and academics often derisively refer to as the Geography of Nowhere: A Target always indicates the presence of a T.J. Maxx nearby; the Pier 1 means you're getting ever so close to a full-fledged mall. This homogeneous world unnerves and occasionally offends Santo-Tomas on some aesthetic level, even as it inspires her and supplies her raw materials. She recalls, as she pushes a wobbly-wheeled cart through Target, that when she first looked at Angie and Jeff's bedroom, "I said, 'Why are we here?' This room is done, more or less. These houses are all alike. The walls are painted, they have their furniture, it looks, you know, like how they would want it to look.

"But see," she goes on, "that's just it: A room like this, you have to really think of something new. I am going to do something, that, okay, they might not like. I'm going to completely change it." She's going for something like a boutique hotel room in Miami. It will be all white, except for the bottom twelve inches of the wall and the floor, which will be dyed orange.

Wilson, who is thirty-seven, navigates his way across the suburban grid, considers his options for the game room, and settles in with his last-minute "barn" concept: green walls, faux rafters, corduroy. He thinks of what the futon frame would look like if he took it apart and rebuilt it.

It was Wilson who designed the chocolate room with the wainscoting that made Puyallup Pam cry. "Once it's over, we're still there," Wilson says. "It's not like I was already on a plane, trying to get away."

I want to know if he ever got to apologize to Pam, or if he felt he should have.

"I liked the room. I thought it worked. So many people thought it worked. I didn't apologize," he says carefully. "I said, 'I'm sorry it disappoints you.'"

We've lost the day's sun. We're also turned around, lost among the starter mansions of Texas. He talks about his own apartment, on Manhattan's Upper West Side—all 500 rent-controlled square feet of it, the bare-bulb fixtures, the spartan furnishings, the lack of color. He hasn't had time to decorate.

■ ■ ■

Early the next morning, the crew is setting up to interview Angie and John Doyen and Angie and Jeff Rexford for an early establishing scene in the Doyens' living room, in which the couples will sit— the men with glasses of beer—and chitchat lightheartedly about their lives and their tastes. "We need to shut that door to the bathroom in the hallway," the camera guy says, looking up from his viewfinder. "Because, as we well know, on television there is no such thing as toilets."

The two days of shooting "Episode 41: Shady Valley Road" unfold with the simultaneous pressures of redecorating the rooms in
each house, keeping the progress secret from each set of owners,
and making television. For every lighthearted, hammy moment on
camera, there is a tense moment off camera between crew members and the designers. *Trading Spaces* groupies have begun turning
up at each location. On a recent shoot, a woman appeared in a wedding dress and asked Ty Pennington to marry her. A teenager burst
into tears when she spied Paige Davis crossing Shady Valley Road.
During the shoot, Plano princesses cruise by in their cars, pointing
and waving. Neighbors hitherto unknown to the Doyens and Rexfords now loiter in the alley and adjoining yards, trying to sneak a
peek at the houses, which are cordoned off with yellow caution
tape. Angie and Angie, separated now and spending thirty-six hours
in each other's houses, seem to be communicating telepathically.
An interesting thread in each *Trading Spaces* is the way the wives
(who are best friends, usually) look out for one another's taste, wag-
ing war for all America against the designer-sophisticates.

Angie Rexford is defending Angie Doyen on the "barn room's"
country look, relaxing only when she talks Doug Wilson into changing fabrics one more time. Angie Doyen stands firm against Hildi
Santo-Tomas's orange carpet dye. As the second day lumbers to a
close, the crew readies the climax. It is here where *Trading Spaces*
betrays reality most, insisting that life is but a series of befores and
afters, instead of all that intermediate gray. In the Rexfords' house,
perky Paige is slowly leading Angie and Jeff up the stairs for their
reveal. They have their eyes closed. Most of the crew is crammed
into one of the children's bedrooms, lights out, not making a sound.
Hildi Santo-Thomas, bags packed, smelling of expensive perfume,
the professional who claims not to care too deeply if the homeowners are pleased with her designs or not, nervously watches on a
small TV monitor.

The couple are led blindly into their bedroom.

It is all white, except where it is bright orange. Long white drapes
with an orange border descend from the vaulted ceiling. Candles

flicker on the nightstand; all $5,000 of their bedroom furniture has been polyurethaned. There are bright orange rose petals (a last-minute Hildi touch) scattered over the undyed carpet. "Okay, Angie and Jeff," Davis giddily commands them. "Open your eyes. . . ."

■ ■ ■

Things worked out okay, both Angies report, a week after the crew has gone. The Doyens loved their moss-green-barn-rafters game room. (John enthusiastically ranked the TV taping as one of the greatest things that ever happened to him.) Angie and Jeff Rexford tentatively and politely appreciated the direction taken in their master bedroom. Angie thinks she'll redo the bedroom, keeping the white and changing the orange baseboards, curtain hems, bed, and ottoman to "something else, maybe a mocha kind of brown?" The Rexfords are thinking of resale value, motion, upwardly mobile restlessness: "We'll probably move to another house in a couple years," she says. (The ceiling fan is going back up there, too, she says. "Hello? Texas in summer?") Curious neighbors have been dropping by; the rooms have taken on celebrity status. "I started telling people to all come by at the same time for a showing. I don't have time to deal with them all. I don't want all these strangers in my house," Angie Doyen says. Except for the millions who will see her house on TV next month and will go on seeing it in rerun perpetuity.

Angie Rexford reports that one of her twins already threw up on the carpet in the bedroom, a peach-colored barf of fruit juice that left a stain.

"The ghost of Hildi," the other Angie remarks. "She got that carpet orange after all."

But then something else happened in the time after they traded spaces. The episode aired six weeks later, and some *Trading Spaces* fans, in an anonymous chat room on the show's Web site, viciously critiqued both Angies based on what they saw—their hair, voices, attitudes, marriages, styles of life. Angie Doyen looked out her window one morning and saw a car parked outside the Rexfords house, and she was pretty sure it belonged to their real-estate agent. She kept waiting for her best friend to tell her about it, but the other Angie didn't say anything. Within weeks, the Rexfords put their house up for sale and bought a slightly bigger house, in a slightly newer subdivision. By the end of the year, the Doyens, too, had put their house up for sale and moved with their three boys into something smaller, in an older subdivision. Living neighborhoods apart now, Angie and Angie worked together to make something of a part-time, freelance interior decorating business, helping other Plano princessess discover warmer tones and post-post-country charm.

The Angies were still having fun, once in a while, but nothing, Angie Doyen says, was ever quite the same.

(2002)

Modern Bride

Albuquerque, New Mexico

I had the weirdest dream. It was a nightmare, really. First of all, I don't have any shoes on. OK, we're all at the house getting ready and I'm in my dress and we are all walking to the church. I'm going, "Don't let Andy see me! Don't let Andy see me!" Then I fall in the mud. I'm not wearing any pantyhose and I have on black underwear and you can see the black underwear right through my dress. Then I can't find my veil. Where's my veil? So we go to a hotel room and there it is, my veil, we find it, and we get back to the church and Mass has already started. And there's Andy up at the altar and he's getting married to some other girl. I can't believe it. I start yelling at him, "Andy! How could you do this?!" and then I throw candy at them. I'm shouting, "Andy, I hate you!"

The phone rings at 6:40 a.m. Her father calls home every morning from work, where he has been since 5 a.m., an established routine to wake up his daughter, to make sure she heard the alarm clock and is getting out of bed. To bring her out of her dreams.

"Good morning, *mi'ja*," Cipriano "Danny" Garcia tells his daughter Darleine. "Only forty-three days to go."

Or thirty-one days. Or twenty-two days, or nine days, or three. Good morning, *mi'ja*. It's one day closer. Danny Garcia marks off the days until Darleine will marry Andy in the church across the street. His daughter will move out, to live ten houses down from his own. His wife probably will cry. He says he won't, cracks a joke about how Andy now will have to take over the service contract on Darleine. Her car needs an oil change? That's Andy's problem. Closet shelves need to be built? Andy's problem. Tires wearing thin? *Andy.* Clogged drains? *Andy.* Meanwhile, a bedroom will be empty. You grow old and your kids move away. Down the street can seem like another time zone. Facts are facts and this is Danny's problem. So he counts.

I'm very close to my parents. When my sister got married, we all cried when she moved out. Now she lives next door. I'm getting married and moving out and I know it's going to be hard. Even though I'll just be down the street. Things will be different.

This is a story about a wedding, one of those runaway trains in life where you set the date months ahead of time and figure it will never get here, only to marvel at the speed with which everything collides. Absolute limits are overspent anyway. Someone could get too drunk and say the wrong thing at the wrong time. It's a North Valley drama as simple as this: A pretty secretary with a spiral perm meets and falls in love with a nice man who drives a pickup truck and coaches Little League. Rings are purchased, a reception is planned, and people wonder how much they're going to cry when it comes time to cry. Tensions surface in the nightmares of a bride-to-be, images of wet hair and jilted lovers broken suddenly by the blare of the snooze alarm and the soothing voice of Daddy.

Good morning, *mi'ja.*

Darleine Garcia, twenty-two, gets out of bed. She has her hair and makeup down to a twenty-minute routine. She always irons her clothes the night before. In this morning shuffle, she talks to her mother, Lucille. They gossip and find each other's car keys. They talk about what to do after work. Sometimes Lucille will zip up the back of Darleine's dress; Darleine will tell her mother which shoes to wear with what earrings, and she'll comb her mother's hair. Breakfast is Fruity Pebbles. They check one another's teeth for lipstick.

Lucille, a small woman with short dark hair and a perpetual giggle, bids her tall, pretty daughter good-bye. They back their cars out of the long driveway on Griegos Road Northwest and head separate ways—mother to her job as a doctor's office receptionist, daughter to her job as a personnel secretary at Ross Aviation. "I think," Lucille says, "I'll miss her most in the mornings. We talk about everything then. Who will tell me what to wear after she's gone?"

Her oldest daughter, Denise, twenty-seven, married Ronnie Nuñez in 1990. Now there is a baby granddaughter, Danielle.

On June 20, 1992, Darleine—Lucille's baby, the smiling princess immortalized in framed photos in the den, a little girl in barrettes, a poised teen in a Valley High School cheerleader uniform—will marry Andy Barboa. A bedroom will be empty. "They never understand," Lucille says. "I tell them, 'When your kids grow up and move away, you'll understand. Then, I say, 'then you'll know.'"

Danny and Lucille: Andy's brothers call them, affectionately but not to their faces, Dick Clark and Zsa Zsa, hanging on to younger days.

■ ■ ■

People have no idea what it takes to have a wedding. I hear about people who get married in just, like, four months. How do they do that? There's no way. I think eight months is barely enough time.

Get the particulars straight. A wedding is details. A wedding is at the center of the story, spinning along the happy edge of a drunk summer, a narrative that begins and ends along a tree-lined sliver of North Valley lifestyles. Two families come together for a $12,000 hoopla of middle-class tradition. ($15,000. No, more. In the end, including the honeymoon, Andy and Darleine's wedding will cost $25,000.) Eight hundred people are on the guest list for the reception, which will be held at the Albuquerque Convention Center. The couple has been duly announced in both the morning and evening newspapers. China patterns, bathroom colors, stemware, crystal, and the whole gift wish list have been registered at American Home Furnishings. Tuxedo sizes have been measured. The color scheme will be royal blue. The white wedding gown, beaded, with veil, will cost $800. Royal blue napkins and match books ("Darleine and Andy" embossed in silver lettering) have been ordered. An off-the-shoulder dress pattern has been selected for seven royal blue bridesmaids' dresses. (Yes, seven. The wedding party—including the starring roles of bride and groom, supporting roles of matron of honor, best man, bridesmaids, and groomsmen, and cameo appearances of a ring bearer and flower girl—numbers eighteen.) The church has been reserved; a choir will sing. Five separate ballrooms at the convention center will be opened onto one another, creating a reception and dance space. A cake will tower eight tiers, with a bubbly fountain beneath and crystal swans atop. The band will play "La Marcha." A limousine will deliver the bride and groom. A honeymoon in Vegas will follow.

There are some people in both the Garcia and Barboa families who will tell you that Darleine and Andy's wedding is out of control. Too big, too much, too many, too this, too that. Others will shrug and smile and say that it comes only once, so why not indulge? A wedding is like that first bite of wedding cake. Love is sweet and $12,000 weddings are a million times sweeter and outdone. A wedding is an icing rush, a sugary get-go, swimmingly sustained with alcohol.

Everyone, in theory, will be happy.

Everything, in theory, will be *just so.*

There will be a wedding photographer and a videographer, hired on a package deal. Even more vérité, hanging so far back that he hopes you forget he's here, there is a newspaper reporter, who asked if he could follow Andy and Darleine, and their families and friends, while taking notes on their wedding experience. It's a summer in which the newspaper reporter happens to also be writing, too often, about multiple homicides, or house fires, or arroyo flooding, or 4-H fairs, or about the foothills on the edge of Albuquerque in which nuclear missiles have been stored for almost half a century. It is safe to say the newspaper reporter has some quiet, unarticulated dread about the future. It is safe to say the reporter feels lonely, or bored, and perhaps too peripheral to life itself, and that he wants mainly to go to a wedding, a big wedding, and see it up close. To know more about love, and about what people think love is.

■ ■ ■

Sometimes I forget I'm supposed to be happy and enjoy all of this. I just want it to be over.

Darleine is sitting at the dining-room table. The wedding is five weeks away. There are 450 invitations, stacked in white boxes, mostly addressed, waiting to be sent out: "Danny and Lucille Garcia together with Celeste Medina and Jerry Barboa, invite you to share in the celebration when their children unite in the Sacrament of Holy Matrimony—Darleine Marie to Michael "Andy" Barboa—on Saturday, the Twentieth of June at Two O'Clock in the afternoon. . . ."

When you open the envelope, blue glitter spills out. That was Darleine's idea. She sprinkles it on with a saltshaker.

A breeze blows through the open window. The sun is starting to set. Cars pass by on Griegos Road. Darleine frequently looks up to watch the traffic. "You can sit at this table and see the whole North Valley driving by." She has never lived anywhere else. The 1988 Valley High School graduate puts in her eight hours a day at work and, not so long ago, spent her nights with a group of kindred spirits—single women with fake IDs and penchants for two-for-one margarita Ladies' Nights, at places like Midnight Rodeo or Denim & Diamonds. Paychecks went to her car or the shopping mall. Guys were for flirting with, and marriage was of course imminent, but far away.

Now it's different, because now there's Andy. He is twenty-five, also a graduate of Valley (class of '84) and a former varsity baseball player. He works at a building supply store downtown and has served six years in the Air National Guard. His truck pulls up in the Garcia driveway. Andy has been at the North Valley Little League fields, across the street, next to Our Lady of Guadalupe church, coaching his team, the Calmat White Sox, a group of hyper, nearly undefeated ten- and eleven-year-old boys.

"Andy," Darleine asks him, "did you take more of the reception invitations?" He sits down at the table, takes off his baseball cap,

and runs a hand over his short, dark hair. She drums her red finger-
nails on the table, waiting for an answer. This is a touchy issue.
While 450 invitations are being sent for the wedding and dance,
only 375 will include an additional invite to a buffet reception. Suddenly, the reception cards are dwindling.

"Andy is giving out reception invitations to just anybody and
everybody," Darleine says.

"Dar, I see people on the street and just hand them an invitation.
They're on my list. We still have enough," he says.

"Andy, I see people driving on this street. I don't hand everyone
I see an invitation. Now we're out."

"Did you see my ring?" she asks me, changing the subject, hand
outstretched. Diamond baguettes twinkle on her finger. "When the
wedding ring is with it, it's going to look huge."

Andy starts addressing envelopes from a legal-pad list his
mother compiled. His careful, neat penmanship spells out names
and addresses. Another wedding chore. Another task. Dar has
dragged him to shopping malls, to discount party supply stores, to
the cavernous excess of American Home Furnishings he doesn't
know how many times. She has a blue folder of receipts and catalogues and a typed agenda of everything they need to buy. She pulls
him away from sports sections to find out, for instance, whether he
likes this kind of blue ribbon or this other kind of blue ribbon better. ("That one." "This one? Are you sure?" and so he'll say, "OK,
that other one.") He just wants what she wants. She says she's the
one who has to do all the work. He goes back to the box scores. She
sighs loudly and ponders this blue or that blue.

Eee, this guy.

It was a warm, early spring afternoon two years earlier, when Darleine went to a barbecue at her friend Gary's house. "Some guy"
kept bothering her. "All the guys had been playing basketball and
they were drunk," Darleine says. "Andy was all dressed in sweats
and coming up to me and talking. I said to my friends, 'Who *is* this

guy?'" She does an impression of him from that day. All swagger and macho, beer in hand. "He was all, 'Hi what's *your* name?' He just kept coming up and talking to me and asking if I had a boyfriend—'*Where's your boyfriend, where's your boyfriend?*' Finally I just said to my friends, 'Why don't we leave now,' because the guys were just being obnoxious and drinking."

Several weeks passed. At an engagement party for Gary and Michelle, Darleine spotted a guy from across the room. "He walked by our table," she remembers. "I said, 'Oh man, look at that guy's lips.'"

That guy? Darleine's friend Valerie Chavez laughed and told her: "Dar, that's the guy who was at the barbecue that time."

"That is not the same guy, Val."

Another time, a few weeks later, Darleine was with her sister, Denise, and her friend Dawn Green at the Guardsmen's Club on Kirtland Air Force Base. That guy with the lips. Again. This time, Andy Barboa came over to their table. "He was being all cool," Darleine says. "He said, 'Give me your numbers, I'll remember you as the Three Ds—Denise, Dawn, and Darleine.'"

He bragged that he could tell a woman's age, Darleine recalls, "by looking at her butt. I don't like a guy who flirts with all the girlfriends at once." He took a swig of his beer and walked away. And Darleine was not impressed: "I said, 'He's cute, but I hate guys who act like that.'"

Later, I don't know how many days after that, I saw him at Midnight Rodeo. And then, I guess that next week, I went to the church fiesta and Dawn poked me and pointed over at him and said, "Look who's here." I told my friends to go on ahead without me. I wanted to talk to him.

■　■　■

They grew up a mile away from each other. The same doctor delivered them. Danny Garcia used to coach some of Andy's cousins in Little League; Andy's mother, Celeste Medina, was best friends with Danny Garcia's cousin in high school.

Many ideas of "valley" converge in this particular part of the North Valley, which distinguishes itself entirely from the South Valley, but also from the valley farther north or the valley areas across the Rio Grande. Its children rarely move far away from the unofficial boundaries we are talking about here—a rectangle outlined by Rio Grande Boulevard and Fourth Street on the west and east, Montaño and Indian School roads to the north and south. This is the valley where everyone knows everyone, or at least knows one of their cousins. It's not the chic North Valley of late, with its sprouting hacienda condominiums, three-car garages, and other well-to-do notions of bliss on the bosque. Rather, it's the Valley of two-bedroom houses with living room built-ons; the Valley of chain-link fences and security bars on the windows, where most everyone graduates from Valley High School and settles into a conventional storyline of work and family loyalties: The men may likely become construction workers or city employees or service technicians; the women might choose to be secretaries, bank tellers, or clerks. Children sail by in swarms of bicycles; dogs bark in every yard. Graffiti occurs in occasional splays across the adobe walls—sometimes to be quickly sandblasted away, other times to linger, which the rest of the city sometimes reads as a sign of slow decay. The tin and tile rooftops shimmer in the day's waning sun, under New Mexico's paralyzingly blue skies. The North Valley is, to anyone who has ever lived there, a walk along the ditch just as the sun wanes, and the cicadas go on nagging the sky, the opening act to the cricket's evening song. Later, it's a shared pitcher of beer at Leonardo's lounge on Twelfth Street and Candelaria Road.

Now. Follow this closely, the constant buzz of activity in the Garcia house, with a confusing ensemble of names: Ronnie and Denise are having a barbecue, unless everyone is going over to Mom and Dad's, in which case Gary asked Andy to call him and Michelle called looking for Gary. Uncle Abel is here, or he was just here. Lucille is making a double batch of *bizcochitos* for a funeral tomorrow and a First Communion on Saturday. Val just called for the third time. Danny (another Danny) and Jerry are over at the other house, so maybe we'll drop by there or they'll come here. Call Denise back. Is the baby sleeping?

No one uses the front door; just pull up to the back. When something happens, everyone knows within an hour. There are no secrets and there's beer in the fridge, so help yourself. You are welcome here, so long as you are welcome here. Danny and Lucille Garcia's brown stucco house, where they have lived all their married lives, bears the telltale seams from where the girls' room was extended eight feet and the den—Danny's dream den—was added onto the back of the house in the 1970s. On the back of the lot, there are three stucco work sheds, a carport, and a sidewalk leading to the house next door, which the Garcias own. Now their daughter Denise lives there with Ronnie and the baby.

Danny Garcia stands in his den and tells of his many hunts—as far north as Canada, deep in the snow. He puts in for his hunting licenses early; he and his relatives spend weeks cleaning guns, planning, imagining future kills. On the wall above the stereo hangs a black bear rug, its head nosing past the back entryway toward the narrow kitchen. Nine mounted heads of deer, elk, and antelope stare all around the room. A pair of stuffed snow geese spread their wings over the color-console television, in permanent midflight toward the wet bar. The carpet is a dark, short shag. A beige, U-shaped sofa takes up most of the room.

Danny sits in a reclining lounger with an afghan thrown over it. Above and around the brick fireplace, crowding the mantel, are dozens of trophies, mostly Danny's from decades as a Little League coach. There are "Employee of the Month" plaques he has been given in his years as a city welder. There are pictures, too, of Danny's beaming wife and daughters, his proudest accomplishment, he says. Look at this one: Danny, Lucille, Denise, and Darleine in the snowy woods a few years ago, posing around a dead deer. The majestic head with antlers is held up, the dark animal eyes turned flashbulb-white, a spot of blood dripping on the snowy ground. This the Garcia family at their happiest.

This is the room prospective boyfriends always saw first, when meeting Danny. All these dead-eye stares. He jokes: "I tell them, this is what happens if you hurt my daughter." Danny has a sad, warm gaze, sarcastic Father-of-the-Bride wisecracks, and a nose broken from too many long-ago fistfights. The beer belly is "muscle, all muscle," he says, sucking it in. At heart, Danny Garcia hunts for what's right. Lack of family, he says, is the root problem for kids these days in the Valley. Gangs happen when there aren't enough fathers out there coaching with their boys, or scrutinizing whom their daughters date, he says. Respect is at a minimum these days. (One afternoon, I dropped by the Garcia house just as Danny had threatened and chased off a Griegos Road pedestrian. He said the man had hit Sheba, the family dog. The message was clear: What's behind my fence is mine. He sat and watched through the dining-room window, waiting to see if the man would return.)

Danny married Lucille in 1964. They had a big church wedding and a reception planned. Four days before the wedding, Lucille's grandmother died. Tradition holds bad omen, not to mention ill respect, for dancing and celebrating so close to a funeral. Tradition prevailed and Danny and Lucille missed their own dance, their own "La Marcha." It won't happen again. Danny told his mother, Felia Garcia, half-jokingly, "If you die before the wedding, I'm putting you on ice until it's over."

∎ ∎ ∎

Two families shoulder the weight of a wedding that they believe will cost a minimum of $12,000. Two families try to work things out and see eye-to-eye. "Can you believe what it costs these days?" Lucille says. And so soon after Denise and Ronnie. Can they afford this?

"Well, everybody's pitching in," Lucille says. "Darleine and Andy are paying for a lot. Andy's parents are doing a lot. You save money, cut back on some things. You want everything to be the best it can be."

Danny speaking, one night outside by the garage: "They get one chance at this. It's worth it. My daughters mean everything to me.

Money doesn't matter." Sheba, the dog he calls a stupid mutt but will defend from anyone who tries to hurt her, lies at his feet, resting her head on his shoe.

I always said I wanted to be a stewardess. I wanted to be a stewardess or an interior decorator. And I didn't do any of those. I always said when I turn twenty-five or twenty-seven, that's when I'll get married. And my mom said, "Well what happens when you turn twenty-five and you don't even have a boyfriend? What are you going to do, just pick anyone?"

My mom always says, "You'll know when it's right. You'll know when you're in love."

One of the first times Andy and I went out, we went to Players, the sports bar. Robert and Tina were there. We were there for I don't know how many hours. I was just trying to impress him, so I sat through two or three football games. The guys got really drunk so Tina and me wound up having to drive them home.

Which I had never driven a truck before in my life.

Darleine is sitting on a brand-new couch she and Andy bought for this three-bedroom rental house they soon will share. She is sucking ice cubes out of one of the many drinking glasses given to her at her bridal shower. Andy sits next to her, feet stretched out. He has already moved in, sleeping on a mattress and box spring in what will become the guest room. On their new twenty-seven-inch Zenith (a gift of sorts, bought on store credit with bridal shower returns and certificates), we are watching one of those real-life rescue shows where some poor soul is in peril and paramedics are frantically trying to prevent death, all captured on video.

The man lives.

Darleine and Andy stare at the screen, blankly, unmoved by rescue drama, four days before their wedding.

They have been fighting, a little, or maybe it's just nerves. Their families have been joking all week, the usual prewedding taunts about being tied down, about the loss of freedom. I talk about this tension. For every moment of happiness I've seen on Griegos Road,

I've also picked up on the tiniest vibes of dread, loathing, jealousy. I want to know if this is part of love.

When Andy popped the question all those months ago, Darleine says she put off telling her cadre of drinking buddies—Dawn, Val, Deb—about her engagement for two weeks. They all went out for drinks one night. "I have something to tell you," she said to them, bringing out her ring. Their response was happiness. Yet there was also, from these single women addressing one leaving their ranks, a half-joking, half-serious jealousy: "I hate you."

Why get married?

Darleine says: "I think people who don't get married by the time they're, you know, like early thirties . . . they don't have much of a life."

Andy tsks aloud, sitting up.

"Oh, sí, Dar," he says, giving her a disapproving nudge on the thigh.

"No, I mean, here they are getting older and they're not with someone serious and all they do is go out all the time," she says. "I just, I just think it's nice to have someone there. Someone just to . . . there's nothing wrong with those people who don't ever get married. . . . There's not really pressure. I don't think. Nowadays nobody is married anymore."

We had talked about it, just like joking around, saying, "Well, when I marry you . . ." But nothing serious.

In October 1991, he took her up to Sandia Peak Tramway, a cable-suspension gondola that crawls up another 6,000 feet through jagged crevices to the crest of the Sandia Mountains and a ski area that is closed most of the year. Overlooking the city, they had dinner at the High Finance Restaurant, which is where people in Albuquerque sometimes go when they want to feel fancy, or see their world twinkle and blink and ripple in the haze and gridded city sprawl far below. Andy said he had a surprise.

"We were waiting for the tram to take us back down," Darleine says. "We're sitting there and I hear this little noise. I said, 'What is that? What are you doing?' He pulled out the ring and said, what was it, 'Will you make me the happiest man?'"

Or something like that.

Andy remembers: "I said, 'Will you make me happy and marry me?'"

Back at the Garcia house that night, Andy and Darleine sat on the big den couch with Lucille across from them, Danny in his recliner, watching TV.

Andy fidgeted. Darlene nudged him. They giggled. Finally, after the ten o'clock news, Danny stood up and said he was going to bed: "Why do you guys look so nervous?"

Andy stood up. "There was another reason why we went up to the tram," he said, taking the ring from his pocket.

Lucille hugged them both and cried.

My dad likes Andy. He said, "Well, if this is what you guys want, we stand behind you."

Andy Barboa reads every word of two newspapers every day, memorizes whole seasons' worth of sports scores at a time, yells at ten-year-old baseball players, fights with umpires, carouses around with friends, makes a funny joke out of seemingly humorless moments, won spelling bees as a boy, and yet he cannot begin to tell you, in words, his feelings. Or maybe he won't tell. Life, he says, is "good." The game, he says, went "good." Work today was "good." And Darleine. Darleine is "great," and so he will marry her. "We always get along real good. Joking around and laughing," he says. "We knew the same people. . . . I don't know. I asked her because we have a good time with each other. She's a good girl."

A bedroom will be empty.

After that October night at the tram, a wedding machine was set in motion. Lucille Garcia, fresh from her role as Mother of the Bride from daughter Denise's wedding, set about planning, with Darleine, a big-budget sequel: Bigger, more, with a returning cast of all the regulars and dozens of extras.

Another bad dream I have is where I'm walking down the aisle and no-
body is looking at me or anything. And then everyone is saying how
they're not going to go to the reception. So we get to the reception and
nobody is there. It's just . . . no one is there. And we don't get presents
or anything. Eee, it's sad.

"Good morning, *mi'ja*," Danny says. "Thirty-six days left."

Darleine is concerned about presents. American Home Furnishings, where all her patterns and colors and styles are meticulously
registered, has called to say her china pattern has been discontin-
ued. With the bridal shower just three days away, the prospect of
not getting any place settings—any at all—angers her. She has an
argument, over the phone, with a store employee. She eats a package of Oreos. She cries. Eventually, a new pattern, "Black Midnight," is selected. Darleine frets that maybe someone tried to buy
her a place setting and couldn't.

On that following Sunday afternoon, some 150 women sit in a
large hotel ballroom and politely "ooh" as Darleine unwraps her
stack of presents. There is a buffet of sandwiches and a large,
white cake with cherry filling and vanilla icing. Lucille has a camcorder; she makes Darleine stand in front of the hotel sign that
reads "Garcia Bridal Shower" for a picture.

Time for a little game. Everyone fills out a "Kitchen Quiz—So
you think you know food? Below are foods and drinks that every
bride should know. . . ." Are shallots a small onion or a seafood?
Gnocchi—is it Italian pasta or a bread made from corn meal?
Vichyssoise—a mild white sauce or soup made from potatoes? The
running joke in the Garcia family, among the women, is that Darleine has never cooked in her life. Getting married has brought her,
so far, a set of sixty-nine-dollar-a-pan steel Swedish cookware,
"deluxe" cutlery, serving platters, and twelve place settings of
"Black Midnight." It has brought her multiple settings of silver-
ware, two pressure cookers, potholders of every shape and size,
strainers, spatulas, slicers, dicers, cookbooks, a food processor, mixing bowls, cutting boards, and so many drinking glasses that "I'm

going to break them if we get any more." Darleine's only claim to fame is macaroni and cheese.

Andy ate four bowls of it.

There is great emphasis on "the take" in this whole affair. Jokes are openly made about gift swapping in this wave of summer weddings, and returns are taken back with the nonchalance of drive-thru. You get, you take back, you get something else, you write a thank-you note—it's all face value. Whole conversations revolve around how much cash will flow into the "money box" that will sit prominently near the gift table at the reception, and how much they'll get for dollar dances with the bride and groom.

Darleine was adamant about establishing an entire household of goods and furnishings before the wedding. With their combined monthly net income of $2,500, and credit from department stores, she and Andy bought two new sofas, a coffee table, bedroom furniture, a glass-top kitchen table, and chairs made of curved, tubular metal. Tall, silk-flower arrangements in black, red, and teal top off the small living room. An imitation Patrick Nagel print hangs on the wall. Darleine's exercise equipment was moved into the house about a month before the wedding—perfect for Andy to hang wet towels and jeans on. Her hundreds of sweaters, shirts, skirts, dresses, shoes, and everything else are slowly migrating from Danny and Lucille Garcia's house to what Darleine refers to as "the other house." In their bright-pink future bedroom, the marital bed is first set against the west wall, then it is decided it should be against the north wall. As soon as the frame is tight and mattresses even, Darleine makes the bed. "The room seems small," she says, tucking pink sheets under the mattress. "This feels strange."

■　■　■

He gets a bad temper when he drinks. He's never hit me or anything like that. But he'll yell. And I can yell. I'm pretty much calm, but once

*I get mad, that's it. Within an hour we'll call each other. What are you
doing? Are you ironing? Are you watching TV, turn to this channel—
it never really lasts. But we don't fight real bad.*

Pre-Cana classes, the Catholic Church's version of engagement
counseling and second thoughts for God, taught Andy and Darleine
the standards:

Never give each other the silent treatment.

Go to church and bring the babies up Catholic.

Darleine and Andy met four times with a Catholic sponsor couple. These sessions were spent talking, praying, and reading from
the Bible. They had cake and ice cream afterward. This probably
will be the extent of Andy and Darleine's church life, as neither is
the Mass-every-Sunday type. The babies will get baptized, receive
First Communion, and so on. The church fiesta comes around
every year. There's always Christmas and Easter. One night, the
topic of divorce comes up. Like all engaged couples, Andy and Darleine swear it won't happen.

Andy's parents divorced when he was five, but he is quick to
point out that his mother, Celeste Medina, has been married to his
stepfather, David Medina, for sixteen years. His brother, Jerry, just
split from his wife of seven years. His stepbrother, David Jr., also is
going through a separation, after four years of marriage.

Darleine sees it this way: "I see my parents, who have been married twenty-seven years, and my grandparents, who have been married fifty years, and see them happily married, and Andy, he has
seen what people do go through when they get divorced, so maybe
it's good for both of us. Maybe he wouldn't want to go through that
like his brothers have."

Pre-Cana offered a series of compatibility tests, which Andy
says he and Darleine aced. They were given a chance to write down
the things they would change about each other, and each gave almost predictable answers: He wishes she didn't shop all the time;
she wishes he wouldn't watch so much sports. "You're not normal if
you don't fight," Darleine says. "Everyone fights."

■ ■ ■

*The guys always have a bachelor party. This is just us girls saying,
"Hey, we can have fun, too." It doesn't mean anything. I am going to
get really drunk. I can't wait.*

"Never fear, Lucille is here!" Darleine's mother shouts as she walks
through the kitchen and into the den with a tray of shot glasses
filled with tequila, Darleine's favorite. Twenty-five women scream
and cheer. Crepe paper has been strung across the ceiling. Two
bright-yellow condoms dangle above, stapled to the crepe paper. A
vat of vodka-soaked fruit punch sits in the kitchen. Danny has
been banished to his son-in-law's house, where he and Ronnie are
watching the baby and the NBA playoffs. An hour into Darleine's
bachelorette party and most everyone is sauced, dressed in miniskirts and heels, ready to party. More gifts for Darleine: Lingerie
and crotchless panties and love oils and, her favorite, a lipstick
that when you twist it, becomes an erect penis, "And look," she
says. "It has little veins."

Squeals fill the house.

"Cake time!" Lucille shouts, bringing out a chocolate-cherry
cake in the shape of a male torso. Coconut hair on the chest. Pink
icing testicles. And the pièce de résistance, the squealing by now so
loud you wonder why the neighbors haven't called the cops: a giant,
erect, chocolate penis.

"Eat it!"

"Eat it!"

OK, Darleine says. But first another shot. Tequila all around again.

She kneels before the coffee table, looking over this obscene
confection, holds her long hair back, and bites down.

Getting loopy now on icing and Cuervo, the party continues and
relocates, via a caravan of Honda Preludes and Ford Probes and
Chevy Luminas uptown along Interstate 40, to Café de Ville, disco
of the desperados, a hovel of high hair and Spandex all set to thun-
dering dance music. While the bachelorette part moves inside to

the core of the nightclub, Dawn, Val, and Denise wait at the door for the stripper.

He arrives wearing a tight-fitting, pseudo-Navy officer's uniform with white gloves, his hair moussed-up in an Andre Agassi mane. He introduces himself (Ryan), and talks over the details with Darleine's friends.

"OK, how does this work?" Val asks.

"Where's the bride?" he says. "I'll just come up on her and start my dancing."

The friends hand him his sixty-five-dollar fee.

Suddenly he's behind Darleine, on the dance floor. He taps her on the shoulder. A hit song by Marky Mark and the Funky Bunch is playing: "Yeah. Canyoufeelitbaby? I can too. It's just a good vibration/ It's just a suhhweeeet sensation!"

Two women at a table across from the dance floor watch as Darleine participates in her own humiliation.

"I can't see. What's happening?" one of the women asks the other.

"Oh, god," says the other. "He's peeling off the uniform now. He's, no way, yes, he's making this woman kneel on the floor. Stand on the table so you can see." The other woman strains for a look. A crowd has gathered around, clapping and laughing.

"He's got his crotch in her face! She's sticking money in his G-string! Oh, god. I would kill my friends if they did that."

"I think," the other woman says, "it's kind of neat."

Back on Griegos Road, in the North Valley, Danny Garcia has figured it's safe to come home by now. He unlocks the door and steps into his quiet den, turns on the light, contemplates the melting chocolate erection, the remnants of a pink-icing testicle on the carpet, shakes his head, turns out the light, and goes to bed.

Darleine dances on:

> I'm too sexy for my shirt
> Too sexy for my shirt
> So sexy it hurts. . . .

Guys are perverts.

A week passes and it is again Saturday night, and forty or so men are standing around in the backyard of Ronnie Nuñez's parents' house, a pink adobe nestled in the maze of narrow streets off Indian School Road. Andy, appearing loose and talkative in a way we have not seen him before, is leaving the edge of sobriety, dressed in black jeans, a green sport shirt, and snakeskin boots.

Jerry Barboa Jr., twenty-seven, who is Andy's older brother and who is one of the groomsmen, who himself eloped seven years ago to Las Vegas, Nevada, and who now has split from his wife and moved back to Albuquerque, wonders aloud if his little brother's wedding hasn't become a kind of Frankenstein monster, a beast no one can control. "Everyone is getting on everyone else's nerves. Little things are becoming big things," Jerry says. "I think everyone agrees it's getting too big. But, it'll all be over soon. I can't wait for it to be over." He's drinking a Coke, the only person in this whole wedding saga who appears, with any success, to be on the wagon.

Danny Garcia, wearing white cotton pants and dark sunglasses, stands over by the adobe wall and talks to his brother Abel. He points to many of the men at the party and explains to me, quietly, which of these men have been in trouble with the law, and which of them he coached in Little League, and which are good kids, and which he considers to be fallen.

A voice, shouting. It is Andy's younger brother, Danny Barboa, twenty-four: "The bitches are here."

"Okay, listen up," he then shouts to the men, who gather around: the "bitches"—two strippers named Christina and Skye, hired for the night from their regular jobs at TD's Show Club for $240 (plus $30 for their armed, surly bodyguard)—are waiting inside. First, they'll dance for Andy and then they'll dance for everybody for tips, and if somebody touches them at all, the party's over. "Get it?" Danny Barboa says, "No touching."

All of the men go into the house. Andy is seated in a chair in the middle of the living room. Those who don't fit in the living room spill over into the kitchen. They hoot and growl and laugh, as the sound of a Guns N' Roses song explodes, with too much treble, from the radio on the counter. It must be eighty-five degrees inside. From the bathroom, Christina and Skye saunter out and begin their routine, under the watchful glower of the bodyguard. They shake and strut around Andy—a blonde and brunette, white lace and black lace, a sleazy wiggle, a shimmy, hands on Andy's shoulders, his face, his arms. His eyes go glassy and scan the room—all his friends whooping and yelling—to rest, momentarily, on the un-blinking eyes of his soon to be father-in-law, Danny Garcia.

The instant lingers. Danny leaves. Sitting in the dark out back, next to the bone-dry beer keg, he explains: "I figured it would be a better time for Andy if I stay out here. He's a good man. He'll be good to Darleine. I don't want to ruin his party." Inside the house, the screams and music get louder. The strippers are now at the tip-ping stage of their ninety-minute routine, which allows for Andy and everyone else to eat whipped cream off their bare nipples, for a price.

The men wait with $10 bills in their fists. Christina and Skye each cup one breast in one hand and squirt whipped cream on with the other hand. Each man then sucks the cream off, but the women have the process down to such efficiency that no nipple barely touches any mouth. They jerk the breast away, wipe it off with a towel, and move on to the next man, all of which goes on for a half hour, the men lining up for this macho communion.

Jerry stands near the kitchen doorway and shakes his head and does bachelor-party mathematics: All these guys drank all this beer, and now with strippers added into the mix—and just then a cal-loused hand reaches from the sofa and slaps one of the strippers on the rear. Christina and Skye angrily retreat to the bathroom and, de-spite Danny Barboa's feverish negotiating with the bodyguard, a rule has been broken and the women are leaving. In the sudden ab-sence of music, there is tension.

"This is your fault," yells Danny Barboa to a drunken-eyed man on the couch.

"Whassht? I, ah, I didn' do nuthinsh," he stammers.

Danny waves his beer at the man. "You have ruined the party. It's over."

By now we are in the front yard, being regaled by beer breath and story after story of how "Andy is my *bro*, you see, he's like a brother to me, man," and, this from another glassy-eyed partyer: "We are like this close, we go back to childhood, you see? I love Andy, you see?" After the strippers leave, but before Andy's friend Gilbert beats up a guy named Robert (whom no one invited), and way before Robert comes back angrily with a group of his bros and way, way before a bigger fight breaks out in front of the Nuñez house, and certainly before someone breaks some guy's jaw, before any of this occurs, I left.

I had gone with my friends to Bennigan's and was coming home and I pulled up in my parents' driveway and there were all these guys, about, I don't know, maybe twenty guys all around my car. And at first I was scared, I didn't know what was going on. And then I saw Andy. And one of the guys, you know, you could see blood on him and I just said, "I don't even want to hear about it." I just went inside.

For a while, Andy and Darleine aren't speaking.

But there is too much to be done. There is a wedding, something that cannot be stopped. There is a twenty-seven-inch television to pick up at the store, Father's Day gifts to buy, a snafu with the remaining balance due at the Convention Center, hair appointments, and rings to be soldered together.

Darleine wanted to go on being mad at Andy, but here is what she remembers from those Bible study sessions in Pre-Cana: Never, said the priest, give each other the silent treatment.

■　■　■

That other dream, that third dream I told you I didn't remember? OK. My mom remembered it. It was really strange. Andy and I were getting in a stagecoach to go to our wedding. And we couldn't find the church. Finally, we get to the church and we're really late and they start doing my makeup and do my eye makeup like a clown. Clown makeup.

Good morning, *mi'ja*. One more day.

These are the final forty-eight hours, and no one has slept. To-day, tuxedos aren't fitting on one side of town and dresses aren't fitting on another side of town and Griegos Road is quiet in the late afternoon. But for a minute, let the story not be about Dar-leine, or Andy, or hairpieces or glitter, or chocolate penises, or any of that. Now hear another voice, soft and calm, sitting at the dining-room table with her caffeine-free Diet Coke, a voice be-longing to a woman with all the time in the world. Someone who cannot bear what she sees on television, all that kissing and nu-dity. "I just get up and leave the room. Kids today, they're so wild now. I remember back when we didn't worry about being raped or nothing."

Grandma Flora Perez, seventy-five, Lucille Garcia's mother, has come from her son's house in Alameda to stay at the Garcias, for no apparent reason other than to hold her great-grandbaby, watch the last-minute wedding hassles unfold, and trade nagging jibes with her son-in-law.

"What's for dinner?" Grandma Perez asks.

"You can't eat," Danny Garcia says, winking. "You haven't cleaned the house yet. We don't have no free lunch here."

She swats the air, makes a face at him.

Danny can't resist.

"When she dies, I'm going to have her buried upside down, so when she tries to claw out of the coffin, she'll just go down deeper in the ground."

"*When* I die," she says, waving a finger at him, "I'm going to come back in the middle of the night and pull on your legs. You just wait."

The phone is ringing and ringing, mostly Darleine's friends, or Andy or Denise or Ronnie, and finally Grandma Perez just takes it off the hook. Feh. The baby is sleeping. Danny goes on the roof to fix the air conditioner. Stomp, stomp, clank, clank. At last, the ninety-degree heat will be broken, somewhat, with a blast of cool air.

Grandma Perez remembers her husband, Frank. He died fifteen years ago. Lung cancer. Left Flora alone, and comes back to her, she says, once in a while, in dreams. They had a nice wedding, she says. 1937. The mariachis followed Frank and Flora through the streets of Martineztown.

He used to take her on hunting trips, with little Lucille and their two sons, Frank Jr. and Fidel, up to northern New Mexico.

Don't say anything, don't make a sound, Frank would tell Flora. *You'll scare everything away.*

She sat on a rock to smoke a cigarette. Frank was looking ahead. Behind him, a giant stag walked out of the trees. Grandma Perez is re-creating this years-ago scene. "I was moving my head, like this, going 'Tsst, tsst.' Ay, that fool! He wouldn't turn around. Finally I say, 'You idiot it's right here!' Well, of course it ran away and he yelled at me."

She looks out the window. He was a good man. He demanded respect. Would their son, she wonders aloud, have gotten a divorce if Frank were alive? Would there be all this cussing and drinking in the world? "If he were alive I think things would be so different," she says. "'Oh Frank,' I say to him, 'Why did you leave me?'"

If you wanted a crazy family, this is it.

Images ebb and flow. Present and past collide. Uncle Abel, Danny's brother, dancing around the dining room with a laundry basket on his head. Four-year-old Darleine falling off a chair and breaking her arm. Danny picking the bugs off his menagerie of beheaded fauna. The family funeral where the corpse fell out of the casket—remember that? Lucille going to the grocery store to get Fruity Pebbles, Cocoa Pebbles, and Cocoa Puffs because Darleine asked for one of them but she doesn't remember which. The big ice chest, the one that goes on hunting trips, is in the garage, full of beer. Two ready-made lasagnas are cooking in Lucille's oven; three more are cooking next door in Denise's oven, all for the rehearsal dinner tonight outside behind the house. Our Lady of Guadalupe Church is stuffy and hot. Everyone gathers outside, waiting for the rehearsal.

Images ebb and flow. The bridesmaids and groomsmen lining

up. Slow down, slow down. Start over. An ornate church-aisle choreography: Danny Barboa, best man, meets Denise Nuñez, matron
of honor, halfway down the aisle. Celeste Medina and Jerry Barboa
Sr. hold Andy's hand. Danny Garcia and Darleine come down the
aisle, pick up Lucille at the second pew and a football huddle of
hugs and handshakes follows.

And then it's just Andy and Darleine and the priest and the altar.
The Reverend Ernest Montoya quickly runs over the Mass with
Darleine and Andy. "Now will be the offertory, and the mothers will
bring up the gifts. . . ." Montoya says. Andy perks up.

"We get presents here, too?" he asks.

"Eee, Andy," Darleine says, knocking him in the shoulder. "He's
talking about the Communion."

They practice the whole thing again, before everyone walks back
down the aisle, out of the church, and back across Griegos for
lasagna, *bizcochitos,* and beer. Andy and Darleine stay behind, for
one last matter with Father Montoya. It has been so long. Neither
knows the Act of Contrition. Or even how to start, *Forgive me Father* . . . Andy goes first, and then it's Darleine's turn.

Andy's confession lasts two minutes and fifty-four seconds.

Darleine's lasts two minutes and twenty-nine seconds.

They walk back to the house alone, holding hands.

■ ■ ■

*Well, you know how all the guys left the party to go drinking at
Leonardo's. I was up all night and I kept calling the house, waiting for
Andy to get home. And there's no answer. It's like three in the morning. I go over to Denise's window and I'm all, "Denise! Wake up! I
need to go down to the house and see if Andy's there." I get her up and
we go down there and we look in the window and he's all asleep on the
floor. I said, "Andy! Why didn't you answer the phone?" He's like,
"Come in, come in."*

*I said, "No, you can't see me on the wedding day. You've caused me
enough bad luck already."*

*I finally went to sleep at five and Dawn calls at seven. Look at me.
I'm shaking.*

Morning. The Twentieth of June, circled on every calendar in the house. Over at North Valley Little League, the Calmat White Sox, wearing black-ribbon armbands because "Coach Barboa has to kiss the bride today," win their game 11–1 and dump an Igloo cooler of water on Andy. Darleine is at the salon, having her long hair twisted round and pinned up and shellacked into place and the veil pinned on securely. She drives home the long way down Guadalupe Trail, sipping a large Coke from Blake's Lotaburger, hoping Andy won't see her.

She sits in her room and looks around at the things that aren't going with her. A Valley High cheerleader's megaphone. Stuffed animals on a high shelf. The alarm clock says 12:30 p.m.

And now the makeup lady is here, lugging cases of Mary Kay. She takes before and after pictures of Darleine to enter in a Mary Kay contest. If they win, the makeup lady and Darleine get to go to Dallas for a Mary Kay convention. The portrait photographer is here, metering light sources and shaking hands. The video lady is here, rounding out the eerie, complete documentary of a house on Wedding Day. Grandma Perez's slip is showing. Bridesmaids are all finally here, nervous blurs of shiny blue taffeta going from the bedroom to the bathroom. Danny Garcia is fumbling with cufflinks. Darleine is eating a bowl of Fruity Pebbles. The baby is crying.

The bride emerges.

The photographer is ready. Now let's have one with the sister. Now the mother, now the father. Now both. Now just the bride. Now with the grandmothers. Good, good. Excellent, good. One more of just the bride. Good.

The limousine is here. Darleine stands in her room and cries for a brief moment and comes into the kitchen, downs a shot of tequila with her bridesmaids, and walks out into the hot sun.

In the sacristy behind the altar, Andy paces. Celeste straightens his tie. Danny Barboa pulls at his own jacket cuffs. There are 300 people sitting in the pews. The church's air conditioner is rattling. The procession song begins, "Que bonita/Que bonita. . . ." Danny Garcia wraps his daughter's arm around his own.

Sweat on Danny's forehead. Tradition over taste. Your kids grow up and move away. An empty room. Good morning, *mi'ja*. Forgive me, Father. A truck backing down the long driveway onto Griegos Road. The big ice chest. Icing rushes: a cliff to leap from, a shot of tequila, a diamond, a blur.

This is it. Oh, god.
Ohgodohgodohgod.

■　■　■

About an hour and a half after the marriage of Mr. and Mrs. Andy Barboa, the newspaper reporter is standing, in his only suit, outside the Albuquerque Convention Center, when, at long last, two white stretch limousines finally pull up with sixteen drunken passengers, having tooled the wedding party all over town, so that traffic could honk at them, and they could honk back. Darleine Barboa emerges streetside and swigs down the last of her Jack Daniel's Lynchburg Lemonade. A glass in the limo breaks and cuts Denise Nuñez's knee and for a minute, right here, it looks as if Ronnie Nuñez and Danny Barboa will erupt in a boozy brawl.

Jerry Barboa Sr., Andy's father, throws himself between the two men: "I'll kick the shit out of both of you if you don't knock it off!"

Andy grabs his brother by the shoulders. "Cut it out!" he growls, "This is my fucking wedding!"

Something always happens. So everybody has to ruin this now for us.

Tempers cool down in the lobby. Ronnie tells Danny to "Never come near my family again!" The mariachis strike up a song and the entire wedding party marches into the reception, smiles, and struts around the dance floor while the crowd claps. The dancing begins, and a band called the Shysters plays for five hours, running the gamut of rock and romance. The cake is cut; the bride and groom do their dollar dances. Teenage cousins gather in corner tables while kids play hide-and-seek in the lobby. Security guards stand arms folded. At six cash bars, a $2,400 quota is met with ease. Somewhere, somehow, Grandma Perez gets her caffeine-free Diet Coke.

Danny Barboa and Ronnie Nuñez meet at one of the bars. Will they fight? A moment passes, and they are hugging, bragging to the woman bartender about something or another. ("Really," says the bartender, Kathy Stephenson, "there was no text to what they said to each other. It was just that *Bro,* I love you, *bro,* you're family' stuff. This is a pretty classic wedding. I've seen a lot of them. A Budweiser wedding.")

Sagging cummerbunds, a tossed bouquet, "Wooly Bully," and a toast, from a very drunk Danny Barboa: "I love Andy and I love Darleine and I love all you guys, and in twenty-five years bring your silver. I love all these people. Bring your silver in twenty-five years. And . . . that's all I got to say."

A wedding is details. A wedding is everywhere in the summer. It's a line of cars covered with pastel balloons and tissue-paper flowers, honking down Central Avenue, all that elusive happiness speeding by the rest of us. The notions, the drinks, the traditions are served. In the same convention center on the same night, you could drop in on the Sandoval-Lucero wedding, or the Herrera-Rodriguez wedding. What are their stories? What was their budget?

North Valley tradition tells that the bride and groom are supposed to sneak away from all this while everyone is dancing and no one is watching.

Andy and Darleine dash out a side door at five minutes to midnight. Lucille chases after them, yelling, "Darleine, your bag!"

But Andy has picked his wife up in his arms, white dress on white tuxedo, and they are through a revolving door and gone.

■ ■ ■

Felia Garcia, Danny's mother, comes to see her own mother, Monica. It is the morning after Andy and Darleine's wedding. She goes past the front desk to her mother's room, in a nursing home uptown. *Is that you, Felia?*

Yes, Mama.

Great-Grandma Monica is one hundred years old this summer, bedridden with a stroke she had long ago, when Darleine was still a toddler. But she knows some things. She knows there was a wedding, and she knows she missed it, and she wants to hear about it.

And was she pretty?

Yes, Mama.

And was there dancing?

Yes, Mama.

And presents?

Lots of presents, Mama.

Oh, you should have seen it. There are things we can tell Great-Grandma Monica about, and things we cannot tell her, things we should not tell her. Everyone danced "La Marcha." They served green-chile meatballs. There were seven kinds of cake.

Las Vegas, Nevada

The bed was shaking. I jumped out of bed and screamed, "What are you doing?" It was the earthquake. The bed was moving like in The Exorcist *or something. We were trying to get all our money and the rings and get out of the room, but by that time it was all over. The water was splashing back and forth out of the swimming pool. . . . Las Vegas was okay, but they didn't give us the room we wanted. They had already given away our honeymoon suite, so they put us way in the back in this 1960s room with an old TV. We didn't win any money. We lost, gosh, I guess about six hundred dollars. But it was a good time.*

We had fun and that's what counts.

(1992)

Invisible Airplane

Prequel Dreams

One thing that happened in the spring of 1983 was that my life un-hinged, slightly, and no one around me noticed. This is a universal story in the galaxy. In the social order of high school, I fell from a middle-tier popularity grace between the eighth and ninth grades, and never reescalated. My body, on the other hand, had shot up nine inches two summers before. I took to wearing a drab trench-coat every day that spring, long before drab trenchcoats meant any-thing at all. I did as Yoda said—hid my feelings, stayed wary of the dark side (to which I was understandably attracted). My parents di-vorced on the twenty-second of March that year, after almost three decades of marriage, and Luke Skywalker and I were both having problems with our fathers. At the Catholic high school I attended, the afternoons always ended badly, in my seventh-period freshman algebra class. I who had tested so highly in aptitude had met a kind of math I could not conquer. Girls in pep club uniforms, previously stupid, had managed to crack algebra's codes and meanings, and yet I could not. Who could expect me to? It was like I was already dead.

D is for dead.

D is what I was making in algebra.

D is for Death Star, which I drew on countless spiral notebook pages, sitting in the far back row on what seemed like thousands of afternoons of algebra in the spring of 1983, a time of my life I can still smell and see and touch. Entire pages were given over to the Imperial armada and the half-constructed Death Star floating over the small forest moon of Endor, a picture of which I tore out of a *Newsweek* magazine in the school library, where I used to dwell during lunch hours. On other spiral pages were occasional attempts to factor polynomials and comprehend basic logarithms. I didn't show these drawings to anyone, because *Star Wars* was old by then. At fourteen, there was no longer any currency to the ownership of action figures. It happens that I still own the textbook from freshman algebra. On the inside back cover of the book, I apparently listed the date of every Wednesday from the middle of February 1983 to the end of May 1983. I underlined Wednesday, May 25, several times. They are all crossed out, my weeks of waiting for *Return of the Jedi*. Finding those hashmarks fills me with a sense of joy and pain. How badly I waited, and what the world felt like then.

Do or do not. There is no try.

I am your father.

It is useless to resist.

One place I liked was the comic-book store, which I visited weekly. They always seemed to be playing Rush or Styx on the stereo. A British guy worked there most days, and that passed for exotic in my town. A copy of the *Return of the Jedi* comic book arrived weeks before the movie—an accidental early shipment from the publisher that wound up in comic-book stores across the land, which set off a flurry of alarms in Lucasland. The British salesguy tacked the comic, swathed in a plastic bag, high above the register with a "Not for Sale" sticker on it. He forbade anyone to read it. "You'll ruin the movie for yourself," he warned us. "Why would you want to do that?"

It disappeared when he wasn't looking; probably when he walked next door to the 7-Eleven. Secrets got out: Luke Skywalker and Princess Leia are brother and sister. Darth Vader gets killed at the end.

The yelling about it, the intrigue of who took it, the accusations, the revelations.

A few weeks later, on May 25, *Return of the Jedi* earned $6,219,629 in box-office receipts in a single twenty-four-hour period, a record which stood for some time, and a record in which I took a certain pride in partial responsibility. I was in line, at the NorthPark 4 in the NorthPark Mall, all day, with my cousin. We were surrounded by kids and adults who had a similar compulsion—people just like me, but to whom I did not speak, generally. What I'm trying to sort out is this: Some kids needed *Star Wars* worse than others, and we went on needing it, for the rest of our lives, almost but not quite ever getting what we required from it. I saw it, and then I saw it again that night, and then I saw it again three days later on the night that my father usually came over to the house to take me out for pizza and a movie. Usually we saw dramas (*An Officer and a Gentleman*) or T & A comedies. That night we watched Luke Skywalker defeat and then reconcile with his enemy father. This seemed to not apply to us at all, but I remember wanting it to.

Houston, Texas: 1998

Smart, anonymous sources report that the hairstyles on the teenage space queen, played by an actress named Natalie Portman, "will put Princess Leia to shame." Then comes not terribly reliable and unofficial news that Samuel L. Jackson, as a Jedi Knight, will be the first character to utter "May the Force be with you." There will be Ewan McGregor and Liam Neeson and Yoda and a nine-year-old boy as young Darth Vader. Snitches sent details and pictures from the film's sets in Tunisia, Italy, and Great Britain, and somehow most of this gossip was first channeled through Texas.

It will come out a year from this point—Taco Bell promotions and all—and perhaps earn $200 million in its first week alone.

Beyond this, who knows?

Scott Chitwood knows, in a spare bedroom of the far northwest Houston home he and his wife just bought, a place quietly hidden in freshly budded subdivisions with patchwork lawns. Scott knows because "Bothan Spy" knows, and Bothan Spy knows because he (or she) worked on a British movie set, got hold of paperwork originating from Lucasfilm Ltd., and developed an itchy fax finger. So Scott knows, and his best friend, Darin, in Lewisville, Texas, knows and, sure, Carl in Atlanta knows, and of course Harry Knowles in Austin knows all, and Harry often claims to have known it first. The Internet gossip Matt Drudge knows. And because these men know, hundreds of thousands of people know, across a virtual parking lot of impatient fans. They know a little bit more every day.

"We're like the kids who peeked at our Christmas presents," admits John P. Benson, twenty-five, a supermarket manager in Georgia who knows.

What, exactly, do they all know?

"We know that it's going to be the coolest thing to ever happen, for one," says Carl Cunningham, twenty-six, from his home in suburban Atlanta, where he conspires with John from a basement crammed floor to ceiling with beloved *Star Wars* junk. Together they publish a Prequel Watch Web site, devoted to finding out as much as they can about "Episode I," the still-untitled, $115-million *Star Wars* movie to be released a year from the time all this flurry was taking place—May 19, 1999. It's hard to know if the fans are ready for the truth, and in struggling with whether or not to tell the secrets of the new *Star Wars,* Carl ponders a picture taped to his computer of himself at age six, in the late 1970s, standing in a church parking lot between somebody dressed as Darth Vader and somebody dressed as an Imperial stormtrooper. "This little boy," Carl says, "is why I do what I do. When all this stuff gets so serious and people start arguing and all the rumors go around, I look at the picture. I don't want to ruin the movie for this little boy."

■   ■   ■

Little boys. Yes. Completely about little boys and their mental well-being. "C'mon, it's just a movie," says Jeanne Cole, a cagey if cheerful spokeswoman from Lucasfilm Ltd., in San Rafael, California, the first and only person to tell me, in the course of writing this story, that Episode I is just a movie—even as it is her job to promote it as something larger than life.

Normally I'd agree that it really is only a movie, except for the hundreds of men, and some women, most of them of a particular age group (mine), who are each afflicted, to some degree, with prequel fever, and who have divulged to me the bits and pieces of dreams they've been having about the prequel in their sleep. After waiting sixteen years on the edge of a confusing and noisy millennium, they have dreams in which they are finally seeing a fourth *Star Wars*. They have bad dreams laced with anxiety and impossibly awful scenes, of stormtroopers singing Broadway numbers, and six-shooting Jedis with John Wayne accents riding horseback. They have tragic dreams of inadequacy and letdown, where they are locked out of twenty-four-screen cineplexes and miss the prequel. They have godly dreams where George Lucas—"the Flanneled One," in fanboy parlance—becomes a personal friend or beneficent employer; dreams where they wield lightsabers and triumph over darkness.

Your basic archetypal tangle of love and anticipation and letdown.

"Whereas we think in periods of years, the unconscious thinks and lives in terms of millennia. So when something happens that seems to us an unexampled novelty, it is generally a very old story indeed. We still forget, like children, what happened yesterday." (Carl Jung right there, in: *The Archetypes and the Collective Unconscious*, 1939.)

A collective unconscious chews its nails. A collective unconscious dreams the movie is a bomb. "Sequel" is a word from the French medical books, *sequelle*, suggesting aftermath. Now comes "prequelle," rooted in another medical term, suggesting "symptom." "All of it very, very interesting," says Charles Dominey, a Jungian analyst, as I sit in a black leather and Scandinavian teak easy chair in his darkened Zilker Park office, just off the Loop 1 freeway in Austin. For weeks in the spring of 1998, I had been posting to Web sites like Carl Cunningham's Prequel Watch asking *Star Wars* fans, young and old, to share with me any dreams they had been having about the impending release of George Lucas's new space epic. I received back more than 200 replies, most from North Americans, and a few from Europe and Australia, and one from Mexico. I asked for Dominey's help—he was one of the few Jungian therapists practicing near where I lived—so I could, in the classic way, sort the dreams by motif, and examine any Jungian "affect" within a generational psyche. When I get to his office, Dominey has dug up his video copy of the original *Star Wars* and has it playing. A rotund air purifier inhales and exhales in the center of the room. ("R2-D2," the doctor says, as a joke, as I open up my manilla case folder of prequel dreams.)

■ ■ ■

Not such a long time ago, not that far away . . . A Saturday in March 1996 to be exact, in the Memorial Student Center at Texas A&M University in College Station. A thousand or so science-fiction fans gathered to talk shop and trade Boba Fett action figures at the annual "Aggiecon," and, almost accidentally, the "spoiling" of *Star Wars: Episode I* began.

Consider the amazed little boy who lives in all men (or the warrior princess who lives in certain women) and you start to understand, breathing in the pulpy smell of treasure: There were tables and tables of comic-book dealers and toy collectors, and the movie-poster vendors, and the heavy-set married couples who peddle bootlegged copies of Japanese cartoons. There were Trekkers (there always are) preaching a different universal gospel, and *X-File*-philes examining UFO conspiracies and freeze-frames of Agent Scully's décolletage.

Two minions of the Empire arrived, special guests, wearing polo shirts and Dockers, dispatched on newsy business from Skywalker Ranch in Marin County, California: One was Howard Roffman, the head of licensing for Lucasfilm Ltd., and the other was Steve Sansweet, the company's head of "fan relations." They ascended a dais in a lecture hall as Aggiecon attendees crowded in—even the disdainful Trekkers, who never trusted *Star Wars*, thematically or otherwise.

The lights went down. A large video screen sizzled, blinked.

"We were the first fans to find out any of this great, new stuff," recalls Scott Chitwood, twenty-five, who was, at the time, a civil engineering grad student at A&M. "It was pretty rare for Lucasfilm to come out and officially say anything." After a nostalgic Luke Skywalker "Underoos" commercial from the 1970s, the fans were shown footage-in-progress of the "special edition" rerelease of the original 1977 *Star Wars* and its enormously successful sequels, 1980's *The Empire Strikes Back* and 1983's *Return of the Jedi* (known as Episodes IV, V, and VI). Each film, it was confirmed, was being digitally spiffed up for rerelease in 1997. Long dormant as both Zeitgeist and cash cow, the *Star Wars* franchise would be brought back from cold storage. There would, Roffman explained, be more and neater toys, multimedia computer games, holographic trading cards, serialized novels, and so on, down to "Spirit of Obi-Wan" giveaways on Doritos chip bags, product tie-ins sailing among the TIE fighters.

Then the men from Lucasfilm said the magic word: *prequel.*

A thousand grownups were suddenly children again. Work on the *Star Wars* prequels—the adventures of Jedi Knights set thirty or forty years before the events of the first trilogy—had begun, Roffman said. George Lucas had written a script. Locations were being scouted, actors were auditioning to play youthful versions of Obi-Wan Kenobi and Darth Vader. A new class of software animators in Marin County would do the heavy lifting of special effects. Episode I was being targeted for the turn of the century. During a question and answer session the next day, Scott—who stands nearly six feet six inches tall and looks like the sandy-haired, next-door ideal—raised his hand. "What would Lucasfilm do if George Lucas suddenly died?"

Several people in the audience turned toward Scott, registering mild shock. ("I thought it was a legitimate question," Scott recalls. "[*Star Trek* creator] Gene Roddenberry had recently died, and [Trekkers] were up in arms about how the characters and storylines were being treated.")

Roffman shrugged. A world without the Flanneled One had never been considered.

Back in his dorm room, Scott fretted that "We had all this cool information, and no one to tell." Naturally, they all logged on. Shooed away from official *Star Wars* newsgroups, and using full computer access at A&M's aerospace lab, Scott and his college roommate Darin Smith soon created a fan page called TheForce.Net, intending to just worship and stargaze on the Lucasfilm universe.

They stumbled into much more. "If I had known back then about all that I would wind up knowing," Scott says, "I never would have started doing it."

"Lucasfilm is known for its tight security. Well, obviously not that tight, because someone got in, snapped pictures, and sent them to us," Darin says, with a pang of regret. "We've probably tapped out Episode I . . . until they have the advance screenings of it. We'd love to get invited to that—snowball's chance in hell, now."

■   ■   ■

Also in the room at Aggiecon that day was a bespectacled, 300-pound Austin toy collector with curly red hair and meaty arms folded—slightly jaded, but also, like everyone else, a bit enraptured. That same spring he would be flattened by a dolly-cartload full of sci-fi collectibles after an antique show in Austin's City Coliseum. He would have to spend months in bed with a bad back, with only his laptop computer to entertain him, along with his many hundreds of *Star Wars* toys. He started his own Web site of Hollywood rumors.

"It's almost like a drug," says Harry Knowles, twenty-six, who has made himself a semicelebrity with Ain't It Cool News, which often gets 200,000 or more hits a day, a significant part of which was built on prequel spoiling. "You say you don't want to know, but you can't help yourself."

Now he dangles the prequel secrets like baubles. Last year, he came into "a lot" of rumors, and posted a message to his readers asking if they wanted him to reveal "a major plot crux" of Episode I that had been sent to him, he believes, from someone at Lucasfilm. The next morning he logged on and had 7,000 e-mails, two-thirds begging him not to spoil it. "I've seen a lot of the designs and I've read the basic (Episode I) script," Harry boasts, when I catch him on the phone after several days trying, in between his visits to movie locations, L. A. premieres, and other pressing media demands (*Vanity Fair,* the *New York Times, Entertainment Tonight*). At the time, Harry had not yet become the household name (in the hyperwired American household) that he would shortly become. He had not yet written his book, or signed correspondent deals with infotainment news shows. But he is busy; during our chat, his call-waiting beeps eleven times.

"Personally, my confidence in (Lucasfilm) isn't quite there anymore," Harry says. "I was a flag waver in the beginning, saying that this will be the greatest day of our lives, and whatever. I think a lot of people are going to be let down. I see a lot of exactly what we feared—a movie being made to sell toys. You see it in the cast lists, the number of aliens, the number of ship designs. . . . They're planning a massive seven-month (marketing) onslaught."

And when I suggest to him that crap has always been *Star Wars's* middle name, he retreats to the sacrosanct: "Yeah, but for some people it's become a religion. This movie is going to be full of religious overtones. For some people, it replaces God."

. . .

"I have a recurring prequel dream," types a thirty-two-year-old man who by day sells corporate real estate in some gridded burg outside Cleveland, and by night, after an hour or two on the Internet as "Chewieboy," often unwinds with a videocassette in letterbox format, on a twenty-seven-inch Magnavox screen, in Dolby Pro-Logic sound. ("Jason," his wife will call from the other room, "are you watching *The Empire Strikes Back* again?")

Later, asleep, Chewieboy flinching: "I am sitting in a very large theater that I've never been to before. My hands are shaking. We can't believe that we're finally getting to see it. . . . The [20th-Century] Fox fanfare logo starts, and then the 'long time ago in a galaxy far, far away' thing. . . ."

But then the dream goes wrong. "It turns out to be a terrible [movie]. . . . Really dumb stuff, lots of Muppets and cutesy songs. It's the worst feeling. . . . I tell myself, 'It doesn't suck, it doesn't suck.' But it always sucks. . . . I wake up and can't believe it. This movie I waited [more than] half my life for. . . . It's like, 'George! How could you let us down?'"

This combination of devotion and distrust is what brings the *Star Wars* generation together. We are like stockholders without actual stock in the company, and yet have a sizable emotional investment in its success. When *Entertainment Weekly* predicted, more than a year before Episode I was released, that the prequel wouldn't outdo the domestic box-office gross of *Titanic* ($570 million), the Lucasbabies were riled. ("I find your lack of faith disturbing," one reader wrote the magazine, quoting Darth Vader.) In their waking lives, there is giddy, childish preparation; some have already asked off work for the entire fourth week of May 1999. But at night, many prequel dreams touch on a contagiously grown-up—often depressing—cynicism. Many of them dream that the prequel opens and they don't know about it, or can't find the theater, or get the show-times wrong; the rest of the world gets to see it and they don't, a common info-techno-geek paranoia. Others dream of a catastrophic event (fire is recurrent) that cancels the show and destroys the cineplex. Still others dream that it is George Lucas's fault. A twenty-four-year-old art student in Long Beach, California, dreams of leaving the theater so disappointed after the prequel that he can't talk to his friends. A thirty-year-old student in Colorado Springs dreams that the movie plays for ten minutes, before the Jedis break out in song and George Lucas suddenly appears to stop the projector. A twenty-eight-year-old carpenter in St. Louis has a similar dream, where the prequel has cheap spaceships clumsily attached to what is clearly visible as fishing line. That dream ends when the Flanneled One rushes down the aisle screaming, "Stop the film, stop the film," and nervously tells the audience that it will be delayed "another five years." Everyone boos. One guy dreams that Lucas asks for his resumé, and tells him to mail it to a bakery. ("I asked why, and he said, 'Trust me, it'll get to me. . . . '")

"One question is why the unconscious presents the (prequel) dreamers with the prospect that they won't actually get to see it," says Charles Dominey, the Jungian counselor I sought out in Austin. "Each dream means something subjective to that particular dreamer. Somehow these people's psyches are saying that it is going to be denied to them . . . or a failure."

One of the dreamers concluded his dream with, "Someone should hear this other than my wife." Well, Dominey says, the unconscious moves on its own. "Whatever the *Star Wars* movies express about life is somehow more meaningful to them than what is otherwise available—institutions, politics, you name it." The prequel dreams have moments of euphoria and joy (especially when the dreamer ordains him or herself a role in the film) but most of them are sad, cynical, fraught. Nothing works. While many of the dreams foretold ecstasy, many more did not. Dominey suggests it could be an unconscious, simultaneous, collective movement—Jung's "synchronicity," a religious body biding its time, anxiously awaiting a kind of pentecost. Christianity's first millennia, he notes, is strewn with similar dreams, fantasies, longing, and loss. Waiting for God is a bitch.

■ ■ ■

For a dose of the bright side of the Force, I drive from Austin down to Scott Chitwood's house north of Houston on the last day of April, a little more than a year before the release of Episode I. It's a sunny Friday afternoon, and he has the day off from the Shell oil company, where he is a structural engineer. Scott had been hanging close to his home computer all day, on a rumor that 20th Century Fox had scheduled a press conference in Hollywood, perhaps to announce a title for Episode I. Scott wants TheForce.Net to be first with the news. He wants to scoop Harry. (If you split them up by orthodoxy, Scott would be a middle-of-the road spoiler, occasionally leaning toward the wild liberalism of Harry Knowles, who digs the way fans have become a ragtag Rebel Alliance against the Lucas Empire. On the conservative end would be Carl Cunningham at Prequel Watch in Atlanta, shielding the child within. And each considers the other to be friendly competition.)

As it happens, the press-conference tip turns out to be another dud, like a lot of prequel rumors. Like the time "they" said Episode I would have a big underwater battle scene. They've since learned it has a little one, if it goes underwater at all. (In fact, when the *The Phantom Menace*—as the movie was eventually called—is released, an early sequence takes place in Otoh Gunga, an underwater city where giant fish chase the protagonists through sea caves.) Like the time "everyone" said it was going to star some unknown fashion model and Harry immediately found and posted a nude picture of her (an act Scott considered galactically crass). "This happens to us a lot," Scott says. "We spend a lot of time getting people to prove that they know what they're talking about." By "we," Scott means himself and the other fans, and "a lot of time" means volunteering for Web-site duties. Darin Smith, Scott's former roommate at A&M, lives near Dallas now and designs weapon systems for Raytheon, and keeps TheForce.Net's engine running. A guy named Brian Linder in South Carolina gumshoes around the chat rooms, feeding little bits of information back to Scott. Another keeps up on toys and merchandise news—a scoop about *Star Wars* Lego toys was considered a banner day. Another source absconded for the big leagues, taking a full-time spoiling job at a glossy sci-fi magazine.

A Catholic priest in the Netherlands named Roderick Vonhogen creates "virtual edition" interpretations of spoiler news that look like real stills from the movie, down to the pilfered Fox logo. Another fan created a short movie spoof of the *Cops* television show called "Troops," and when word of that spread, TheForce.Net got so much user traffic—30,000 hits a day—that the server crashed.

It's hard not to be taken in by the weenie-ish intrigue of it all. I am briefly fourteen years old again, hanging out at my old comic-book shop. I am elated when I start getting e-mail from "Yodave," who claims to be "inside" the Frito-Lay headquarters in Dallas, privy to some Episode I promotional logos and toy designs under way for potato chip bags, Pepsi cans, and Pizza Hut giveaways. But later I get crafty. Just as I was preparing to drive 200 miles for a secret meeting over secret Fritos to see secret Xerox copies, Yodave tells me the film is going to be called *Star Wars: Genesis,* the lamest rumor afloat, Scott says, and when I confront Yodave on it, he vanishes, and I don't hear from him again.

"You're not actually believing any of it, I hope," says Jeanne Cole, the Lucasfilm spokeswoman of steel, referring me to the *Star Wars* Official Web site and *Star Wars Insider* magazine, the company's house organs (which helpfully include lots of advertising for current toys, trading cards, books, you name it—but only carefully modulated prequel news). "Sure, we're well aware of those guys in Texas, and all the others like them," she says. "The excitement of the fans is very important. . . . But the rumors get pretty crazy. If it's not on the official site, then it's not official."

I ask her if it's pretty there, out at Skywalker Ranch, officially. Gorgeous, she says, laughing—all the magic I can't see. Forested, wine-country hills and tall security fences, dairy cows and horses grazing amidst the wired-up, whizbang, Victorian-inspired ranch houses where absolutely nothing is going on, unless Lucasfilm Ltd. confirms that it is going on. The spoilers are a headache George is officially not having.

"I think my view towards Lucasfilm," Scott finally says, "would be a lot like their view towards us. They really like the stuff we do that is fun and imaginative. But the reckless previews, the posting of prequel news that has gone out of their control, they don't like it. Well, same with my view of them: They make the most creative stuff out there and I love it. At the same time, it's run by lawyers (who) don't know who Jabba the Hutt is. They're businessmen, and that's how *Star Wars* is run." Scott shuts off his computer and we spend some time in the other spare bedroom, where his wife lets him keep his several thousand dollars' worth of tidily arranged, unopened *Star Wars* toys he has obtained at various science-fiction conventions. There are framed posters on the wall. He has the original action figures he played with as a kid, each wrapped in a Ziploc sandwich bag. When something like a rapport has been established, Scott shows me some of the Bothan Spy's prequel faxes—call sheets and scene descriptions from the final days of principal photography on the set of Episode I.

"I don't know who Bothan Spy is," Scott says, "Honestly, I don't. But you can see here"—he points to a place where Bothan Spy did not fully cross out his own name—"that he's putting himself at a pretty big risk."

I leave Scott's house and follow the winding roads back to the freeway, knowing how Episode I ends. (Knowing, that is, if I choose to believe in a Bothan Spy. It would turn out the fax was true—calling as it did for a funeral scene after the death of Liam Neeson's Jedi Master in a lightsaber duel.) "Even after everything," Scott had said, a true Jedi of optimism, perhaps by way of lessening the blow, "nothing compares to actually seeing the movie. It's going to be great."

Still, I feel spoiled. A thought occurs to me, and it occurs to me after each encounter with the spoiler guys: The Flanneled One— holed up in his bucolic fortress—controls all. Maybe the Flanneled One starts his own rumors, spreads them out there, sends the spoilers—and I quote Han Solo here—from one end of this galaxy to the other. Glumly using the Force, I get from one end of Houston to the other in rush-hour traffic, and knock on the apartment door of Chris Filson, a twenty-four-year-old computer salesman. A few days earlier, Chris had sent an e-mail detailing two of his prequel dreams. His visions were common to others—the anxiety dream, leaving the movie theater in despair. His other dream fell into a common category the Jungian therapist and I refer to as the "George and Me" dream, in which the Flanneled One invites Chris to Skywalker Ranch to play with gadgets.

But it was Chris's own analysis of his dreams that struck a nerve: "First, I would like to say that I am amazed that this many people are (also) experiencing this phenomenon," he wrote. "This is going to sound completely crazy, but for the past ten years, I have had a fear that some cataclysmic event (like the end of the world, or my death) would prevent me from seeing any further *Star Wars* movies. There is not much else beyond that I am looking forward to. I know that sounds pathetic as hell, but these movies are something I know will happen. Everything else is either questionable or unimportant to me. . . ."

I find Chris to be the kind of person who would not keep his action figures in their original boxes. You wouldn't find him seeking Chewbacca's autograph at a sci-fi con. He is more the everyday *Star Wars* Kid. He lives with his girlfriend and an enormous dog in a small apartment, and thinks he should get his act together and go back to college, from which he dropped out a few years ago.

We drive by the Alabama, a movie theater in Houston's Montrose district, where his dad took him to see *Star Wars* in 1977, the first movie he ever saw. He remembers it clearly, even though he was barely four at the time. The Alabama has been turned into a Bookstop superstore. We spend a better part of the evening at a taqueria, talking about movies, and life, about why he dropped out of college, about the future, about prequels. (*Prequelle,* that French word again, "the symptom.")

Fear of death, fear of letdown: Carl Cunningham, for example, finds himself driving more safely, especially next to semi trucks, because wouldn't that just beat all—crushed to death and *boom,* no prequel. His daughter, Taylor, will be five when Episode I is released—"the exact age I was when *Star Wars* came out," he says. He considers it an important part of his life to hand down to her. Or Scott Chitwood, who remembers having his first loose tooth in the summer of 1977, and his father saying, *Let me see it, open your mouth.* And then the sweet bribing, "If you let me see that tooth, I'll take you to see *Star Wars.*" And later, Scott recalls, in the dark theater, reflexively touching his tongue to the meaty strings where the tooth had been, the movie unfolding before him.

And me, of all people, feeling older than Yoda, eating tacos and telling Chris that no one has the world figured out at twenty-four. We are all just Jedis in waiting, with mortgages and toddlers and

lawns to mow and Web sites to tend, scoping out cineplexes, counting down. "And it's, like, after that . . . after the prequel," Chris
says. "Then what?"

Then it really is just a movie. Then it is just one hundred more
action figures and spaceships to stick them in; the plastic talismans
of revelations, revealed. *I am your father,* et cetera.

(1998)

The Josie Problem

Scarsdale, New York

Josie herself answers the door of the split level house in Scarsdale wearing a leopard-spotted blouse and black pants, her hair cut in a snowy bob. Her eyes are wide, her smile is giant, and you think, yes, of course, this is what the old man has been drawing all these years: her. All those Bettys, all those Veronicas. And the pinup girls conjured for stag magazines, the secretaries getting spanked by their randy bosses; Josie and those groovy Pussycats—they're all his wife. This is what va-va-voom looks like at seventy-six. And that French accent—"Hal-lo, I am Josie," she coos. Does it still drive him wild? One night, about forty years ago, they were invited to a costume party on a yacht. She wore a skimpy cat suit, with ears and a long tail. "She looked great," Dan DeCarlo says. "Just great." (He went dressed as a hunter, in a pith helmet, carrying a musket.) He draws comic books. You can always spot a DeCarlo girl. Her hips tilted, or arms akimbo, with a hormonally agog Archieland suitor about to drive his jalopy into a fire hydrant from looking at her. DeCarlo is an old man, and not famous. He worked freelance for Archie Comic Publications for more than four decades—up until three months ago, when the company fired him.

Once, in happier times, they asked him to come up with a costumed all-girl rock-and-roll band for a comic book he'd been drawing called *She's Josie*. That was 1969, when there was big money in bubblegum pop. The Archies had scored a number one hit with "Sugar, Sugar"; the back end of Hollywood's television machine suddenly needed more singing cartoons.

DeCarlo thought of his wife in that cat suit.

Which was a wonderful idea, and which is where the Josie problem started.

■　■　■

This story can't happen for you unless we're both sprawled on the carpet, in our footsie pajamas, under a sofa-cushion fort, watching cartoons at an exact moment in time. ("Saturday morny, they make me horny," the comedian Mike Myers once said, exalting *Josie and the Pussycats*.) A DeCarlo girl isn't real, but you want her to be. (Also there is this: Girls wanted to be Pussycats. They wanted to rock like that, and some of them grew up and did. "Everywhere the action's at," sang the cartoon Josie, "we're involved with this 'n' that.") Something burned hot here, into the Apple Jacks devout. Another piece of the Josie problem: Let any cartoon sit around long enough, and it is suddenly worth a whole lot more money, for no particular set of reasons. *Josie and the Pussycats*, which debuted on CBS on September 12, 1970, was a study in Saturday morning superfluff, with mod teenagers thwarting the plans of evil scientists and playing their musical instruments while doing it. How silly but wonderful, how naively sexy. The target audience was about five years old and given to fits of leaping around the living room. It's a narrow demographic, situated somewhere after *Jonny Quest* and yet before pediatricians popularly prescribed Ritalin. The show ran only two seasons (and another two seasons under a more absurd permutation, *Josie and the Pussycats in Outer Space*), but it continues to percolate as a piece of postboomer nostalgia. DeCarlo can't exactly explain it. Grown-ups come up to him at comic-book conventions to profess their *Josie and the Pussycats* devotion. The truth is he really didn't like the show, which was adapted by Hanna-Barbera from his comic book. Even so, he will smile, sitting at an autograph table, drawing the Pussycats over and over.

One guy wants them naked.

"Naked, he tells me, but still furry," DeCarlo recalls, shaking his head, taking that request in stride. Whatever its influence, something Josiesque can still be sensed in pop culture—in today's alternative rock bands, or in Britney Spears; you can also see its vibe in the jet-set background pastiches of European fashion magazines. Hollywood, again turning to TV reruns for fresh kill, released a *Josie and the Pussycats* movie in 2001, retooling the concept as a campy, sexy comedy about grrrrl power.

Even in 1970, DeCarlo says, he wanted a cut beyond his freelance rate, which at the time was $23 for each comic-book page he drew. A lawyer advised DeCarlo then that even if he could get more money for creating *Josie,* he'd most likely lose his job drawing for Archie. He says he kept quiet, and kept drawing. Thirty-one years after *She's Josie* became *Josie and the Pussycats,* DeCarlo, at age eighty, sued Archie Comics Publications for $250,000 compensation for the company's continued use of the *Josie* characters. At the time he filed the lawsuit, in March 2000, he was still drawing *Betty and Veronica,* and a few other Archie titles, a job from which he was promptly canned, after three decades of working for Archie. The publisher struck back at him four months later, suing DeCarlo for $6.5 million.

■ ■ ■

Which is how, on a muggy August afternoon, I came to be standing in Dan and Josephine DeCarlo's small garage. Dan flips a light switch and points toward some shelves in the corner, on which original storyboards are neatly stacked. He says he rescued most of them years ago from the trash Dumpster behind the Archie Comic Publications office in Mamaroneck, New York.

DeCarlo—who has a head of thick, white hair and a sweet, devilish grin, and is dressed in a grandfatherly brown, short-sleeve shirt and high-waisted slacks—removes his glasses and sorts through the drawings. Here's one of Melody, the shapely blond drummer from Josie and the Pussycats. They are terribly cute. In this panel, dated

1972, wild Indians have ambushed the Pussycats tour bus in the desert. Oh, look, now they're tying the girls up . . . with . . . rope.

"That's a nice one, huh?" DeCarlo says.

. . .

"The characters are Mr. DeCarlo's," says his New York attorney, Whitney Seymour Jr. "The theory we are pursuing is that he has underlying ownership. Archie owns the comic books, but [DeCarlo] owns the characters. Archie has sold the characters for use as something besides a comic book, and all Mr. DeCarlo is saying is, 'Hey, wait a minute.' . . . We wrote a letter demanding they sit down with us. Archie basically told DeCarlo to get lost." (Through an attorney, the chairman and publisher of Archie Comic Publications, Michael I. Silberkleit, declined to comment on the DeCarlo flap, with both lawsuits pending.)

As the lawsuits were working their way through court, filming began that summer on Universal Pictures' live-action *Josie and the Pussycats* movie, starring a vixen-of-the-moment, Rachael Leigh Cook, as the redheaded band leader. Anticipating a release in April 2001, Universal's publicity reps fanned out at a merchandising convention in New York in the spring of 2000 to give away drumsticks and furry ears, hoping to whet the appetite for new *Josie* toys and clothing aimed at 'tween-aged girls. "The Pussycats are fun and sexy and adorable and totally hot right now," Allison Brecker, a vice president at Universal, told me. "We didn't want to make just another adaptation of a cartoon. This is something different. It's about an image, or an idea. . . . People really get a picture in their minds when you say 'Josie and the Pussycats,' and we're using that to make a comedy. Little girls are going to identify with it, but so are people who grew up with the old show." In the movie script, the Pussycats are a pop-punk trio who sign a deal with a diabolical record executive who wants to control young minds with bad music. "It's a satire on commercialism and the music industry," says writer-director Harry Elfont. "They live in a city in the not-so-distant future where society sort of mindlessly follows trends. It's up to Josie and the Pussycats to save the world."

Wasn't it always?

For a show that was moderately rated, and had only thirty-two total episodes, and was based on a comic book that finally petered out in 1982, *Josie and the Pussycats* is a case study of one of those pop artifacts that live far, far beyond their original value. What it's worth—financially, culturally—is difficult to determine. Archie Comics owns the Josie image, but the cartoon was created, through a licensing agreement, by Hanna-Barbera, which came to be owned by Ted Turner, who came to be owned by Time Warner, which came to be owned by America Online—and yet another corporate entity, Universal, has the movie rights as *Josie* comes in for its perihelion. (That it originated with a work-for-hire artist in love with his wife is almost irrelevant.)

A woman in the elevator, upon hearing the words "Josie and the Pussycats," begins singing the peppy theme song: "Long tails, and ears for hats/Guitars, in sharps and flats." A rock band remakes the song. A deejay turns it into a ten-minute remix at a rave. Something clicks every time. Our memories are worth millions, if the right buttons are pressed. For every *Adventures of Rocky and Bullwinkle* dud at the box office, there's an inexplicable hit, such as *George of the Jungle*. (Note that all those involved in making the *Josie* movie are in their thirties: "Older white guys who play golf did not get it," says studio exec Brecker.)

The Josie fetish shows how almost anything can go to cult status in the eBay landscape. At every Ramada Inn by the interstate there is a convention of devotees of whatever. A copy of the original *Josie and the Pussycats* record album—"the Holy Grail for bubblegum pop fans," according to one LP collectors' guide—recently auctioned online for $350. *Josie* paper dolls, jigsaw puzzles, and free forty-five-rpm records that came with "specially marked boxes" of Froot Loops routinely fetch high prices. DeCarlo's original comic-book pages can sell for $200 per story. Other fans make and sell their own Pussycat CDs, T-shirts, and cigarette lighters—all of which feature pilfered copies of DeCarlo's girls.

Brad Nelson, thirty-five, a Louisville computer technician who started a Josie Web site, says he was driven to do so the moment he saw a rerun on the Cartoon Network. "Every once in a while, I'm suddenly reminded of a cartoon I'd forgotten about," he says. "I was like, 'Oh, my God.' I was immediately hooked." (He recently paid $200 for a working Pussycats wristwatch; if anyone has the jigsaw puzzle—"in the tin can," he underlines—please get in touch with him immediately.)

There are also the casual references. On NBC's *Will and Grace,* Grace tries to cheer Will up in one episode by saying she found the birthday present he's always wanted. "You found a *Josie and the Pussycats* lunchbox?" he asks hopefully. And no working female rock band, from the Go-Go's to Shonen Knife to Sleater-Kinney, has escaped a snide Josie comparison from mostly male rock critics. Is it the women in spotted fur, is that what does it? Is it Alexandra Cabot, Josie's friend and nemesis, with that alluring white streak in her hair? Josie and the Pussycats tops the list of one man's Cartoon Girls I Wanna Nail Web site: "Don't even get me started," he writes, "on what I'd do if I got those three. . . ."

■   ■   ■

He is up in his home studio, a spare bedroom, where a stained-glass rendering of Betty and Veronica, sent to him from a fan, reflects blue-green color across his drafting table. Since being fired by Archie, Dan DeCarlo considers himself semiretired, although he recently took a freelance job with another publisher to work on an issue of *The Simpsons* comic book, busily teaching himself to draw Homer, Marge, and Bart and the rest of Springfield in the trademark Matt Groening style.

Josie is downstairs, at the kitchen table, looking at the love letters Dan used to send her during World War II. She has fetched them from the box where she keeps them. On each envelope, Dan drew funny pictures of her, or of himself in a soldier's uniform, pining away for her in a swarm of little red hearts. "Everyone used to wait for his letters, even the postman," she says. "These are the one thing I always keep." The Josies on these envelopes have the eyes and noses and mouths that came to be the DeCarlo girl. He worked as a graphic artist for an Army information office in Europe. He's most proud of having designed and drawn the sexy pinup girls on the front of bomber planes, as per the instructions of the squadron pilots. He met Josie in Belgium, dated her, was reassigned, and asked her to marry him in 1945. After the war, the couple and their twin sons moved to New York, where De-Carlo worked regularly for Timely Comics (which later became Marvel), drawing westerns, romances, *Millie the Model*, and *My Friend Irma*.

He also drew one-panel gags for men's magazines. "I'd take the drawings into the magazine office, and the guy says, 'Make the breasts bigger,'" DeCarlo recalls. "So I take them back, I make the breasts bigger, I bring them back to the office, guy says, 'Bigger.' So I take them back, make the breasts bigger, bring them back to the office, guy says, 'Bigger.' I said, 'Forget it. You want them bigger, you make them bigger yourself. I've made them as big as they're going to get.'" Most of his work, by the late 1950s, was coming from Archie. The comic book was originally drawn by Bob Montana, and DeCarlo struggled to draw in Montana's style, which the publisher required. "I finally told them I quit, that I was tired of looking up and looking down," DeCarlo says. "There was something about Betty and Veronica's lips, with the cleft right here"—he points—"I just told them I'd had it. And they said, 'Okay, you can draw it your way.'"

DeCarlo's way became the Archie template. It was here that Betty got a ponytail; Veronica found miniskirts and sports cars; both girls filled out considerably "I love girls," DeCarlo shrugs. "I used to go to the high school to look and see what the girls were wearing, and draw that."

He drew those girls for half his life. A few days after his attorney filed the first lawsuit, DeCarlo recalls "sneaking" into the office one May morning to drop off some pages of *Betty and Veronica* and running into Archie publisher Silberkleit—who fired him on the spot. (Although Silberkleit wouldn't comment for this article, he did respond to a news item in the *Wall Street Journal* about DeCarlo's firing, in a letter published June 19, 2000: "Mr. DeCarlo has been handsomely compensated for his artwork on *Josie* and other comics," he wrote. "We firmly believe that we have always treated [him] fairly.") DeCarlo bristles at the notion that *Josie* was, in the end, just hack work. "At the time I was doing it," he says, "I was just trying to feed a family. I drew anything, just to get paid. Now, looking back, I figured I better try and get more credit for it."

I saw Dan and Josie one more time, by surprise, a year after I first wrote about the *Josie* lawsuits. They were at Comicon, an enormous comic-book and collectible-toy convention held every summer in San Diego. They were sitting at a folding table with some of Dan's old Archie Comics boards for sale, or custom drawings that he would do on the spot. Josie collected the money, and Dan looked tired, and more frail. He died a few months later. Universal's *Josie and the Pussycats* opened at theaters and bombed. A couple years later, a judge ruled in favor of Archie Comics, saying the company owned all rights to the characters.

A comic-book historian once told DeCarlo that the Josie problem is a little like the Sistine Chapel problem. "Pope gets Michelangelo to paint the ceiling of the Sistine Chapel," DeCarlo had told me, in his living room that day. "So he hires the guy and the guy paints it, right? Who owns it? The pope or the artist? The pope owns the ceiling, but who owns the pictures? And who is really the 'creator' of it? The pope or Michelangelo?"

Still, what a gorgeous and bizarre thought: angelic Bettys and Veronicas splayed across all that ancient plaster, backed up by a choir of electric Josies, and jiggly Pussycats. Girls and girls, bending over, or drinking malts, dancing by the jukebox. Foiling plans for world destruction, pretending to like one boy in order to make another jealous. Once again we are staring up, lost in images he made.

(2000)

Evil Queens

In the summer of 2000, CBS put sixteen of the most ambitious Americans they could find on an island in the Pacific, and let them be mean to one another in the name of reality television. They competed for survival, voting one another into nonexistence, until there was just one person left, who would win a million dollars. That person was an unlikable gay man from Rhode Island named Richard Hatch. By the show's August finale, the press about Richard went out of its way to overlook the obvious. To judge by various write-ups, Richard was "mean" and "scheming" and "fat"; he was a "conniving nudist" (oh, the worst kind) and he was, according to the *New York Times,* "a manipulative Machiavellian egomaniac."

But these are minced words. Richard was and perhaps still is an Evil Queen, and that is why viewers were drawn to him. His homosexuality was rendered nearly irrelevant on the social microcosm of *Survivor,* but in his twisted way, Richard did more for gays than a thousand Wills, with their attendant Graces, could ever do. He proved what the military and Boy Scouts of America must on some level have always dreaded, and it is this: The power of one determined gay guy—the archetypal Evil Queen—could collapse a nation. Absent anything to be gay about (neither a love interest nor a rainbow-striped porch flag presented themselves), he set out to do what all Evil Queens do best: He colluded and gossiped and forged the show's morally fraught "alliances" that he proceeded to bend to his will. He stabbed. He clawed. He was wry about doing so; when confronted, he was contrite or aloof. He referred to himself as an "FNF" (Fat Naked Fag), defusing any slurs that might have been hurled his way.

He was the key provider and producer of the ersatz castaways' dinners, which are so important in gay culture; what were Richard's daily catches of tropical fish if not a metaphor for the full-on homosexual sit-down brunch for eight? The Evil Queen always lets you know how hard (s)he worked. What a wonderful meal, her guests will say. *Oh, it's nothing,* the Evil Queen says, deceptively, *just a little something I whipped up.* (Inside, the Queen broods: *You idiots. Without me, you'd be eating only rice and rats.*) Watch as poor, heterosexual, chest-shaving Sean staggers out of that ocean empty-handed. Watch truck-driving, tough-talking Susan come back with a fish, yes, but with a nasty sting requiring bandages. They cannot "fish," in the sense that fishing stood in metaphorically for survival; the Evil Queen can.

One is never quite sure if enslaved children or winged monkeys are busy toiling in the Evil Queen's lair. That Richard was arrested for allegedly overpunishing his chubby adopted son on a 4:30 a.m. "family jog" around their Middletown, Rhode Island, neighborhood is only too in line with what we know about Evil Queens. (Richard countersued the city, for wrongful arrest.) There was something a little too *Mommie Dearest* about all that, calling to mind the Evil Queen's motto: No More Wire Hangers, Ever! The straight world is conditioned to think of homosexuality as a handicap, a weakness, a fey stereotype. The gay-rights movement tries to present a warm, united front and yet somehow amplifies the notion that gay men and lesbians are marginal, lacking in power.

And it is from this perceived weakness that the Evil Queen finds his opportunity to strike. How many neighborhood associations have voted Bob—a nice older bachelor who lives down the street and who has such a pretty yard and bakes tasty brownies—into the chapter presidency, only to find themselves soon living in a totalitarian state that forbids driveway basketball hoops? The gated community is now ruled by Bob, who has morphed into the Evil Queen. (She wants to turn the Dalmatian puppies into a coat!) There is no doubt that the Evil Queen is capable. Witness the David Geffens, the J. Edgar Hoovers. See how, in one of my favorite episodes, Richard—apparently unconstrained by his flabby torso, the physical affliction of many an Evil Queen—dives deep and straight down into the coral to seek out and spear the delicious stingrays he prefers. In the hands of an Evil Queen no task is unsurmountable: the stockholders' meeting, the final legal details of a megamerger, the choreography for the Super Bowl halftime show.

But there will be casualties. Some people won't hack it with the Evil Queen. The Evil Queen praises the weak, even as they toil, while thinking of a way to unload them. (Personally, *Survivor* makes me want a Xanax. All those people being awful to one another, and for what?) Maybe it's comforting to know the Evil Queen never quite wins, that somebody always discombobulates him. ("You fools! The prisoners are escaping!") In our Disney consciousness, it is safe to root for the Evil Queen, because good will prevail. Americans, ever in love with a bitch, started to root for the Fat Naked Fag. They wanted him to be cruel; they liked him more the meaner he got. Gay bars, for the duration of the show's Wednesday night sensation, made a happy hour out of *Survivor*-watching. In Washington, D.C., a gay newspaper ran an editorial cartoon praising Richard's EQ-ness, elevating him to a level held by the likes of *Bewitched* mother-in-law Agnes Moorehead. Barfuls of men stared raptly at TV screens on Wednesday nights (with drink specials, of course, e.g., a mai tai), cheering for their Evil Queen. It's easy to identify with the Evil Queen; it hurts, actually, to watch Richard in action. Gay men have all either dated an Evil Queen, or befriended one. They have been on the receiving end of his wrath, and finally, each must admit that he himself could be an Evil Queen.

Almost anyone in an office or retail store has worked for or with an efficient Evil Queen. You tell the Evil Queen your secrets and wind up wishing you hadn't. (But the Evil Queen has such good advice, offers such trust!) Anybody on a cheerleading squad or in the drama club production of *Oklahoma!* was possibly coached by an Evil Queen. Do not, however, solely rely on these cliché sightings: The Evil Queen is also the CEO or the systems operator, or the department chair, or the guy in charge of purchase orders. Richard is a "corporate trainer" by trade. That sounds like flip charts and overhead projectors and motivational speeches. (Such evil.) Watch what you say around him and know this above all: Until it plays out differently, Evil Queens are in control.

(And a special PS to the fine folks at the Gay and Lesbian Alliance Against Defamation: I know. I know and I'm sorry, but it had to be said.)

(2000)

I Don't Know How to Love Him

Albuquerque, New Mexico

There's this woman who follows the show from city to city, like some *Superstar* Deadhead, only you need to know that the cast and crew are a little spooked by her devotion, especially when she follows them to dinner at restaurants. Or shows up at the hotel with a camera and needs to see Jesus. Other times she insists she's been hired to join the production staff. "She's *nuts*," says the tour's publicist, who half expects the woman to show up any minute now at the University of New Mexico's Popejoy Hall, where a long-running touring company of *Jesus Christ Superstar* has arrived on a crisp September morning.

Then there's the reporter who broke down and cried when she met Ted Neeley and Carl Anderson backstage at *Jesus Christ Superstar* a few weeks before in Salt Lake City. She had urgent things to tell Jesus: Her father had died when she was a little girl, and her mother took all the kids to see *Jesus Christ Superstar,* the 1973 movie version starring Neeley as Jesus and Anderson as Judas, three times a day, for several weeks.

"Three times a day. This show has *baggage*," Carl Anderson says, with awe. "The first thing, when she met us, she lost all professionalism and she just hugged us. I say she was unprofessional, but I don't mean it was a bad thing. She waited twenty years to meet us and thank us. I get that ten times a day. At least."

At this point, it had been twenty-one years since Anderson appeared in the *Superstar* movie, and people were still thanking him for betraying the Lord so rockingly. We're sitting in a studio at KLSK, the classic-rock station in Albuquerque, where Anderson and two other cast members are appearing on the morning show to promote *Superstar*. Listeners are calling in to beg for tickets. The deejay says more people want *Superstar* tickets than, for example, the time the station gave away free passes to Crosby, Stills, and Nash. One guy calls in to tell Anderson how he saw the touring production at Popejoy in 1972, a few days before he went to Vietnam. "Now I rent the movie for my family every Lent," the caller says. "It's become a family tradition."

"Thanks for calling, man, come see the show," Anderson says.

"We'll be there Thursday night," the man says.

"Come backstage and meet us, then, okay?" Anderson says.

There's more: Consider the kooks, like the one-man protest movement who picketed the show every night in Phoenix. Or the member of the Historic Baptist Berea Church in Bloomfield, New Mexico, who fired this angry missive to the management of Popejoy Hall: "We aren't at all interested in supporting a coven of faggots and lesbians who blaspheme the sinless Lord of Glory! Please remove our name from your mailing list." Or consider all the people who come to the backstage door every night after curtain call, when Neeley takes his final bows in a robe so Clorox miracle white it's like he's not really from here: those piercing eyes framed by a sad, soft brow, the scraggly beard with a strand here and there of gray, the Texas twang that becomes a sonic scream in the garden of Gethsemane. Of all of Hollywood's hypnotically tragic and cute blue-eyed movie Jesuses, Neeley still has *it*. People come backstage and want to meet him, touch him, talk to him. They have problems, or questions, or tears, and he listens. Up close, he's small, diminutive, shy, which depending on your theology, is Christlike or underwhelmingly so. Neeley will sometimes talk to them for hours, outside even, when the security guards have locked up the theater. "These are the people," Carl Anderson notes, "who need to talk to Jesus. If you know what I mean."

> After all, I've tried for three years,
> Seems like thirty, seems like thirty . . .

It begins with the "brown album," so named for its plain, chocolate-colored jacket, the original Decca recording with Murray Head as Judas and Ian Gillan as Christ, written and produced in London by two freaks named Andrew Lloyd Webber and Tim Rice, and released in the states in 1970, eventually selling 2½ million copies, a mere eighteen months after *Time* magazine declared "God Is Dead" on its cover. The brown album is the stuff of cellophane lamps and dorm rooms, of sitting in a bean bag chair wearing padded Radio Shack headphones, of days when the stylus would set down scratchily on the vinyl, side one, side two, side three, side four: *"My mind is clearer now. . . ."* You can get it at any flea market, or you can have it on CD, in a half-dozen versions: the London stage cast, the Broadway recording, the excerpted highlights, the movie version, the twentieth-anniversary CD. At the video store, you can rent the movie, a searingly psychedelic hodgepodge filmed on the deserts of Israel, with Roman soldiers carrying machine guns, disciples wearing frayed bell-bottoms, and army tanks symbolizing temptation. You hear it in strange places: *Superstar* cover songs by punk-rock bands, or toned-down and hymnlike in certain churches, or "I Don't Know How to Love Him" piped in on waiting-room Muzak. (And I still don't quite know how to love Him, after so many nights of playing the brown album or the movie soundtrack—we owned both—on the small record player in my boyhood bedroom, dying for everyone's sins with my arms stretched across the closet rod, perhaps the purest religious longings I'd ever had.)

The rock opera, with much of the libretto lifted verbatim from gospel readings of Christ's final days, created a fashionable theology all its own. It is a gritty, depressing, argumentative passion play, which thrived in an age of rebellion. That was a long time ago, and these guys are still singing those excruciating high notes, dying every night, all year. In theological tradition, Christ died at age thirty-three.

The week *Superstar* pulled into Albuquerque, Carl Anderson was forty-nine. Ted Neeley was about to turn fifty-one.

Between them, they have died onstage—Anderson from the Judas noose, Neeley on the cross—a couple thousand times. They were young, unknown singer-actors who got their breaks when they were cast in the Los Angeles stage production of *Jesus Christ Superstar* in 1972. They got screen tests for the movie, Anderson recalls, more as a professional courtesy than anything else. The movie had already been unofficially cast with bigger rock stars. But Norman Jewison decided to cast them anyway. Before the L.A. production even opened, Neeley and Anderson were flown to Israel to shoot the film.

Twenty years later, a production company wanted to stage a new production and put it on the road. They wanted Anderson to reprise his role as Judas, but he said he would only do it if Ted Neeley signed on as Christ. The new show would emphasize the singing and music. The sets and choreography would be understated; the nostalgia value—and the Andrew Lloyd Webber namesake—would be the hook. "We planned to be on the road a few months," Anderson says. "We just had no idea. . . ." Now it has been twenty-one months, with five months to go after Albuquerque. They have made 102 stops with a dozen or more performances at each stop, returning to some cities two and three times.

Playing several nights at each stop in 2,000- to 5,000-seat auditoriums, this *Jesus Christ Superstar* has earned $62 million so far, according to industry trades. (That put it, for comparison, a mere notch below Guns N' Roses and Janet Jackson on the list of highest-grossing concert tours in 1993.) So something is still there. "It still gets people to stop and think about it all," Anderson says. He is sitting in the front seat of my car (the limousine is late picking him up from KLSK, and show-business people *detest* waiting for courtesy) and we are talking about God. It's like giving a ride to an overactive teenager. He sings spontaneously, drums on the dashboard, interrupts himself to make a call on his pocket phone.

Since *Jesus Christ Superstar,* the movie, was released, Anderson has had the most visible career of the original cast. He has recorded eight R & B albums and had a number one ballad,

"Friends and Lovers," in 1986. Neeley has written and performed in various theater productions, and eventually moved back home to Houston. It is likely the two will always be Judas and Jesus, forever typecast in the Greatest Story Ever Told, whether on stage or in cultural consciousness.

That's okay with Anderson: "There was a time, when I was younger and playing Judas, that I considered it a stepping stone to becoming a big star. I never took time to enjoy it back then. Now it's a part of me. If I go down as the guy who was Judas . . . OK, then. That's fine." (He'll go down as Judas. And, interestingly, Judas will, for many people raised on *Jesus Christ Superstar,* forever be a black guy.) Anderson belongs to a church in L.A. called Science of Mind. It's full of people in the Industry, he says, who first congregated in hotel ballrooms and later built a church of their own. They believe in God, Jesus, Buddha, Mohammed, among others. They emphasize the power of positive thinking. "The way it worked, see, God sent Jesus, but there were no airplanes. So Jesus couldn't fly to Japan. That's why God put people all over the world to tell people what was happening. . . ."

The show's publicist, Ann Rippey, is riding in the back seat of the car. She worries aloud that Anderson may have been too emphatic on the air back at KLSK, when asked about the handful of fundamentalist Christian groups who still protest *Superstar* as heretical. Anderson launched into a brief tirade about how, "If Jesus were alive today, he would not even be a Christian." She worries about damage control; Anderson worries about ignorance. "I'll bet you a dime to a doughnut that the people who complain about the piece have never even see it," he says.

> If you knew all that I knew,
> My poor Jerusalem,
> You'd see the truth, but you'd close your eyes. . . .

From a letter dated September 1 and addressed to Paul Suozzi, Popejoy Hall's marketing director, from Larry D. Cox, pastor, East Mountain Assembly of God in Edgewood, New Mexico:

"From the stand point of our congregation, *Jesus Christ Superstar* is an attack upon the foundational beliefs of the Christian faith and the basis of our society. . . . We will be in opposition by every means possible, from announcements in our congregation, and through our community by word of mouth and other means. . . . Your reconsideration of this event is highly advisable and requested with the utmost regard. Thank you for your help. In His Service, . . ."

> Jesus Christ, Jesus Christ,
> Who are you, what have you sacrificed?
> Jesus Christ, Superstar,
> Do you think you're what they say you are?

The union guys have spent all day unloading the semitrailers and assembling the black, metal scaffold *Superstar* set. The band has run through its sound checks. The cast members have checked their microphones. Carl Anderson is in his dressing room backstage, where he has unloaded his wardrobe locker and set out pictures of his wife and teenage son. He lights a ceramic candle and a bowl of patchouli. He has lined his many bottles of herbs and vitamins along the makeup table. A teapot is ready to warm his herbal tea. He puts several drops of high-powered Chinese ginseng under his tongue. His Sony boombox plays jazz. He begins singing along to the music and his powerful voice shakes the fixtures. The cast and crew mingle about the cluttered green room, hugging each other and jumping up and down, a family that prays together stays together, checking sign-up sheets for hotel accommodations in Nashville and Washington, D.C., the tour's next two stops.

Jesus is not here yet. Tonight—opening night—is his fifty-first birthday. He is coming down with bronchitis. The cast says Ted Neeley never takes a day off. The publicity people wonder if an announcement should be made to tonight's audience that Mr. Neeley is feeling under the weather so the audience will be forgivingly aware if he misses a note or two. Carl Anderson frowns at the suggestion. "They'll never know. Ted will go out there and do it and they'll never know."

In Neeley's darkened dressing room, now just twenty-five minutes to curtain, his three Jesus tunics hang sublimely on a rack. A worn pair of leather sandals sit on the tile floor below. The cast has strung Happy Birthday crepe paper across the room. They left him cards and presents, a grocery store Jesus candle. The publicist has fetched Neeley's requisite tequila for the evening. Carl Anderson bought him two bottles of expensive wine, a picnic basket, a piece of Santa Clara pueblo pottery, and tickets to the Eagles concert in Nashville next week, begging him to take a night off, with a note satirizing a line from the show: "On Wednesday night / In Nashville / I don't wanna see your ass / in Jerusalem."

Anderson, being interviewed by a television reporter, is asked if he and Neeley can play these parts forever. Out in the house, the band is warming up with "Superstar," Judas's signature number. "No, I can't," he says. A tear falls down his cheek and he weeps. He says he would like to be considered for a Broadway revival of the show, if that ever happens. "Every night I can't wait to go out there and do it. That's my song. . . . I could listen to it forever, but I can't do it forever."

Neeley shows up at eight, with fifteen minutes to spare, as calm and serene as Anderson is bouncing off the walls. He takes off his wire-rim glasses and begins to put on his mesh garments and tunic. He puts flesh-colored bandages over his fingers to hide his rings. He spritzes his long Jesus hair with a spray. Anderson is dying to show Neeley the bathroom, where cast members have wrapped the Happy Birthday crepe paper around the toilet paper.

Neeley laughs and holds out his hands toward the sight gag, then clasps his hands together, and smiles that smile, a gesture that reminds me of what, a priest, the pope on the balcony? The Dalai Lama? Oh no, of course: Jesus.

When the tour is over, if it is ever over, Carl and Ted call each other up a couple of times a year. "I always hear from Ted when the Redskins play the Cowboys," Anderson says. "The Redskins are my team. And Ted is crazy about the Cowboys." The two men share a private moment together before the lights go down. Neeley always whispers a one-word cue to Anderson before they go on. It is their word for the show.

The word tonight is "birth."

And two hours later—after the lights and sound and spectacle of another performance of *Superstar*, after a standing ovation and a birthday cake for Neeley at the curtain call, with the audience singing "Happy birthday, dear Jesus, happy birthday to you"—the cast and crew steal away to the Monte Vista Fire Station for a private party. Jesus doesn't meet the people tonight. He must rest his voice. Some of the people mill about in the parking lot for a while anyway, not unlike church members after a particularly rousing service. There is a palatable level of nostalgia in their conversations, scratchy LPs, and embraceable beliefs. These are the people who don't turn out for theater so much. They seem to be here for other reasons. After so many years, there still is, to quote the show, talk of God.

(1994)

Recallifornia

Like almost any temporary visitor to Los Angeles, I arrived there happy, in the overbaked bliss of summer, and left slightly creeped out. This was a seven-week trip in which I'd hoped mainly to write stories about the movie and television businesses. (My secret hope was to write about, or at least glimpse, the enigmatic and almost mechanically virtuous teenage-mogul twins Mary-Kate and Ashley Olsen.) Instead I got swept up, on Day Four, along with the thirty-five million or so citizens of California, into a parallel drama that was, fittingly, about showbiz and soundbites and perception: An emergency statewide referendum had been scheduled for the first Tuesday in October to decide whether or not the governor, Gray Davis, a lifelong politician, should be removed from office.

California was behaving like a celebrity gone off her meds, broke and bipolar, babbling incoherently into an invisible phone, toothless and trespassing and asking for help. Orange jumpsuit, darkened roots, dumped by both her agent and her publicist. The state—billions of dollars in the hole—was as obsessed as ever with fresh starts and extreme makeovers, and the recall was frequently compared to some neat, new summertime reality TV show with 135 player-characters, each of whom wanted, sincerely or half-jokingly, to take over the governor's office. As more sober citizens worried about the

event becoming, in the eyes of the rest of the nation (the mass market), "a circus," "a disaster," and a "terrible statement about democ-
racy," there remained a feeling that it could nether be helped, nor
stopped. There were characters to dislike: Firstly, the namby-pamby
governor. Then the scheming car-alarm magnate, a San Diego Re-
publican congressman named Darrell Issa, who—with some of his
own fortune—engineered the petition drive that prompted the
recall initiative. (Later, tearfully, he held a press conference to announce he himself would not run. He had been overwhelmed by
the unraveling of politics as usual.)

Most of all, amassing the biggest bulk of media attention, was
the special effect known as Arnold Schwarzenegger, the former
bodybuilding champion (five times Mr. Universe, seven times Mr.
Olympia) and action-movie star, who announced his candidacy on
the set of *The Tonight Show with Jay Leno,* at NBC's compound in
Burbank, late on a Wednesday afternoon in early August. Before
the taping, the dozens of reporters who'd shown up were admon-
ished by an NBC spokeswoman to embargo whatever the news
would be until the show aired several hours later. There was lots of
shouting back and forth about this, and those of us with East Coast
deadlines assured her of our defiance; we'd file as fast as possible,
come what may; and we did.

"When I moved to California in 1968 it was the greatest state in
the greatest nation in the world," the actor said. "Now it is totally
the opposite. The atmosphere is disastrous. There is total disconnect of the people in California. [They] are working hard, paying
taxes, raising families, and politicians are not doing their jobs.
They're fiddling, fumbling, and failing. . . ."—he paused slightly
here, and this is where the conventional wisdom had assured those
of us trying to figure out the nervous breakdown of California in
the summer of 2003 that Schwarzenegger was going to concede that
he could not run and win such an election, when he said—"And
this is why I'm going to run for governor of the state of California."

I sort of wanted the heads of everyone in the audience to explode at this point.

Blood everywhere.

I wrote "heads explode in audience," and filed from my laptop, thinking that Hollywood could add in the computer-generated effects later, in postproduction.

■ ■ ■

Every day in California this summer is now control-alt-delete, a state of constant rebooting, and it has this obnoxious, impatient feeling. A lot of the action seems to take place in hastily reserved Courtyard Marriott hotel meeting rooms off the 805 Freeway, or the Ventura Freeway, or in the Inland Empire, where one or another group of upset Californians seems to have a limitless and cranky urge to gripe to reporters about their car taxes, their property taxes, or the problem with Mexican immigrants. At community centers for underprivileged children, or in makeshift campaign headquarters in empty storefronts, or at breakfasts with chambers of commerce, the candidates are made to answer to perceived past sins: Davis has to defend his record in office; Cruz Bustamante, the also-running lieutenant governor, is asked questions about his involvement in the Movimiento Estudiantil Chicano de Aztlan when he was in college in the 1970s, back when MEChA somewhat militantly argued for the return of California to Mexico. Schwarzenegger dodges questions about allegations that he groped, fondled, pushed, kissed, and otherwise harassed a series of women in the movie business or entertainment journalism business; and also he is daily pressed about statements he'd made in the 1970s to *Oui,* a nudie magazine, about group sex he'd bragged of having in the legendary Gold's Gym of Venice Beach during his buffest days.

The operative word, for journalists covering the recall, is "meanwhile." What does not change—not until the very final days, when everyone seemed fed up with a series of injunctions and appeals that threatened to delay the vote another six months—is the sense of wild possibility. Schwarzenegger vows to take over (and fix) his beloved, adopted "Cullyfornia" by detonating the hive of bureaucrats whom he perceives, in his speeches and ubiquitous fifteen-second TV commercials, to "have a stranglehold on Sacramento." Others see an opportunity to put forth other messages, or merely to put forth themselves. There are days during the recall that any of them appear to make some sense. The pornographer Larry Flynt is around to remind voters that deep down, anyone in front of the camera can't help but succumb to a certain sleaze. The eco-minded Brentwood pundit to the stars, Arianna Huffington, fights terrier-like up until the week before the election, railing in a Zsa Zsa accent against the very nature of politics. There is a porn star, a bounty hunter, and Peter Ueberroth, the man who steered Los Angeles's hosting of the 1984 Summer Olympics.

Also there is Angelyne, a mono-named woman famous only for wanting to be famous, known to most Southern Californians for the many years she has rented Hollywood billboards that feature her ageless, platinum blond ampleness. She tools around in a pink Corvette. She's available in every way. She stands for nothing, except for one thing, in the widest possible abstract: *California*. She would be nowhere without it; and it would be somehow less without her. The candidates running for governor each have this similar, if differently packaged, California ideal: reinvention, image, connection, spirituality, altruism, sunshine, the allure of the new. In between campaign ads, I keep hearing an ad on the radio for a TV show about plastic surgeons; a show that has also briefly occupied a place in the conversation Los Angeles is always having with itself. "I hate my nose, I hate my breasts, I need liposuction!" screams a woman from a scene on *Nip/Tuck*. ("Where desire," the announcer growled, over and over, "meets desperation.")

Or the people can simply vote for rock and roll. Three days before the deadline to file as a candidate, I speak for a half hour or so one afternoon with Jack Lloyd Grisham, the forty-two-year-old lead singer of TSOL (True Sounds of Liberty), a seminal band in the Orange County punk-rock scene of the 1970s and 1980s. (They'd reunited in the 1990s on the power of such largely unknown hits as "Abolish Government/Silent Majority," "Sodomy," "Terrible People," and "Property Is Theft.") Grisham is on his cell phone, maneuvering his truck through traffic, gathering the last of sixty-five registered-voter signatures required of each candidate. A father of three, he lives in Huntington Beach, and seems mostly upset about his own lack of health-care coverage. (He'd thrown his back out surfing, which had affected his ability to work at his side job, in construction, and also cramped his punk rock; he'd had friends go to prison, or die of drug overdoses. He was battered and torn out there, in the heart of Nixon country. I came to think of him, and not Schwarzenegger, as Mr. California.) "One thing I got a little upset at was all these people saying that the recall election is going to be a 'madhouse.' Well, oh no, God forbid!" he says in mock horror. "I think it's just what we need. It's a chance for every citizen to get involved with what's going to happen next. I have just as much experience as Ronald Reagan did when he became governor of California," he says. "My whole thing is that there's California the business and then there's California the people. I'm just tired of seeing people who work so hard just to get by wind up getting hurt. You know that Verve song, the one with the line that goes 'I want to hear a song that recognizes the pain in me'?" (I didn't, but he sang a line of it for me anyhow, slightly inaccurately.) "That's what I'm thinking of, doing this. I just want to recognize that people are hurt. . . . [The state] put this new budget out and who got the worst of it? People who need health care."

If you want to register to run for governor and you live in Los Angeles, you must drive south along the Santa Ana Freeway, past a hypnotic array of power lines and telephone wires, exiting in Norwalk, wending your way through a particular kind of afternoon drabness. This is an L.A. you never see much on television shows—too unhip to suggest any kind of glamour, and too clean to portray the sinister. At the corner of Imperial and Volunteer is a series of blocky, Marcus Welby-esque, civic buildings. In the biggest of these, the Harry L. Hufford Building, you brush past all the people who, for a fee, will help you register for fictitious business names. Room 2013 is mostly quiet, and decorated with a bit of patriotic pep in red and blue foil streamers. There is only one man in line trying to be governor of California. His name is Robert C. Mannheim, a fifty-five-year-old retired attorney from Agoura Hills. He is wearing a bright-green-and-pink-flowered Hawaiian shirt and navy blue walking shorts. He tells the clerk that his eighty-three-year-old mother managed to get thirty-seven of his necessary sixty-five signatures. "She's taking this way too seriously," he says.

"Aw," the clerk says, in a cutesy-wutesy voice. "She wants to see her baby boy be the governor." On the steps of the Hufford Building, there was a long line of average Californians snaking around to the entrance, where life's little thresholds are taken care of: marriage licenses, property titles, domestic partnerships, and, finally, death certificates. This was the curious, overlooked detail about the state of recall madness. For all appearances, contrary to rumors of its demise, California appears to be working as normal. No one has curtailed or slashed or petitioned against the goldenness of it all. The suffering is the same as before, and so too the slightly exultant sunshine vibe. The palm trees still tower just so above the multiethnic strip malls. The freeway overpasses throb under the weight of speeding trucks. In Los Angeles, people still ignore me in the nicest way. The beaches are crowded. Everyone is grabbing for their piece of whatever California is to them. Everyone would like to own it, for a little while.

Two days later, normal business becomes impossible at the Hufford Building, because Schwarzenegger arrives, with his celebrity-journalist wife, Maria Shriver, in tow, to hundreds of screaming fans. He is here to file his own papers on the dream, and stage his first, postannouncement public appearance. He is asked, simply and repeatedly, about the budget, the environment, the schools, and after a while he snaps, slightingly, into cyborg mode: "Don't you worry about that. We will have a plan."

By deadline, 135 people have similarly filed this week.

One of the candidates who also passed through the Hufford Building, and attracted not nearly as much attention, was only fifty-six inches tall.

∎　∎　∎

Gary Coleman has not spent a lot of time imagining himself in the governor's chair, but he has spent considerable time thinking about an altogether alternate fate for himself, how his life might have been blissfully perfect as a nobody. In this fantasy he still allows for the loss of his kidneys as a toddler, and the failure of the two kidney transplants that followed over the years, and the continual doses of immunosuppressants that kept him alive but halted his growth.

In this other scenario he never struts down the runway of a Montgomery Ward spring fashion show in Zion, Illinois, in 1975. Therefore he never hears the delighted screams of the Midwestern crowd that does not happen to be watching a cute, black seven-year-old perform an impromptu shuck and jive in a three-piece suit. Therefore he never becomes addicted to that kind of attention, and his mother never takes her ailing, sweet-natured, wisecracking child to a casting agent, and so Gary Coleman never gets picked to star in a Harris Bank commercial that amuses Chicago television audiences, and so he never catches the attention of producer Norman Lear, and so his fate doesn't involve characters named Mr. Drummond or Mrs. Garrett. The best part of the fantasy is that he never once says the line, "Watchoo talkin' 'bout, Willis?" because there is no Willis, because there is never a sitcom called *Diff'rent Strokes*.

Somewhat sacrificially, in Coleman's fantasy, there is no earning of eighteen million dollars that will ultimately vanish in medical bills, family feuds, bad decisions, lawsuits, agents, and greedy managers. There is never a vast collection of model trains for young Gary to obsessively collect. He never sues his parents, and they never ask a judge to find him mentally incompetent. In the fantasy, there are no Gary Coleman epilogues because there are no Gary Coleman prologues. There is no hubris-rich E! documentary about his stardom and downfall, or the overpublicized, brief time spent in his late twenties working as a security guard. There is no mention of the autograph-seeking fan he allegedly assaulted in 1998, because there are no fans. There is just the story of a boy who grows up short. (In the fantasy, it is Emmanuel "Webster" Lewis who has to run for governor of California.)

What Gary Coleman, now thirty-five, wishes for most is that he never left Zion. "I would be working in Kmart, or—what was

that five-and-dime called?—Ben Franklin," he says. "And I would
be happy."

■ ■ ■

Instead, Coleman became one of those exotically unhappy citizens
of Los Angeles who live up to or down to a permanent condition of
striving, in a carefully cultivated limbo called *former child star*. Like
many other Californians, he's worried about his next paycheck, unhappy about his taxes, abstractly concerned for the environment,
and ticked off when the power goes out. He frets over the water
supply that leads to his faucet, the hungry immigrant mouths who
he says sap the state's resources. He gripes about backed-up freeways and mass transit. ("There is not a bus in California that takes
me anywhere I want to go," he says, in the trademark huff he ex-
hibited playing Arnold Jackson on *Diff'rent Strokes,* but hearing him
say it evokes a larger sense of being stranded in life.)

Sharply cognizant of his marketing potential as a punchline, he
throws himself into his gubernatorial campaign with seriousness
(or at least a serious larkiness), getting up before 6:00 a.m. in his
modest West L.A. apartment and readying himself for another
round of media appearances. Except for the two days a week he
receives hemodialysis, Coleman has honored a steady stream of
requests for TV, radio, and newspaper interviews. In the days
around the time I spoke to him, he made promotional appearances
for the Game Show Network's spoofy "Who Wants to Be Governor
of California?" competition and it is at the news conference to
publicize the game show that reporters discover that Coleman indeed has limits to his own self-parody: He declined a photo-op request to nuzzle into the bosom of fellow candidate and porn
actress, Mary Carey Cook. ("I'm not gonna make you money today," he sassed to the photographer who asked, according to *LA
Weekly.*) Similarly, he now has nothing but contempt for a local
deejay who goes by the name of Big Boy: Coleman says Big Boy
tried to trick him into saying "Watchoo talkin' 'bout?" and other
things that could be edited later into humiliating gags. He also

soured on Sean Hannity, the Fox News talk-show host, who he says
was mean and "bombastic . . . a jerk."

Some of these campaign obligations involve a network sending a
car to pick him up, in a manner befitting trips to and from the Land
of the Has-Been. Most times, though, he drives himself to these
appointments in his 2000 Mitsubishi Eclipse, as he does when I
met him at dawn one Wednesday at the Fox 11 building at South
Bundy and Olympic. His car, he says, had not yet fallen prey to
Gov. Davis's much loathed "triple tax" on vehicle registration that
some Californians take more seriously as a threat to their daily existence than they do crime, economic calamity, or natural disaster.

As a teenager, Coleman made nearly $70,000 an episode to play
little Arnold Jackson on *Diff'rent Strokes,* but that money got away
from him a long time ago, and so he came to believe that he would
not be able to afford triple the cost of registering his car. "But that
is the kind of thing that qualifies me for this job, isn't it?" he says.
"I'm mad." Like the state, he has known something of a deficit (he
filed for bankruptcy protection four summers ago, with $71,890 in
debt against $19,850 in assets) and worked his way in and out of
solvency. He has been lonely almost as long as he can remember.
He believes himself to be a man of the people, even as he wonders
what it might be like to be "a normal person."

Shortly after seven, on the set of *Good Day LA,* a loose and
gabby news show at Fox 11, Coleman arrives on time, prepared to
participate in the hype and punchlines of his own existence. He is
cleanshaven and gentlemanly, wearing a creamy tweed sport coat
seemingly cut for a boy's Easter church service, with pleated olive
dress slacks, and a blue button-down shirt and tie. He steps over to
a corner of the set, holds a mirror to his face, and touches himself
up with cocoa-colored makeup. He murmurs talking points to himself about California's fiscal and energy crises, a few fragmented
sound bites about "the people" and "the politicians."

And now the news: Police chases in L.A. are significantly down
(thus threatening an iconic Southern California image: the aerial
shot of hot pursuit). A house burned down. The alleged Belmont

Shores rapist appeared in court yesterday. Madonna had J.Lo and Britney over for her forty-fifth-birthday luncheon. *And Gary Coleman is here with us this morning!*

As always, the first question for him is whether this is all a mere stunt. He refuses to admit that. "I'm still running. I haven't pulled out and I'm not going to pull out," he says, but also musing that he might endorse Schwarzenegger as the vote neared closer and his campaign appeared futile.

"What if you win?" bubbles Jillian Barberie, the weatherwoman and fashion reporter with long, Farrah-feathered Valley hair. (God bless Southern California for still having its weather gals, in the absence of serious weather, who stand full-bodied against the chroma-keyed Baja frontal systems and show off their long legs.) "If I win, I'm going to make a lot of phone calls after I pick myself up off the floor from fainting," Coleman says.

"Okay, Gary," barks the anchor, Steve Edwards. "Let's go through a couple of issues and see how you stand on them. The car tax?"

"Uh, it's necessary, but it doesn't need to be that high."

"How high?"

"I don't think it needs to be tripled. You don't want to balance the budget on the backs of the people."

"Okay. Gun control."

"Necessary," says Coleman, who once told Geraldo Rivera he carried a pistol for protection, "but it's still a Second Amendment right."

"Okay. Do you think there needs to be a right for illegal immigrants to get, er, social and medical help here in California?"

"No, I do not."

"What would you do about immigration?"

"You can't stop the floodgates," Coleman says. "But you need to come up with new ways to stop people from getting across the border."

"You know," Barberie coos, "I like him."

"Great," Edwards sniffs. "You just got the Canadian vote, Gary."

(Barberie, alas, can't vote here.) "So what's your platform," Barberie then asks, "on people who say, 'Watchoo talkin' 'bout?'"

Uh-oh.

She had to go and say it.

This is usually the point where Gary Coleman reveals that he doesn't exactly appreciate his singular contribution in the world; yet the world is unsatisfied if he stops contributing the one thing they desire of him. Since August 6, when Coleman gave an alternative weekly newspaper in the Bay Area permission to jokingly nominate him for governor (the paper also spotted him the $3,500 filing fee, and gathered the necessary sixty-five legitimate signatures in support), Coleman is walking a line of believing in his own legitimacy and at the same time lampooning it. This is harder than it looks. The newspaper, the *East Bay Express,* deployed the stunt to mock the effort to recall Governor Gray Davis. It naturally followed, in terms of identifying with its Gen-X demographic, to pick a child star who ascended in the glorious days of late-1970s television, the Happiest Days, as it were. Despite his innermost desire to be viewed as a tough, profane, sharp-witted man about town, Coleman is forever reduced to the lovable rascal he played on television and in a few movies: He is still sass-talkin', folksy, and marketable in a "black" way that plays unthreateningly to Middle America. In the spectacle of the California recall election, it would seem to almost any observer that Coleman's sole purpose as a candidate is to be on hand to "watchoo-talkin" his diminutive heart out, to pop some one-liners about the mess the state is in, and to pose for pictures with all manner of quasi-celebrities, voters, the buxom, the marginalized, the masses. Only recently has an unsettling reality sunk in to those around him: Gary Coleman, *in Gary Coleman's mind,* is seriously running for governor of California. Step one, *in Gary Coleman's mind,* is to schmooze his way to Sacramento, to let himself be patronized.

"You're cute enough," he purrs back to Barberie. "You can say it."

"Do you have a girlfriend?" she asks.

"No. Are you making me an offer?" he asks back. "I can take you away from weather maps."

"I, uh, um, no," Barberie stammers. ("First lady of California," anchor Edwards leaps in. "Or director of communications!")

She changes the subject.

Rejection is a recurrent theme in the life of Gary Coleman, so it's actually no problem, he says later, to put himself on a ballot of 135 candidates and take his chances in the statewide psychodrama. In a recent celebrity dating show on E!, he is seen trying to get a home phone number from his setup date; she is seen physically running from him; the camera records him taking it all in stride. Implied in all this is the subtle refrain: Gary Coleman Can't Win. This is also the obvious point of his campaign. Gary Coleman Can't Win, and yet the electorate (and a bemused world beyond the state line) is repeatedly tantalized by the mere notion that Gary Coleman *Could* Win, with only a fraction of the votes. In some way, this is what the recall movement has stirred up in the people—the frightening idea that a government can now shift much the same way people flip TV channels, or the way the famous descend to obscurity. California is at once smitten and embarrassed by it all.

■ ■ ■

He is shown through a hallway toward the studio exit, but not before a station employee comes up to him and asks to have her picture taken with him, hugging him and telling him he's so cute. Another employee, a camera operator, comes over to reminisce about their days working together on the *Diff'rent Strokes* set, during the first season, 1978–79. (Coleman doesn't remember the man, but he remembers the studio.) The two men talk about the old building, where *Soul Train* was also taped, and when Coleman learns that it is being torn down, he seems genuinely sad for a moment.

Then it occurs to him he was promised breakfast in all this. "Wasn't there something about a breakfast?"

"Did they tell you that you could get breakfast?" a station employee asks. And Coleman insists, so he is led to the back end of the studio, where an intern-aged young woman sits guarding a picked-over buffet table of grocery-store bagels, a few Danish pastries, and an almost empty tray of scrambled eggs. Coleman makes himself a plate of eggs and covers them with salt and pepper. He eats rapidly, standing up, and patiently explains to us where he's "been," what he's been doing all these years: "Unless you've been living under a rock, you'd know I've been right here, that I've been busy." He's designed a video game. He is the spokesman for an Internet site called UGO.com, which has assigned him to various publicity tasks, such as writing an online advice column, and escorting models to awards shows. He says he recently had a part in a small independent film called A *Christmas Too Many,* currently unreleased, about "a dysfunctional family who has a vegan Christmas." Earlier this year, in another expression of American television's love for its recent past, Coleman and *Strokes* costars Todd Bridges and Conrad Bain reunited in March at the TV Land Awards, to present the prize for "Funniest Food Fight."

Coleman prefers to live by himself. "Family," he says, "never meant anything to me but a whole lot of trouble that I don't need," although he is on speaking terms with his own, after years of protracted court disputes. A 1993 settlement awarded Coleman an amount believed to be several hundred thousand dollars, maybe a million—but almost all of it going to legal fees. He says he never wants to have children. This is not to say he isn't a warm, friendly person, because he very much means to be; testiness, however, has always been his trademark. As a ten-year-old overnight sensation being interviewed by the *Washington Post*'s television critic, Tom Shales, he was similarly snappish, petulant, at least in print:

"[The episode titled] 'Goodbye Dolly,' the one we're working on now, I think is going to be a FLOP," he said, while eating a slice of carrot cake. "I don't particularly like that show. All the dumb lines they threw into it! It's about a doll that I sleep with—who wants to see that? Why can't it be something important, like it's always been? A doll! Who wants to see that baloney?"

Do studio audiences always laugh at the right time? Shales asked him.

"No, they're as dumb as we are."

Does he like signing autographs?

"No. I remember one night when I had to sign at least 300 of them. I got writer's cramp! My hand was like THIS [he scrunches his hand into a gnarl]." (In fact, it was the request for an autograph that resulted in an assault charge against Coleman twenty years

later, for which he was sentenced to anger management classes—
which in turn angered him, because they focused on domestic violence, which only reminded him that he had no love life.)

Arnold Jackson, Coleman's sitcom character, was one of the last
Norman Lear creations to at once confront and then gloss over an
American pop-cultural exploration of race. Phillip Drummond
(Bain) is a white millionaire who adopts the two sons of his deceased black housekeeper. ("Real boys!" exclaims Drummond's
prep-school teenager daughter, played by the ill-fated Dana Plato,
in the pilot episode, which aired in November 1978. "Hi, big
brother! Hi, little brother!" To which Arnold snaps, "What's she
smokin'?")

"Watchoo talkin' 'bout, Willis?" followed soon after and it would
never leave him. The show lasted for 189 episodes, as Arnold Jackson learned life's little lessons from a revolving cast of guest stars,
including Nancy Reagan, who told him to stay off drugs, and Mr.
T, who answered his "watchoos" with a "pity the fool." His exhaus-
tion with the role, and another failed kidney transplant in 1984,
sapped him of a requisite level of cheer that audiences expected,
and producers brought in another child to play his new stepbrother.
(An early episode for that character revolved around bed-wetting.)
Finally, around the time the call sheet ominously touted "David
Hasselhoff as himself," the show was canceled, wrapping its last
episode in February 1986, when Coleman was eighteen (and still
playing an eternally twelve-year-old boy). By 1990 he had fired all
his agents and managers, and sued his parents in an attempt to lo-
cate his lost fortune.

He describes his twenties as "boring"—a constant yearning to
find himself and finding nothing, and no one. He left California
and lived in Denver for a while, but show business drew him back
in. He believes in working for a living, and so he has taken almost
any job he could stomach. He spends a lot of time doing "nothing,"
he said, but he still has model trains, and he spends a lot of time on
the Internet. He likes go-karts and bowling. His favorite restaurants are Hamburger Hamlet, Tony Roma's, and Chili's. It's a nice

life, he said, and it is a manhood, despite how people sometimes treat him. He is able to laugh about himself, but you should be careful not to humiliate him: Don't pet him, don't lift him, don't tell him what to do.

You could, if you lived in California, vote for him. He'd like that. "My slogan is I'm the least qualified guy for the job, but I'd probably do the best job. I have no ambitions or any motivation at all to be a politician," he says, getting ready to go back to his car. "I am going to be a private citizen who happens to be governor. I'm not going to be political about anything. I'm going to make decisions. I'm going to decide things that are good for the state as a whole, not a left-wing or right-wing or no-wing kind of thing. You've got your senators and representatives and they're going to be fighting me tooth and nail, because I'm going to be going after their little honey pot way too often. So I'm about being a public servant. Career politicians have forgotten that their job is to make life better for their citizens. . . ."

And on he goes, auditioning for the part—any part.

Going back to Zion, he says, is not an option. He is stuck in L.A. If it could happen all over again, he would never have come to Hollywood as a boy. He would have said no to the commercials and the sitcom. He doesn't think children should be allowed to perform in television or movies. "They can make dinosaurs in movies now," he says. "Then they can make children, too." He is also aware of the special effects of California's overbudgeted politics, and he still wants more than a bit part. He wants to be bigger than they think he is.

October 7 comes and goes, and for whatever reasons, absurd or not, 14,235 Californians place their faith in, and vote for, former child star Gary Coleman.

(2003)

Wonder Woman's Powers

New York

"You boys shouldn't get so excited—it spoils your aim!"
—Wonder Woman, to thugs, in
Sensation Comics No. 26, 1944

Is it the star-spangled panties?

Maybe. Let's just think about the star-spangled panties for a while.

There. Okay. Something happens when you look at her now, reminding you of what she used to be. (And what you used to be.) Several buttons are pressed in one tangled subconscious: America, patriotism, but also ancient Greece, the gods, democratic ideals. Warrior women shaving their armpits and legs. Quiet women wearing librarian specs who duck into closets and become something else. Human flight, leaping off a window ledge toward a brilliant fabulousness. Feminist boot-kicks to the stomach. When it comes to deconstructing Wonder Woman, how much of the day can anyone (should anyone) spend thinking only about her power cleavage, or being helpless in the cinch of her kinky golden lasso? Where else to begin?

With a pencil. First, he sketches her face, then neck, bare shoulders. He then moves down to the double-Ws emblazoned across her thrust-out chest. (For reference, Phil Jimenez keeps handy a three-ring binder of pages clipped from women's lingerie catalogs and lady bodybuilder magazines.) Yet, as the current illustrator and cowriter of DC Comics' monthly *Wonder Woman* comic book, Jimenez comes to the task understanding, as a gay man, that his heroine is ultimately about so much more than her ta-tas. She is endlessly complex and she can be distant. "Sometimes you can't relate to her," he says. "Wonder Woman has no problems and who can relate to that?"

She does have one problem, and in a way, it's also Jimenez's problem: Most of the world has forgotten about Wonder Woman. Sixty years ago, she stirred imaginations and helped vanquish Hitler. In early 2001, in a trade magazine called *Wizard,* which runs a list of the one hundred top-selling comic books, *Wonder Woman* ranked eighty-sixth. Still, we'd know her if we saw her. This is what happens to spent icons. They become easily recognizable Halloween costumes with no context, aging reference points to outdated ideas that may have once been metaphors for something. Which was what, exactly, in her case? Feminism? Love? Sacrifice? Try this on for size: The man who invented Wonder Woman, a psychologist, wanted little boys to access the female archetype within themselves. (Suffering Sappho! It's Jung's beloved anima! See if the panties fit. . . .)

"She's a very difficult character to write, so people have tended to write around her instead," Jimenez says. "For a lot of people, she winds up being about the costume." He loved Wonder Woman as a boy. (His mother, a working single parent, would tell him to sit down and color, to wait for her to finish her appointments, to be good.) He loved Wonder Woman still as a young man, leaving his Orange County, California, home after high school and setting out for New York in the early 1990s to draw comic books professionally. He slept on a friend's couch for a year, after dropping out of art school when he couldn't pay the tuition. Jimenez's first boyfriend, Neil Pozner, who was also his first editor at DC, taught him the value of story economy: Stories are simple. Stories unfold one panel at a time, leading to bigger panels, two-page spreads, building toward some unexpected bang. Love stories can be that way, too. Pozner died of AIDS in 1994, a little more than a year after he and Jimenez started dating.

Six years after that, at age thirty, Jimenez was assigned his dream job: the care and feeding of Wonder Woman. Coincidentally or otherwise, the more reverent of Wonder Woman's stewards and loyal fans have tended to be gay men. Many women artists, leery of typecasting themselves, have steered clear of the assignment; straight men, agog, transformed Wonder Woman into "a Terminator babe," Jimenez says. "Which is so not like her."

■ ■ ■

Some things you may or may not need to know about WW:

1. Her Amazon bracelets, which she uses to deflect bullets, are actually symbols of her all-female tribe's enslavement under Hercules. Sometimes, one of her enemies will cut them off her wrists, and Wonder Woman goes berserk. On the other hand, if you solder the bracelets together, she becomes weak.
2. She used to have an alter ego, a secret identity: Diana Prince, nerdy Pentagon employee. They wrote that part out years ago.
3. She hasn't had sex in fifteen years.
4. There is no more invisible airplane.

That pretty much catches us up to Wonder Woman. Phil Jimenez wakes in the morning, has a Diet Pepsi, watches the all-female coffee klatch of Barbara Walters et al. on *The View,* as a kind of addictive procrastination. Then he works, at the drafting table in his living room, in his tidy apartment on Manhattan's Upper West Side. Bound editions of his favorite comics line the bookshelves, next to a clunky Sharp photocopy machine. Old Wonder Woman toys and gewgaws line the windowsill; traffic bleats below. Comic-book artists tend to occupy themselves with background, much of which the reader never sees. They fantasize about the contents of superheroes' refrigerators, or their laundry routines. Jimenez is doing that exact kind of thinking about Wonder Woman's day, giving her life: Should she wear a Chanel suit to a U.N. fundraiser? If she moves to New York, should she get a penthouse on the East Side or West Side? If you tell a joke, does Wonder Woman get it?

"Oh, she gets jokes," Jimenez says. "She actually loves humor, but you have to remember, she's not from here, so maybe she doesn't always appreciate the joke. . . . She's reading a book on gender theory right now. She thinks it's fascinating and kind of funny."

Wonder Woman fans tend to be adult, generally male, though the female segment is vocal. Many are gay men, some lesbians; Jimenez, who chats frequently with fans on a Web site, says he was most surprised at the number of black men who appear to have a Wonder Woman thing going on. In the first story line he wrote and drew late last year, Jimenez decided that Wonder Woman would use little besides harsh language to defeat Ares, the god of war, after he tries to take over Batman's Gotham City: "These people need the voids in their lives filled with love and self-respect and hope," Wonder Woman shouts to Ares. "Voids you cannot fill, War God." Ares then goes away; there's no climactic battle scene, and some longtime fans complained. They'd grown so used to those kicks, the hair-pulling, the grimace of womanly violence.

> *The picture-story fantasy cuts loose the hampering debris of art and artifice and touches the tender spots of universal human desires and aspirations. . . . Comics speak, without qualm of sophistication, to the innermost ears of the wishful self.*
>
> —William Moulton Marston, pop psychologist,
> in the *American Scholar*, 1943

In 1941, William Moulton Marston, a Harvard-educated psychologist who was secretly writing comic books on the side, gave the world Wonder Woman. She was anything but accidental, and as long as she has been around, her fans have felt that no one ever got her quite right. Marston was one of those deeply complex men who are in their own way genius, and perhaps just a bit nutty professor. He seemed particularly drawn to three subjects:

1. Women. (Smart women, often in some sort of sexy bondage.)
2. Truth. (And scientific ways to catch people at lying.)
3. Stimuli. (Pictures, movies, color, stereo sound, infotainment. It's as if Marston heard the multimedia buzz machine decades before it existed.)

At Harvard, he pioneered research that led to the polygraph. His favorite test subjects were sorority sisters: He would attend their clandestine initiation parties, at which the young women would tie one another up and sometimes wrestle. Using the lie detector, Marston would carefully monitor the rise in their fellow sorority sisters' systolic excitement while they watched the hazing rites. The coeds would never admit that seeing other women in bondage turned them on, if just ever so slightly. (He found it necessary to repeat the sorority sister experiment—dozens and dozens of times, it seems.) An outspoken publicity hound, Marston was a bad fit in academic environs. He wound up working as a sort of consulting shrink to Hollywood producers in the early 1930s. He tested moviegoers' response to colors (red, yellow, blue) and sound effects, using his data to point to the human need for subliminal stimuli. He adored the eroticism coded into horror flicks. He also wrote randy pulp novels about Greco-Roman mythology and history. In *Wonder Woman: The Complete History,* comics historian Les Daniels excerpts what Marston had reimagined for Julius Caesar and the goddess Venus: "His soul was lost in beautiful, palpitating dreams of serving her glorious womanhood forever. . . . Those wonderful feet!"

According to Daniels's biography of Marston, the psychologist fathered two children with his wife, and also two children with his research assistant Olive Byrne, who lived with the couple. He became something of an ardent feminist, telling the *New York Times* in 1937 that America would become a matriarchy within one hundred years, where "women would take over the rule of the country, politically and economically." At some point, everything in Marston's world merges into the making of a modern goddess. Under the pen name Charles Moulton, he dubbed his creation Paradise Island,

and his Wonder Woman first appeared, curvily drawn by Harry Peter, in *All-Star Comics* No. 8, a month before the Japanese bombed Pearl Harbor. In that opening episode, the Amazon princess Diana rescues a downed Air Force pilot, Col. Steve Trevor, and is chosen by her tribe to return to man's world and fight evil.

As a 1940s bombshell, Wonder Woman struggled not to swoon over Steve, brushing him aside, putting her mission first. After a typical rousing fight with negatively portrayed ethnic stereotypes, she would stand arms akimbo and preach justice to a cruel world, looking like an American flag with great gams. The press nicknamed her Wonder Woman and before long she was battling Nazi baronesses, the vainglorious Cheetah, and, eventually, gooey space aliens.

After Marston died of cancer in 1947, the idealism began to weaken. She constantly fretted about her secret identity (a powerful McCarthyism vibe runs through these issues) and whether she should chuck it all and marry Steve. A standard scenario had Wonder Woman walking down the wedding aisle, only to be interrupted before vows by would-be world dominators. Although endowed with superhuman strength (and that transparent airplane), Diana would rely mostly on love and common sense to settle disputes. She used her bracelets to deflect gunfire and her lie-detecting lasso to coerce confessions from thugs.

The premise still holds, though some would say Diana strayed even from the very beginning. Feminists wished for her to be less hung up on Steve, more concerned with fighting patriarchal evils. Lesbians have always longed for a more direct approach to some of Wonder Woman's obvious Sapphic subtext. Scholars heaped dissertations and analytical essays upon her persona, and still do. As for your basic classic-rock-listening, garage-apartment-dwelling, still-single male comic-book fan? (Vicious stereotype? Oh, well.) So long as Wonder Woman keeps washing her ever-shrinking costume in hot water, she's fine by them. Her high-minded dialogue has often seemed empty or preachy. The fanboy world pretended to listen, staring at her breasts.

. . .

Not even girls want to be girls so long as our feminine ar-
chetype lacks force, strength, and power. . . . The obvi-
ous remedy is to create a feminine character with all the
strength of Superman plus all the allure of a good and
beautiful woman.

—William Moulton Marston, 1943 (from *Wonder Woman:*
The Complete History, by Les Daniels)

Is it the twirl? We should consider the twirl, and pay homage to
actress Lynda Carter, and the way she did it on *The New Adventures*
of Wonder Woman, which ran on ABC, and then CBS, in the mid-
to late 1970s. Remarkably, I spent part of the autumn of third grade
dressed, in heady anticipation of Halloween, as Wonder Woman,
until the culture of my suburban Oklahoma City boyhood suggested this wasn't the best way for an eight-year-old boy to get back
and forth to the 7-Eleven. Also, my father drew a line here, and I've
not crossed (or cross-dressed) it since.

While it lasted, I had a costume made from one of my sisters'
tight red tube tops, a blue green pair of swim trunks I'd outgrown,
and aluminum-foil bracelets. I found a long, yellowish gold extension cord in the garage—a magic lasso—and forced my five-year-old
neighbor, Paige, to stand still while I practiced lassoing her. "You
will tell the truth," I commanded, double- and triple-knotting the
extension cord all around her body. My mother yelled at me every
time she caught me tying other kids up with the cord. The patio
table was my invisible airplane; a pair of red knee-high socks stood
in for my Wonder Woman boots. One afternoon my father pulled
into the driveway as I fought crime and lassoed little girls and
twirled around in long red socks, and it was in this moment, seeing
his angry face, that I realized there were things little boys could not
be. I could watch it on TV, but no more spinning around in the tube
top. I could have a cowboy lasso, and cowboy boots, but not a
golden lasso, not long red socks, not with swim trunks, never with
panties, not in the front yard, and probably not even in the back.

This is only one of the reasons I went up to New York to watch Phil Jimenez work for a couple of days, on deadline, to produce the next issue of *Wonder Woman*.

He laments that she has not twirled, in the pages of the comic book, for years.

But sometimes certain little boys find things on television and can't stop thinking about them. Long before these certain little boys know or realize what being homosexual even is, they will often fix-ate on some strong or larger-than-life female idol, and she won't let go. The diva inside unfurls. It could be triggered by a movie god-dess, a pop singer, a chick on a scooter escaping secret agents. It could be as unlikely as a *Life* magazine spread of Pat Nixon show-ing off the White House.

Or, in the specific case of Phil Jimenez, as well, it was Lynda Carter, twirling around and around and exploding into such inexpli-cable gloriousness as to make one wish to leap off a jungle gym at recess. Jimenez was about five years old for that. There is some-thing still very much boyish about him. "The Lynda Carter Wonder Woman turn was kind of big for a lot of gay guys I know," he says. "Some people talk about it a lot, the transformation of her doing it, spinning around, going from this dowdy, secretive woman and sud-denly she's this gorgeous superheroine. I practiced the spin when I was little. Probably because I was gay."

Too bad about all that debunking Carl Jung took from academia in the last twenty years, because it seems that his anima/animus theory runs strong in things like the Wonder Woman story, which basically shows men a path to the anima, the woman in themselves. It's as if she's right in there, this cartoony Jungian archetype of a good and protective and heroic and beautiful mother. The official line on Wonder Woman's history was that she was created to be a superhero for girls, a worthy partner to the male characters. But for Marston, she was also an entry point to the anima in little boys.

"This is a drawing of Wonder Woman I did when I was seven, and gave to my mother," Jimenez says, picking up a framed picture that is propped against a wall. It's a colored-pencil drawing of Wonder

Woman looking exactly as she did on *Super Friends,* a Saturday morning cartoon series, wearing a kind of Marlo Thomas flip. "My mother recently found it and had it framed and gave it to me as a gift. What I'd like to do is take one of my current drawings of Wonder Woman and have them framed together, and give it back to her."

■   ■   ■

In the late 1960s, with sales of the comic book waning, Col. Steve Trevor was assassinated and Wonder Woman lost her superpowers. She learned kung-fu and ditched the star-spangled panties for mod miniskirts and white pantsuits. Gloria Steinem saved her that time, by putting Wonder Woman on the cover of the first issue of *Ms.,* in 1972, spangles and all, reiterating Marston's original profeminist intent. Steinem recalled in a 1994 essay how a male editor at DC begged her to back off: "'Okay,' he said, 'She's got all her Amazon powers back. . . . She even has a black Amazon sister named Nubia. *Now* will you leave me alone?'"

It is the TV show—Lynda Carter in the plexiglass airplane—that so many people will forever equate with the character. But in a jumble of strong pop culture heroines—bionic women, police women, "Charlie's Angels"—Wonder Woman had outlived her usefulness to the collective unconscious. She stopped being the exception to the rule. When the TV show was canceled, things got worse for the comic book. She married Steve (he came back from the dead), seemingly out of boredom. Longtime readers, including, by that time, a teenage Phil Jimenez, drifted away. The men in charge of writing and drawing her (most of them were men) didn't seem to love her. Having run for 329 consecutive issues, *Wonder Woman* was temporarily shelved in 1985.

■   ■   ■

Before his contract with DC ends, Jimenez hopes to deal with each of Wonder Woman's many guises in a multilayered story line, a discreet sixtieth-anniversary nod to the heroine. The current version of the comic book was rebooted in 1986, obviating much of Wonder

Woman's cheesier past exploits. "She has transcended forty years of bad scripts," says DC publisher Jenette Kahn. "She's had a lot of high-profile artists and writers working on her over the years, and she has defied many of their abilities. Sometimes she languishes." DC, part of the Time Warner empire, is also duty bound to Wonder Woman; she's an important trademark to the company's repertoire, and a perpetual agreement with Marston's estate stipulates that a *Wonder Woman* comic book must be regularly published in order to keep the rights to the character. ("That's certainly not how we think of it, as a legal obligation," Kahn says, declining to discuss *Wonder Woman*'s contract. "I feel it's an honor.") In Phil Jimenez, Kahn hopes, she has found the rare person who can not only write and draw a crucial character, but also take the icon elsewhere. "All of our characters eventually get into lulls," Kahn says. "When someone is able to reinvent them, I get excited all over again. I actually start to read it again."

In the afternoon, over a late lunch at a restaurant not far from his apartment, Jimenez stabs at a Caesar salad and wonders why Wonder Woman keeps falling for men who aren't available to her. "For years, there has been this whole thing going on between her and Superman, this crush she supposedly has on him, their unrequited love, but he's married to Lois Lane. Wonder Woman doesn't *need* a man, but she . . . needs a man. She needs to explore." So Jimenez has based a potential boyfriend on an amalgam of real-life friends of his friends, a U.N. staffer in particular. "A normal guy," he says. "A normal, available guy, who isn't intimidated by her."

In the afternoon, he continues progress on rough pencil storyboards for an upcoming issue, in which Wonder Woman will let Lois Lane write a *Daily Planet* profile of her. Lois's motives here are suspect (she wants to find out if Wonder Woman has designs on her husband, Superman). In a "day in the life of Wonder Woman," Lois will follow the heroine to play basketball at youth shelters, then to Africa to hold infant refugees, then to a science lab to work on a cure for diabetes. After the long day, the two women go to a bar and shoot pool and Lois tries to pick Wonder Woman's brain, and get her to confess some of her hidden truths.

This sounds like what William Moulton Marston, all those years ago, might have had in mind. It might assist the subconscious to see them tie one another up for some light bondage play. Marston was always finding a way to get Wonder Woman tied up, sometimes spanked. That would have pressed the late professor's buttons, but these are comic books. They go everywhere indirectly, but they do not go there.

(2001)

Everything
Must Go

Other People's Stuff

Austin, Texas

Sooner or later, you'll come back for that which you'd stored away, and sometimes it isn't there. "Honey Bear's coming," one of the ladies in the front office screamed, "and he's got a gun!"

Well, well, well, Debbie Billington thought, looking up from her desk.

Honey Bear crashed in like a big boulder tumbling off a hill of his own accumulated rage, waving his gun and bellowing, "What'd you do with my stuff? Where the hell is my stuff?" Honey Bear was way behind on the rent for his unit at the Austin self-storage facility where Debbie Billington got her start, back in the early days of this weird and sometimes emotional business of leasing space to a world with extra junk and nowhere to put it.

In her defense, Billington had left messages for Honey Bear. She sent Honey Bear certified mail. Eventually, and legally, she sawed off the lock and auctioned everything Honey Bear had. What choice was there? She sold Honey Bear's lumpy mattress and box spring. She sold his love seat, his coffee table, his Barry White albums. She made her peace with this last-resort recourse, and released the space. "But I always knew, one day, Honey Bear would be back," she says. "And that he'd be mad."

Now she was trapped. *Surely one of them will call the police,* she thought to herself, watching her employees dash out the back door. They ran across the street. None of them called the police. *I'm going to die at the storage units,* she thought, her mouth going dry, her heart pounding, *but first, I'm going to give Honey Bear a piece of my mind.* "Honey Bear," she said sternly, standing up, both hands on the desk—and this is small and soft woman with amber-colored hair who once ran a day-care center, who looks like your aunt, who looks like she would bring you a casserole. "Honey Bear, I'm so angry at you. You put that gun away. Now I want you to sit down, because you know good and well that I tried to find you so this wouldn't happen."

Honey Bear froze. "Really, what Honey Bear was mad about was that his wife had run off with another man," Billington recalls, having lived to tell it. "The thing he really wanted back was this old bed he had." So it was like the song "Hey Joe," except it ended at the storage unit, and no one got shot. Twenty minutes later, Honey Bear sat in Debbie Billington's chair, put his gun down, and cried. "Now, there," she said, trying to cheer him up, putting her arm around his massive shoulder. "You didn't want that bed anyway. She probably slept with that other guy right there on that bed, all the time."

"Yeah," Honey Bear blubbered. "And she probably did it with him on the couch, too."

I. Nine Billion Seven Hundred Million Cubic Feet

When, exactly, did the American crap crisis begin? Think of the pioneers abandoning those oak chairs and milk pails when the horses began to wheeze, before the trail diverged to white-capped mountains and everyone wound up eating one another. Think of all those Italian grandmothers who managed to get to Ellis Island without last year's Christmas decorations. Think of the Russian Jews. All that moving and misery—*Anatevka, Anatevka*—without any Rubbermaid laundry baskets.

(What, without beanbags?)

(Without a NordicTrack?)

Once there was a rationale: We can live without it. But we got to the promised land, and promptly ordered double prints of snap-shots we took along the way. Then we needed a place to put the snapshots. We divorced and fought over particleboard furniture. We had our teeth X-rayed and made laws that these records can never be discarded or destroyed until many years after we are dead. Now there is no rationale, which is one of the reasons why, by the mid-1990s, there were approximately 9.7 billion cubic feet of self-storage in the United States, and growing. In the American Else-where, developers stopped building homes with basements. Criminals needed to hide things. People kept moving to new and better jobs, emotionally and physically itinerant, dragging their things along with them for comfort, loving their jobs a little bit more than they seemed to love their mothers, or their hometowns.

Storage units are the gray areas in our lives. It can be on the other side of town, it could be on the moon. It's the place where your stuff is, and you're not. There's an old here and a new there and all those interstate off ramps in between.

Some real-estate analysts believe the self-storage warehouse concept began in California in the mid-1970s, during the New Dis-location, the transient search for careers and love and sunshine. New York's gritty wharves were retrofitted decades ago as spare closets, to accommodate the clutter of apartment dwellers. Texans, naturally, believe it all started in Texas, in rural areas, in sheds sur-rounded by barbed-wire-topped cyclone fences. Debbie Billington is almost certain it started on North Lamar Boulevard in 1974. That's where it started for her, anyway, when she got into the busi-ness as a bookkeeper for a man named Charles Basquette, who had space to spare in his lumberyard and decided he'd rent it out.

Self-storage facilities are the among the last inexpensive land ventures, cheaper to own than single-family dwellings, factories, or strip malls. Ten years ago, there were fewer than 7,000 self-storage businesses nationwide, but they've multiplied at a rate of 10 percent to 20 percent every year since. No one's counting precisely, but it was thought, in 1997, that there were 30,000 extant facilities nation-wide, each averaging 400 units. (In Texas, the market was believed to have peaked that year at around 3,000 facilities.) Storage units are at once cheerful and somber and no fun to look at, from the outside, and frequently appear on freeway frontage roads, next to the chain restaurants and motels. They are stark places that fade into the grid, and are often arranged in neat croplike rows of putty-colored, cinder-block buildings. Some are stacked four and five stories tall and gussied with neon, proclaiming themselves "Climate Controlled." They can be such quiet places, serenity and concrete, laid out like mausoleums. Your stuff is resting in peace. About 60 percent of what's stored, according to consumer surveys, are personal items such as clothes and furniture; the rest of the spaces are leased commercially, to businesses that store supplies, inventory, and equipment—and boxes upon boxes of old documents.

Behind every padlock and brightly colored rolltop door, there is our history, the life and times of the Permanently Temporary People. Earlier this summer, I moved most of my belongings into a storage unit, for the second time in two years in two different states. You need an eight-digit secret code to open the gate. Then, if you want to talk to people about what they keep here (and why), you face another real hurdle: hours of silence, where no one comes to visit their stuff. Just when you're ready to leave, there is at last the sound of life. A salesman drives up and loads the trunk of his Infiniti with the latest gizmos, which he keeps there, in bulk. Someone's ex-girlfriend has gathered her gumption and her cousins, and there is wicker and a microwave oven and bedspreads and then nothing, poof, she and the cousins are gone. A family readies itself to move to Florida, a happy assortment of tricycles and floor lamps. Next, a fellow renter rolls by on his Harley-Davidson, which he keeps here in the storage unit, and visits, furtively, like he's having an affair with a mistress, and this is the bland apartment complex where he keeps her hidden from his wife.

"You know when times are good and times are bad, by what people store," says Will Farrar, a storage-unit developer in Bryan-College Station, who is president of the Texas Mini Storage Association Inc. "Some years it's jet skis and boats. You see people at the happiest times in their lives or people who are absolutely down on their luck."

"Your storage unit is not your castle," says Rich Elmer, who owns Cypress Storage Stalls on East Ben White Boulevard in one of the ugliest parts of Austin. "It's important to people, but in a different way." The self-storage trade associations, and the spokeswoman of the local organization of mini-self-storage owner-operators, and the Public Storage Inc. corporate Web site—all of them tend to speak in measurements of square feet.

As in how much floor space, per unit—total square footage.

Did they forget we can stack things?

Cubic. (Piled, crammed.)

I kept my sofa turned up on end.

I have many times considered myself an ingenious nomad.

II. The Quiet Sheep

One afternoon this summer I am talking to Doris, a thin and strong and somehow angelic woman who runs a small, weathered, but reliably locked-up storage complex on Ben White Boulevard, where I am keeping most of my belongings in a ten by ten for about two months. I am between overpriced Austin apartments in the heyday of the high-tech boom, and not entirely convinced I want to go on living in Texas (and some days, not entirely convinced I want to go on living at all).

Doris has lots of motherly advice: An open bag of charcoal in the corner will reduce the humidity in your unit. Ants hate mothballs as much as the moths do. Doris has stories, too. "Ooh, I hate when I have to cut the lock off and throw open that door for the first time," she says, in a campfire-tale tone of voice. One time she came face-to-face with a cougar. It was stuffed. Then there are the rolled-up carpets. "I see a rolled-up carpet and the hairs on my arms stand up on end," Doris says.

"Dead bodies!" I squeal.

"Never saw one, thankfully," Doris said.

Later, another customer, a man signing his lease, chimed in: "It's like that scary movie, what's-it, *The Quiet Sheep*."

The Quiet Sheep? I tell him I don't think I ever saw it.

"Yeah," he says, "where she finds that head in a jar?"

Ah. *The Silence of the Lambs,* I think he means. Early in the film, FBI Agent Clarice Starling (Jodie Foster), on the trail of Hannibal Lecter, checks out a storage unit leased by one of Lecter's former psychiatric patients—also a serial killer. She crawls underneath the jammed door, and eventually finds, by flashlight, a head in a jar. Every storage-unit manager has seen the movie, but the discovery of human remains in storage units is, in fact, relatively rare. So says the man from the Self Storage Association in Cincinnati, to my complete disappointment. ("I have a guy who stores English muffins," he offers, as a consolation.) Storage units are hardly ever as foreboding as they are in movies. They're better lit. Security cameras and gate codes prevent the newly homeless from turning into storage-unit residents. The managers develop a sense for spotting trouble. Earlier this spring, a newspaper report out of Tulatin, Oregon, blessed me with a gross storage-unit story: A young man named Lloyd Stephen Solomon, then seventeen, fatally bashed up his buddy and fellow bogus-check writer, Eric Chambers, eighteen, with a baseball bat. Solomon then allegedly cut Chambers into 150 pieces. He put some of Chambers in an ice chest and some of Chambers in a garbage can, and put all of that in a Public Storage unit on a frontage road. Almost three years later, he missed one rent payment, which is the only reason he got caught.

III. The Auction (Always Count Your Cushions)

Like photocopy shops and greasy-spoon diners, storage units have been revolutionized and made somewhat cheerier, if less adventuresome, by corporate ownership. Moving-truck companies such as U-Haul have joined the game, making it harder for the mom-and-pops. The industry's biggest chain, with 1,400 US locations, is Public Storage.

Public Storage has fifteen sites around Austin, painted purple and orange. For two days every month, it sloughs off delinquent tenants by selling their belongings to junk collectors. Sherice Reid, one of the local sales managers, saws off the padlocks and takes a brave look inside each abandoned unit, at each Public Storage location in town. "It's just a job, but I'm a Christian, too," she says. "You hate to have to sell people's stuff." Legally, she cannot rummage through the stuff. She jots down what she sees, and replaces the lock. Public Storage then turns to public notice. Lengthy but fascinating classified ads are placed in the newspaper eight days before the sale, listing each tenant by name and unit number, and briefly describing what's stored:

Paul Atkinson: Sofa, bike, trunk, boxes.

Mary E. Martinez: Fur, TV, boxes, clothes.

Janet Youngblood: Sofa, boxes, sewing machine.

At nine on a depressingly sweaty Tuesday morning, which happens to be the twenty-second anniversary of Jimmy Hoffa's disappearance, I join the cliquish and competitive storage-unit scavenging scene, which commences at a Public Storage location off Research Boulevard.

Patrick Sauer, the district manager for Public Storage, shows up to begin double-checking the paperwork at the first of thirty-eight sales at nine Public Storage locations on this day. He's young and has sideburns and looks like he played football in school. He smiles to everyone waiting outside. Among the dozen or so auction customers clustering by the front office is Kay, a retired school principal, and her husband, Joe. They own a thrift store in Prairie Lea, Texas. There's Brian, a flea marketeer. There's Larry, and there's Terry, who travel together in the same pickup. There's Nellie, who describes herself as "bitten by the bug" of one too many garage sales and now wants to branch into junk's big leagues. She's brought her mother, Alameda, and they both appear dressed for church. There's Michael and Maria, a young couple who called in sick so they could go to their first storage-unit auction just for fun. "We're thrill seekers," Maria says.

Eventually, Patrick and Sherice step out of the office and go over the rules. Most everyone has heard them before, but just in case: The curious twist to a storage-unit auction is that the purchaser has to buy the unit's *entire contents*. You can't bid on a single item; you are bidding on the whole mess. If the unit is filled with cardboard boxes, you cannot know what's in each box until you've bought it. Sometimes, Sauer will lift open the door to the unit up for auction, only to reveal that it contains one small mysterious suitcase—which cannot be opened until it is sold. Sometimes it's a three-bedroom house's worth of cheap furniture, old towels, framed pictures of hot-air balloons. If you buy it, you get it all.

"It's a gamble," Kay says. Some units sell for a few bucks and some for a few thousand, depending on visions of hidden treasure. "There was one load we bought in San Antonio, and we were just embarrassed once we had it. It was trash. . . . We almost wanted to just roll it off into a river." Once the contents of a unit are auctioned, the buyer has two days to remove it all. According to Public Storage's rules, personal items like photos and letters must be returned to the office. (But the original owners rarely come back for them. And the bidders rarely turn them back in.)

"Get the golf cart," Patrick says. He and Sherice and a couple of the more elderly would-be bidders tool along the asphalt, past rows of storage units. Everyone else walks.

The first unit of the day, and the only auction at this location, is D-34, belonging to someone named Becky Hudson. Sherice rolls opens the door.

Whoever Becky Hudson is or was, she left a lot of stuff. The junk collectors collectively go ka-ching, with poker faces. They see a dishwasher and, better, a pool table.

"Hmmmm," Kay says.

"Oooh," Nellie says. "Lotta good stuff in there."

"Always count your cushions," Kay says, pointing to the sofa.

"Who wants to start the bid?" Sherice says, tossing her braids, tracing at the pavement with her penny loafer.

"Twenty-five doll'rn," says a man through a wad of tobacco.

"Twenty-five," Sherice hollers.

$40, $50, $60 . . . $100, $120 . . . $200.

Within a few minutes, a man in a red shirt buys the unit for $230.

While he fills out paperwork, everyone goes back to their cars and drives to the next auction, at a different Public Storage off In-

terstate 35. There, we dicker over Susan Delgado's boxes and vacuum cleaner. We bid low for Linda Hardaway's sofa (another ingenious nomad—sofa on end). Gregg Moore had a lamp, and those
cheap, chrome-metal dinette chairs that bend when you lean too far
back in them. "Quality, quality," Patrick says with a snide smirk,
when he opens the door.

"Hey, doesn't anybody want to go for the briefcase?" Kay quips.
"You never know! Diamonds! Krugerrands!"

Walking back to the gate, amid the bleakness, Patrick turns serious. It's a sad world, he says, if you think about it. "Somebody's losing," Nellie says. "We benefit on someone's hardship."

In a unit off Lamar Boulevard, the door is pulled open and Kay
can instantly sense what happened here: The unit is half-empty,
and left behind are a worn-out recliner, camouflage netting, tackle
boxes, an ugly lamp, a little cube fridge. Pistol bullets and shotgun
shells are scattered on the floor, a nice touch. "It's a divorce," Kay
proclaims. "She came and got all her stuff and left his."

"And looks like she did it pretty quick, too," Terry (or is it
Larry?) adds.

The unit goes for $60. Another unit contains nothing but paper:
newspapers, junk mail, dozens of plastic postal tubs full of useless
paper. It spills out into the breeze. It takes three guys to help
Sherice and Patrick push it all back in and shut the door. No sale.

As the golf cart heads through the long labyrinth of cinder
block, and the temperature past noon reaches into the high
nineties, we see a man watching a small, black-and-white TV in his
storage unit. He's messing with piles of wire on his work table. He
is sitting in an old kitchen chair, surrounded by little shreds of
everything you could think of. He peers out at us like a weary Geppetto, and then looks back down. "He's here every day," Sherice
says. "A sweet man. He just comes and sits in his storage unit."

IV. Time Capsules (Stevie Ray)

A check is sent from a Los Angeles address every month to Top Hat
Storage on South Congress Avenue, to cover the rent on a unit kept

by the estate of Stevie Ray Vaughan, the famous blues guitarist who died in a helicopter crash seven summers earlier, in 1990, and who was a customer for many years here at Top Hat Storage, and still is, in a way. Vaughan is a local, tragic hero in this town. People leave flowers at the statue of him near Town Lake. What treasures might be in his old storage unit, and how many Texans would love to have—or merely glimpse—Stevie Ray Vaughan's stuff? You think of old cassette demo tapes and guitars, jottings, musings. Diaries, receipts.

Then again, what if it's still more Christmas decorations? Another broken vacuum cleaner in a world of broken vacuum cleaners? Stevie's old tinsel, layers of dust? "The check comes," says Sandra Northrop, with a shrug. Of course, she's never checked inside it, because that would be wrong. A manager's knowledge stops at the gate. Enough months go by that a storage unit becomes a time capsule. "They did come and get his old tour van, pretty recently."

Sandra and her husband, Keith, have found a small paradise at Top Hat. They live in a cozy apartment behind the office with Wolf, a German shepherd/mix who is their guard dog. In the front, they have a collection of exotic pets: a rattlesnake, a boa constrictor, a tarantula, two baby crocodiles. Keith rents out Ryder trucks and private mailboxes on the side. Sandra's teenage son lives with them, and Keith happily shows me the kid's winning science-fair project about gravity. "That's the kind of thing people would put in a storage unit," I say, admiring the work.

"It is," exclaims Keith. "It is the kind of thing they'd put in a storage unit."

The final auction ends up at the Vegas-bright, but somehow still creepy, even prisonlike, five-story Public Storage facility off I-35 at Forty-first Street. This is the mother ship. Patrick Sauer proudly shows me the James Bond layout of the place, with its computerized sentry and climate command center. Michael and Maria, the thrill-seeking couple on a date to storage auctions, buy the last crap of the day, for $31: a suitcase, a gym bag, a CD player (the prehistoric kind), and a pair of muddy workboots, which all belonged to another faceless mystery man, James Cummings. Michael rummages through the clothes in the bag. "That's some good stuff, right there," Patrick says, with exhausted sarcasm.

We smile and laugh. It already is archaeology. (What will the petrified Cheetos in the cracks of our abandoned sofas mean in a thousand years?) We examine these flint tools of some poor sap, in the ancient fields of the quiet sheep.

V. Nine Billion Seven Hundred Million Cubic Feet and the Widow and the Cheeto

Rich Elmer had a customer at his storage units, a man who was a lawyer. When the man died, his widow put off going through the unit for many years. She never touched it. That was another check that always came on time. "A lot of our business is customers who just don't want to face it," Elmer says. Because we're lazy. Because we're sentimental. It feels better to keep the stuff somewhere else, somewhere locked and private.

Sandra has learned about people who have too much. People who run storage units become, opposite to their jobs, the advocates of junk reduction. "You fill up every closet you have," she says. "It's human nature. . . . You get burdened down with all these things. But your stuff is important to you. We get the estate sales, where Mom passed away and the kids have every intention of coming back and going through it. But a lot of times, they don't."

Sandra has learned, and Keith has learned.

Doris has learned, and on the day I move out, into a living arrangement where the furniture sits flat and the books are on shelves, she tells me she doesn't want to share any more of her stories about storage. She wants to keep them to herself, save them for her book. Debbie Billington has learned, and maybe Honey Bear learned when he lost his stuff. The junk collectors learn every time they get their hands on those boxes, which they, in turn, have to store somewhere. They've learned that time and space have actual value.

(1997)

Scooch Over

There's something about the plastic patio chair.

No, there's not.

And that's what it is about them. Plastic chairs, plastic chairs. Stacking plastic resin chairs. Four high, five high, twenty high. Wipe 'em down, have a seat, stay a while. Sit a spell on a petroleum planet. Resistant to the jaws of overbred Dobermans, contrary to all feng shui, airborne in tropical storms, swirling about in the Wal-Mart-flattening tornadoes of American notions of taste, landing God knows where. They remind us there's cheap living, here, outside, in our plastic chairs. In March you unstack them and admire the filth that collected on them over the winter, the shadows of grime in the seat pan. You spray them with 409. There's now an antiseptic smell layered atop their blessed plasticity. Last summer is gone. They gleam again.

These are not the good chairs; these are the chairs that, engineered for low expectations, will do when life is nothing special.

Plastic Patio Chair Scenario No. 1: Do you want to sit outside? This is an easy question. Of course you want to sit outside, have a nice lunch, and so you carry your tray out to some piece of sidewalk in front of that Middle Eastern kabob place. See if there's a table out there and we'll sit outside. There: table and chairs, molded resin plastic, a study in unassuming nonstyle, invisible but for the fact that they exist. So you sit. You deconstruct office politics. You badmouth everyone in town.

Plastic Patio Chair Scenario No. 2: She's having some people over, some friends of Greg's from work, also her sister and her sister's husband, and they're going to be cooking out, do you want to come by? This question is not quite so easy. Yes, you want to come over, *in theory*, until you're there, and then for some reason you wish you could leave. You spend three hours in a plastic patio chair, listening to people you don't really know talk about buying their second house. You sit in the plastic chair and do something painterly on a piece of Chinet with your plastic fork and the orangy brown residue of pork and beans. Swirls, then crosshatching. Five more people show up. Hi, yes, we've met before. No, come over here, there's room, you can have my chair. Greg, get the extra chairs; there's three more in the garage. The white ones.

Someday, when you spend more than $300 on patio furniture made of wood or wrought iron—into which you've put considerable thought about cushion color and pattern—you will know that you've left a certain part of your old life behind: the salad days, the plastic chair days, when it was still possible that you would meet new lifelong friends, instead of just shaking hands with people and making small talk and getting by with nanoglimpses at the peekaboo flesh on somebody else's spouse. You owned plastic chairs when you were hungry about ideas and thought there was more to figure out about the world. Before you knew about style, and knew more about philosophy; back when these things were still sorted out and mulled over aloud, with beers, the domestic beers, kept in a red plastic Coleman cooler. Before anyone expected you to hold a new baby, and back when you never asked to hold a new baby. (There were no new babies.)

The cheap chairs date back to when you were a nicer but possibly less refined person who didn't require people to RSVP for your barbecue or brunch or whatever you're calling it. People just came over, and there were places to sit. A tiki torch seemed like the ultimate expression of your sense of summer exotica. The citronella candles burned like your desires.

Plastic chairs. If you went to Vietnam now, you'd see them

everywhere, a new twist on the corruptive West-East bumper-car
notions of tacky aesthetic, Asian tropic, bourgeois comfort, jungle
stickiness, the ricey cleanliness, the sin, and the infectedness. You
would notice that they're smaller, made for Vietnamese men, who
sit in them while their wives work. Plastic chairs show up in news
photos of troubled, other nations: They are strewn after a suicide
bombing at a café; they are the chief furnishing in the mullah's
camp; stars are shuffling by them at the Cannes Film Festival.

White, or forest green, and then suddenly a little more fancy,
now in "cashmere granite," or "pewter blue." Nobody's written a
book about them. Michael Graves has not redone them as a kind of
iconic, wink-nudge, $29 version. Target has not dolled them up
with red-bull's-eye logos. The cable home-and-garden networks and
Real Simple–type magazines have yet to sing their praises. ("Plastic
Chairs: Too Simple?") Consider the $800 stacking chair, however,
in magnesium, sci-fi shaped, and marketed by unbearably snotty
Germans dressed in ribbed cotton and Lycra T-shirts and tiny spec-
tacles. (The *New York Times*'s "House & Home" section is talking
about those chairs: "This Chair Hates Being Ignored," reads the
headline, so it costs $800.)

But plastic chairs that cost $4.88 at Home Depot: They love be-
ing ignored.

Honey, the chairs are in the pool again.

■   ■   ■

Sometimes the plastic chairs are inside, in the living room, or at the
dining table. This is unsettling. It starts to feel like the set of a porn
movie, or the apartment of a guy whose wife kicked him out. He's
got golf clubs, a big-screen television, and three plastic chairs.
Sometimes plastic chairs are a menace: "Attention all residents," a
photocopied notice in an Arlington apartment elevator admonishes.
"Please remember during severe weather (thunderstorms, etc.) to
bring all chairs inside off the balcony. Its hazard [sic] for people below to avoid." The idea of them, thousands and thousands of them,
falling from the sky, like biblical mystery frogs.

The resin stacking patio chair is the Tupperware container of a lard-assed universe, and like Tupperware, you can always use a few more pieces. Forty plastic chairs arranged around a lawn that has been freshly mowed in seductive crisscrosses. It's a party. Plastic chairs with matching plastic tables, each with a plastic centerpiece that disgorges foil confetti, a karaoke machine set up to one side, a sheet cake that says "Congratulations!" adorned with Crisco-icing roses. An entirely plastic party, with plastic champagne flutes, and everybody wearing sunglasses and flip-flops. Kraft Miracle Whip. Paprika on deviled eggs. Sunscreen with bug repellent already in it. Thighs on resin plastic.

Scooch over: Grip the plastic chair by the seat, or the curved arms, and scooch over, the sound of its four V-shaped legs dragging across the patio pavement, the slightest wobble to the whole affair. Make room for more. The plastic chair fits almost anyone, but not everyone: "Not intended for use . . . by persons weighing more than 250 pounds," says the fine print on the sticker. But there is ample room for such a person. Lots of places for the fat to push through on either side and through the spaces along the back. A nice, American-fanny-size seat pan. One factory that makes them reveals the use of a 400-pound test weight that it drops into the chair to see if it cracks. Looks good. The 400-pound weight, attached to a robot arm, also tilts the chair back to see how far you can go before it's Flip City, and the whole party is laughing at you.

Scooch over for some history: It's 1927 in France. Auguste and Jean-François Grosfillex open a factory in Arbent, north of Oyon-nax. They're brothers. They make only wooden handles for tools. One of them has a son, Raymond, who inherits the company and hears what the gods of plastic are telling him, in 1954, and the company thus focuses only on plastic, starting with kitchen utensils. Grosfillex manufactures what is believed to be the world's first mass-market plastic chair, in 1959.

But this is not the patio chair we are now sitting in. The 1959 Grosfillex chair is wondrously French, modern. It is bright red plastic snapped onto a black metal frame, with quarter-size holes all over it. This chair hates being ignored. By the 1970s, Grosfillex is selling products in the United States—soap dishes, toothbrush holders, and plastic outdoor furniture. By the 1980s, the patio class of America has seen the coming and going of several pieces of the furniture of various futures: the aluminum folding chair with nylon weaving in the seat and back; the hard metal patio chairs of the 1940s and 1950s that added a classic panache to tract living; teenagers sunning themselves in back yards on those plastic and metal trifolding chaise lounges; Eastern blue bloods and their beloved Adirondacks; cheap deck chairs of all sorts.

Then came the plastic stacking chair. Some people say it was 1988, 1989. Resin technology took off. Europeans had embraced plastic. Americans certainly had no aversion to it. Someone put together a clean-lined, benignly elegant chair's chair—shaped somewhat like a midcentury desk chair, only slumpier. The true ubiquity of the plastic chair emerges from the facts that no one takes credit for having made it, there is no patent on it (only patents on techniques of making it), and no one knows how many have been made, or who sold them, or who likes them. They simply are. (Plastic, triumphant.)

In the patio furnishing retailing world, these chairs are thought to be the lowest of the low. Which is why they are everywhere. Scooch over for the utterly fascinating details of how they are made: There are around a half-dozen manufacturers of plastic patio chairs in the United States. Plastic chairs, it seems, are so cheap to make that no one imports them or exports them—Mexican plastic chairs are made in Mexico; European plastic chairs are made in Europe; Taiwanese plastic chairs are made in Taiwan. Grosfillex, one of the biggest producers of plastic chairs, has a factory in Robesonia, Pennsylvania, where they make plastic chairs twenty-four hours a day, nine months out of the year. (The other three months, July to September, they make plastic chairs only twelve hours a day.) The most familiar model is the Miami Lowback, but there are many permutations, each trying a little harder to transcend the plastic chair paradigm: the Modulis Classic, the Bora, the Aquaba, the Colombo.

To make a plastic chair, you need a press that is roughly the size of a freight locomotive. Grosfillex has "several," according to a spokeswoman, who declined to say exactly how many. A plastic chair begins with an exact combination of thousands of tiny pellets of an oil derivative, a specific blend of resin, mixed with pellets of anti-ultraviolet additives, color, and anti-static magic. A computer shoots the pellets into the mold, where they are heated to a molten state. A huge screw—"I mean really huge, like two feet in diameter and twenty feet long," says Grosfillex's marketing director, Karen Klein—presses the mold together and a chair is formed. Water jets immediately start cooling it. A robot arm lifts the chair into a cooling sling. The whole process takes anywhere from forty-five to ninety seconds. And so, if the press is running all day and all night, every day for nine months, and there are untold number of these presses—*More Doritos?*

More Doritos?

What?

Your hostess is snapping you out of your zombie sunshine distraction. For a moment, you'd gone someplace else, where plastic stacking patio chairs outnumber the Americans. The chairs were crawling across the burbs like insects, but now you're back, making polite small talk, crossing your leg over your knee, the gentle unpeeling of your thigh from uncelebrated resin.

(2001)

The Faster Lane

Akron, Ohio

The headquarters of the Professional Bowlers Association is located exactly where you'd hope to find it—in a low, boxy, 1960s optometrist-esque building on a quiet commercial strip along the broad waistband of the nation's Sansabelt, next to a Mexican restaurant that is temporarily closed. On the day before Thanksgiving in 1999, the sport's commissioner, Mark Gerberich, a calm, deep-voiced, forty-year-old man who stands six feet four inches tall and begins his day by attending a men's Bible study group, told his staff of nine employees to go home early. The commissioner then went into his office, shut the door, sat down at his desk, and began to weep.

Sometimes it feels as if the world is unraveling thread by thread, and there are theories that it may have to do with the state of bowling. People have loved bowling for five millennia, but they are also unfaithful to it. It's no surprise that pro bowling has long been infected with a terminal case of disrespect. Gerberich had been shouldering most of the burden in secret. There were things even his wife didn't know. He realized, last November, that he wouldn't be able to make the Professional Bowlers Association's next employee payroll. Already the board of directors had unwisely dipped into the last cookie jar—their players' pension fund—to make ends meet. The PBA Tour was $3 million in debt. Sponsors were bailing.

Money wasn't the only problem. The less-than-mythic stereotype of the pro bowler, with his Flintstones DNA and pleated-
Dockers worldview, hasn't transitioned gracefully to modern sports
glitz. By the turn of the century, bowling alley owners had to turn
their lanes into retro-style disco nightclubs to draw crowds. League
membership was down by half. In the age of the Tostitos Fiesta
Bowl and the Chevrolet Player-of-the-Game, bowling was the only
professional sport still lacking the Nike swoosh or a suitable equiv-
alent. (And yet so primal, so seemingly marketable—so fixated on
man's urge to destruct.)

Gerberich sat, crying to himself and feeling, he recalls, "like the
man who will be remembered for killing the PBA." Then the phone
rang. A millionaire in Seattle was on the other end. In one of those
happy midlife crises that Seattle millionaires seemed to have with
increasing frequency in the late 1990s, this man had discovered
that he had a bowling jones—after sixteen years of sitting in front
of a computer writing code and moving up the ranks of Microsoft
Corporation.

He and two partners offered to buy the entire league, reportedly
for about $5 million. It was almost divine. Bowling and computers.
Yes, of course: Internet wealth in the form of three former Microsoft whizzes offering to reach down and rescue a blue-collar religion from its outdated doldrums. It would be a love story for and
about certain kinds of not-terribly-exciting guys who deeply understood one another. A deal was finalized in April 2000, after a players'
vote, born of a struggle between what's old and what's new and
what is, simply, nature.

Nature is a round thing knocking stuff over. Everything else is
strictly business.

On balls, Jorge Luis Borges:

> He felt the incessant weight of the physical world, he
> experienced vertigo, fright and solitude, and he put his
> feelings into these words: "Nature is a fearful sphere,
> whose center is everywhere and whose circumference is
> nowhere."

Borges wrote it in 1959, which happens to be the same year a bunch of men gathered in the back of a bowling alley in Paramus, New Jersey, and listened to instructions from a man named Eddie Elias, who was going to put them on a television show called *Jackpot Bowling*.

In the ongoing obsession to resell, repackage, and relocate American leisure, even bowling has gone West Coast. Something so Erie, so Akron—so very Akron—will now be masterminded from hiply decorated offices in downtown Seattle. When the 2000 PBA Tour began on June 11 in Albuquerque, it did so with a new, tech-savvy marketing plan, with the ultimate goal of making the sport cool. "This is our chance," Gerberich says. "Bowling will never be the same." No one involved seems to want bowling to be the way it was. The new owners are a former Microsoft executive named Chris Peters and two other Microsoft alums: RealNetworks CEO Rob Glaser and former Starwave Corporation CEO Mike Slade. They are taking on the PBA's considerable debt and pop-cultural baggage, with the deftly calculated assumption that bowling can't get any worse.

"It might seem like a good idea to sell bowling on its nostalgic value," Peters says. "But when you look at what happens when you do that, all you get is a nostalgia trip. It would actually be a sure way to kill it. All we want to do is Normal Sports Marketing 101—promoting the players, explaining the game, showing the excitement. No one ever did that for bowling."

Once a pioneer of televised sports, pro bowling is now preparing to go Internet bonkers, with visions of fans clicking in every day to watch live tournaments. Players will compete for more money and—one day, in line with its owners' Microsoft upbringing—stock options. Peters likes bowling for a lot of reasons, not the least of which is its artful science: "Spheres and planes, right, exactly," he says, believing the key to respecting bowling is to understand the tricky and ever-changing physics behind it. (This will involve lots of keen graphics.)

The sport is also looking for stars. The New Bowling may come to resemble a hybrid of pro wrestling, pro golf, and *Mission: Impos-*

sible, with good-versus-evil narratives, gadgetry fixations, brand-name advertisers, and perhaps better-looking guys. Something more macho, within gentlemanly confines, in which athletes will ascend to elevated bowling lanes in laser-lit arenas packed with thousands of fans. There might be babes. The crowds, everyone hopes, will begin to become the kind of people who chant. Before any of this can happen, bowling must confront a profound identity crisis: At a time when nerds came to rule the planet in terms of technology and commerce, are pro bowlers the right kind of nerd?

Dundalk, Maryland

In the basement of his mother's row house, Danny Wiseman is digging around for some piece of memorabilia from his life in bowling, but it's easy to get distracted by the visual tour of his shirts: Dozens of polos in every hue and stripe hang from two clothes racks, with the PBA and other brand logos stitched on, and his name embroidered on the back. Wiseman, thirty-two, has worn them through an up-and-down decade as a pro bowler, through the nadir of a divorce from his teenage sweetheart and another breakup with a girlfriend who also bowled pro, through the death of his father, of cancer, in 1995, and through a career with earnings totaling $723,568, not counting an endorsement deal he has with Brunswick's Revolution balls: "I never wear this one anymore, never wear this one anymore. In fact, I never wear any of these anymore. Do you wear polo shirts? What size are you?"

On a Monday morning a few weeks before the PBA season commences, in the well-worn Baltimore suburb of Dundalk, Wiseman is the picture of the bowler who thrived in the latter-day PBA. He's quick to address his up-from-nowhere roots: that he didn't go to college. His curly hair is short on the sides and long in back, and dyed a deep, unnatural red. He wears a gold chain around his neck, and also wears his father's old ring—he never takes it off—two fingers away from his "300" ring (bowling's secular grail).

When the new season starts, Wiseman wants to reassert himself as one of the stars of the New Bowling, though his story firmly adheres to the old. Among other things, he wants a whole new wardrobe—less nerdy, a little more style. "I've got some really good ideas," Wiseman says, and this includes a theme song: something from the heavy-metal band Pantera, he says, but, "They would never let me do that."

"He's still a Dundalk boy," says his mother, Dorothy Potter, sitting on a couch covered with a Lord's Prayer throw, not far from bowling trophies. "He can be a world-famous bowler, but he'll always be a Dundalk boy."

That is the story of this ancient sport, trying to fit into a new world where the de facto national anthem is "We Will Rock You." Bowling never learned to rock you. In its unchanging nature, it sings to Dundalk boys.

■   ■   ■

The PBA's story quietly turned publicly tragic about four years ago. Complaining of poor ratings, executives at ABC dropped bowling in 1997, after thirty-five years of less-than-scintillating television. Advertisers were afraid of bowling's aging demographics. (Bowling drifted to CBS for a stopgap season, then found a more permanent home on ESPN and sometimes on Fox.) In Akron, you start to understand where Seattle might be able to help. Along a wood-paneled stairwell that leads to the basement of the PBA offices, there is a Wall of Fame, a shrine of framed eight by tens of its demigods going back to forever, in order. Mark Gerberich, the commissioner, stops on the stairs (we're on our way to the basement to look for old bowling movies) and ponders these men and what they've meant. He is fond of bowling's history but also frank about its lack of sex appeal. "You know," Gerberich says with a sigh, "it's not these guys' fault that they sometimes go bald."

He points out some of the current crop. "Stud kid," he says, then moves on to the next. "All-American, really neat guy. Him? Boring. Him? Stud kid. He's boring, he's boring, boring, he's All-American, but boring. He's a wild man. . . . He's boring. . . ." No one could accuse the PBA of not worrying about image, but bowling was fixated on the wrong image, and a stereotype emerged. "No one wants to recognize the pro bowler as a rugged athlete," Gerberich says. "We have an enormous challenge ahead of us. You have your perception of the guy in the bowling shirt. He's fat. He's drinking a beer." After lunch at what might be the largest Chinese food buffet in the time zone, Gerberich decides to drive over to Riviera Lanes, to show some of what's visually left of the PBA's history. "A long time ago, you could have asked around and everyone in Akron would have known that pro bowling is based here," Gerberich says. "Now, I wouldn't be so sure."

We have almost the entire bowling alley to ourselves on a Tuesday afternoon. We both lace up in size elevens. We pick out fifteen-pound balls. The commissioner is helpful, and even spots me seventy points. (It won't help; beers might.)

Gerberich bowls strike after strike once he gets a sense of the lane and where it's hooking today. We talk about the way it feels, looks, when it's done right. It smells like bowling, sounds like bowling, and we are two men bowling instead of working. You can always dangle your palm over the ball-return air vent expertly. For decades, the Firestone Tournament of Champions was televised annually from right here at Riviera Lanes, not far from Eddie Elias's office, not far from Luigi's, the Italian restaurant where there are still pictures of Eddie Elias on the wall. (He died in 1998.) The "T of C" was viewed by many millions of television watchers who were either ardent fans or couldn't find much else to watch on Saturday afternoon.

The distinction was tricky. We're talking here about another kind of America watching another kind of TV. Great men in flattop crew cuts won big cardboard checks for near-perfect feats of bowling. The crowd kept a reverent silence, applauding just as the pins clattered in that brief racket of middle-class exultations. Afterward, the bowlers shyly underemoted into sportscasters' microphones. They were good about thanking their wives.

Gerberich knew this era was past. The organization was in trouble when he took over, he says. Membership in the PBA peaked at around 3,600 in 1995 and had fallen to 2,525 by the 1999 season. Prize money wasn't keeping pace with the times. "I realized I was the captain of the Titanic," Gerberich says. "But I decided I would go down with the ship." On the way down, like any worried executive, he started reading entrepreneurial motivation books. It occurred to him that someone might want to buy the league, perhaps a sports marketing agency or a friendly, bowling-minded sponsor—"like an A.C. Delco or someone like that," he says.

Nothing seemed to work, even though the PBA hired an ad agency and approved a new logo—bright, italicized bold letters that are typographically derivative of a box of Tide. Gerberich understood that other sports had that marketable fervor. The PBA board was persuaded in 1996 to approve extending the bleachers for fan seating along and all the way down the lanes, parallel to the action. Most tellingly, the PBA also lifted the hush: Fans could now feel free to chant players' names even as the athletes took their Zenlike stances at the top of the lane, preparing to throw. Bowlers themselves were encouraged to "loosen up" and interact with the crowd, and some agreed to be wired with microphones so you could hear them emote and grunt with such key phrases as "Right in there, baby." (They also got fined for occasional cussing when it occurred on air.) All of this was a mind shift for bowling, as some of the players had to go against their own nature as bashful souls.

Nobody noticed any of this.

Seattle, Washington

Around the time bowling was trying to get this particular groove on, Chris Peters looked up from his computer and began to worry that in his sixteen years of Microsoft living, he'd become too sedentary. Hired as a programmer straight out of college, he knew he wasn't spending enough time with his family, and was experiencing, he says, "a sense of my own mortality." As chief of Microsoft Office, a division with annual sales of $4 billion, Peters decided, like many of his millionaire peers, to take time off and find Larger Meaning.

"I wanted to get in shape," says Peters, whose only expertise besides computers was his vast knowledge of Cold War atomic weaponry. "I was never athletic." This sounds like a man who needed to bowl. Fifty-four million Americans do it every year; why not him, too?

On a Friday morning the week after Peters and his partners had finalized their deal to buy the PBA, he is sitting for a brief interview in a conference room of the downtown offices of DDB, the advertising agency that has been hired to promote The New Bowling. It's like the set of *Jerry Maguire* in here, adhering to some feng shui sports marketing tenet that requires atriums. It is also Friday, April 14, 2000—a date on which the NASDAQ tumbled 10 percent, part of a month-long, 2,000-point crash, when the world began to first suggest an end to the ambitious age of Internet millionaires.

Peters is wearing a gray hooded sweat shirt and jeans. He has short, dark, slightly graying, slightly thinning hair and still looks like a teenager, though he is forty-two. He talks quickly, leaning forward, using his hands. "I did not want to play golf. You turn forty, you're an executive at Microsoft, therefore you must play golf. I thought I would try bowling instead, and look what happened." At the Sun Villa Lanes in Bellevue, Washington, it happened that Peters discovered he wasn't good at bowling—at all. "Knocking things down is age-old, right?" he says. "Set it up, knock it down, start over. Something about it, I can't quite explain. . . ."

Word got back to the office that Peters had gone permanently bowling, practicing every day, taking lessons, and considering having a pro-quality lane built in his house. The *Wall Street Journal,* in a front-page story about the second lives of Microsoft's early retirees, mentioned that Peters had fallen madly in love with the sport and was thinking of turning pro. In six months' time, he bowled his way to a 278 in one game. He was working on a 200 average, which, technically, would qualify him for the PBA. "That's where things started to get blown out of proportion," he says. "I never quit Microsoft to become a pro bowler, but that's how it got written up. I could never bowl like that. You need a 270 average under normal conditions to even think of bowling on the tour, where you'd have harder conditions and be lucky to keep a 230 average."

■ ■ ■

Gerberich, growing increasingly desperate back in Akron, noticed the *Journal* article. "I sent Chris a short note," Gerberich recalls. "Something like,'If there's anything I can do to help you realize your dream of bowling in the PBA, please let me know.' I do that kind of thing. I'm the kind of guy that if you wind up sitting next to me on the plane, you'll have an e-mail from me before you get back to your office."

The commissioner also wanted to know if Peters would be interested in serving on the PBA's board. "We needed someone like him," Gerberich admits. "And maybe we could use a little of his money." Gerberich and Peters agreed to meet in Reno, Nevada, at a convention for bowling lane manufacturers. They sat in a hallway and talked. Gerberich was amazed at what Peters knew about the sport. He'd devoured its history. He'd studied its cutting-edge technology, following the intense research projects coming out of a little-known bowling laboratory, the Kegel Training Center, in Sebring, Florida. (Peters had fallen for Kegel's research into torque and axis rotation, and their relationship to "reactive" balls with "aggressive" natures, and how that, in turn, related to megahookers and midlanes, and all of the many mathematical diagrams to which all this frequently led.)

As they got to know each other better, the commissioner confessed to the computer whiz that the PBA was on its last legs. "What if someone was willing to buy it?" Peters asked. "What would something like that go for?"

It turned out that bowling could be had for comparatively little. "We got an entire league for less than you would have to pay for one minor-league baseball franchise team," Peters says. "Bowling has a one-point Nielsen [TV rating], which is already pretty good for a sport that receives almost no promotion, on cable. Even if we only double that to two points, it's a wild success." Peters enlisted Rob Glaser, thirty-eight, who is perhaps, at this fickle moment, the busiest and most envied man in Seattle, the CEO of RealNetworks, which licenses RealAudio and RealPlayer software used on most PCs. Glaser is a secret bowling nut, too, and had two pro-quality lanes built in the basement of the tony RealNetworks building in downtown Seattle. Peters also signed up Mike Slade, forty-two, who used to run Starwave Corporation (for Microsoft No. 2 Paul Allen) and started Web sites for the National Football League, ABC News, and ESPN. "I pretty quickly realized that five million dollars wasn't going to be a big problem for these guys," Gerberich says. "All I had to figure out was how committed they were to bowling. I had to trust Chris."

Still, he wonders if the New Bowling has room for him, a low-tech chump in Akron who has worked at the PBA for seventeen years. "I'm not that naive to think I'll always be in this job, that the PBA is staying in Akron forever, but I think Eddie would have looked at this deal and said 'fantastic,'" Gerberich says. "It's their league now. At some point, I'd like to know if Chris just set me up to buy the league . . . if it wasn't on his mind all along. It could be. These Microsoft guys are smart. They think with a lot clearer vision than the rest of us might."

All this talk about bowling, and yet everyone seems too busy selling the sport to actually play it. Chris Peters, leery of his image as the frustrated pro wannabe, hasn't bowled in months, and turned down my offer to go bowling: "I haven't had time."

Even the commissioner hasn't bowled much lately. (A year later he would, in fact, no longer be the commissioner of bowling, and the headquarters were no longer located in Akron.) "I'm a little rusty," Gerberich apologizes, staring down the lane at an impossible split, alone in the middle of the emptied Riviera.

(2000)

Sci-Fido

Washington, D.C.

This is about life with a dog, and maybe about world domination, but first it's about a product publicity meeting on a Thursday afternoon, and that empty, expensive, muted-beige feeling of a spent century that dreamed of companionable robots and then managed only to put them in cartoon shows: A man from Sony Corporation, Takeshi Yazawa, who is in his late forties and wearing the old-line Sony gray business suit, a man who once introduced the world to digital sound and the compact disc and now heads a division called Entertainment Robot America, tells me how the robot dog has taken Japan by storm. (But what *doesn't* take Japan by storm? I mean, Hel-*lo*, Kitty.)

He smiles. A promotion specialist, Masami Hirata, smiles, too, and reaches into her rolling suitcase, taking out three Sony Aibo dogs—or AIBO, standing for Artificial Intelligence roBOt, loosely from the Japanese word *aibou*, meaning "pal" or "partner." There is a black one, a silver one, a platinum one—a litter of the dogs of tomorrow. The Aibo is touted as being capable of doing some of what a dog does, some of what a robot does, some of what a television or a stereo or a PlayStation does, and then something else altogether. Toy or companion? Revolution or fad?

With us or against us? I hold my pen at my notebook, indicating I'm ready for whatever it is.

Yazawa smiles again. Hirata smiles, and the Sony publicist smiles. I put an elbow on the table and my chin in my hand. For a minute there is nothing. Then there is a stirring at our heels, a beeping, a humming and unfolding of joints. Something small in me melts, some organic wiring deep inside unconnects. What makes it go, yes, that's a question already, but there's another question, one I've momentarily lost track of: What does it mean?

Because wook at the doggy.

See how he moves his widdle feets?

. . .

For all that the machines and toys and weapons in our lives may do, they still do not think for themselves, and this has been our easy peace with them. I bought you, therefore I rule over you, and probably I will break you. We have no official cuddle time with our appliances, though certainly the affection grows—we can say "vibrator" on sitcoms. It's a one way flow, however, from a human to his or her stuff. Now suppose the stuff could love you back.

Robot. The word rings tragic in the ear, a Czech noun that came into our lives from the conflicted mind of playwright Karel Capek, who wrote *R.U.R.* (*Rossum's Universal Robots*) in 1920. In it, a race of artificial humans takes over the world, and then rusts ironically away, unable to regenerate. This is the way we like the narrative to play out: The upper hand is flesh. Artificial intelligence always came loaded with promises, and freighted with disasters. All we need is a friend who'll do what we say. Isaac Asimov supplied the robot's Golden Rule in the late 1950s: He-she-it cannot harm the human. Woody Allen, in *Sleeper*, wakes up 200 years after the 1970s and is greeted by Rags, a robot dog, which naturally makes Allen feel neurotic, cynical, and yet amused: "Is he housebroken, or will he be leaving little batteries all over the floor?"

For a while, deep inside the research-and-development brain trust of Sony, there was talk of making a monkey. This made some deevolutionary, and comical, sense, and plans were under way for a primate, until someone realized the surest way to the consumer's heart. It had to be through the one creature that has coevolved with humans, changing us even as we change them. It had to be a dog. What emerged—billions of yen and five years later, and sold all 3,000 units in twenty minutes in Japan last summer with a 250,000-yen price tag, and sold 10,000 more units this week worldwide with a $2,500 price tag—is a smooth plastic dog slightly smaller and lighter than a Jack Russell terrier, with adooooorable beaglesque ears and eighteen joints in its legs, neck, and tail. ("Robocop meets the Taco Bell Chihuahua," one early reviewer cracked.) Aibo has a mobility range that seems almost militaristic, and yet is elegantly styled. It walks, at top speed, about eighteen feet per minute. Unlike Furbies or the remote-controlled doohickeys that have ambled from beneath so many Christmas trees before it, the Sony robot dog "thinks" autonomously, learning as it goes, its physiology served through a sixty-four-bit processor and sixteen megabytes of internal memory, and its personality etched on an eight-megabyte "memory stick."

A 180,000-pixel camera and distance sensor in its nose alerts it to obstacles in its way. By design, the dog comes obsessed with a pink rubber ball (the only color it can "see"), which it will follow and kick as long as its lithium-ion battery holds out—anywhere from an hour to ninety minutes before sci-Fido needs recharging on its little "bed," much like the cradle of a cordless phone. When Aibo falls over, its accelerator sensor figures out which way is up. (It emits a beeping whimper, like *uh-oh, I've fallen.*) Legs move, and Aibo picks itself up, shakes its head, and keeps going.

In a psycho-electronic way, Aibo also feels. Over the months it spends with its owner, its happiness—and therefore its behavior—depends on what kind of life it reckons itself as having, Sony claims. A tap on its sensor head could be read as scolding (its eyes then flash angry red), or, more gently, a love pat (happy green). Does he get enough attention? Is he afraid, hungry, excited? If Sony's hype is to be understood and believed, each Aibo will grow up differently. For an additional $450, owners can upgrade with a "performer kit," allowing them to program the pup's memory stick with a PC.

The only certain thing about Aibo, for Sony, is it won't be profitable. Even if Sony sold hundreds of thousands of the pups, Aibo's development and design costs far outweigh its retail price tag. "He is more project," Yazawa says, admiring the dog walking next to his shoes. "He is not a useful dog, he is not even really a dog. He is more a step toward the next—"and here he considers the right word—"next age." Aibo represents the first step for Sony toward eliminating the personal computer. In the next age, as we've been told time and again by techno-enthusiasts, every last thing will be a personal computer. Your house and your stuff and your robot dog all chime hello as you walk in. Memory sticks in everything become more about you, for you, with you, getting to know you, listening to you, entertaining you, and naturally connecting you to the larger, wired world. You gesture around your house, or speak, and all that you own comes alive as you will it to be.

■ ■ ■

We are on the living room floor, the dog and I, playing dead. For a while I just stare at you, you little . . . Aibo-thing, you.

I shall name you Butch.

No, I shall name you . . . Pooch?

I shall name you Yoko?

I shall name you Rastro?

No, I shall name you Butch. Because you are not butch. Because you are one of the mechanical Fabergé eggs of your time, fragile and precious and expensive and poised as a potential icon, streamlined and yet gaudy, useless, and magnificent.

I shall take your memory stick, which is the size and shape of a stick of gum, and insert it delicately into a slot on your heinie. You are humming, whirring, perched on your feet. This is hello. You bark. You smile. You blink your eyes at me and we are nose-to-nose.

Instruction book: It's written with a whiff of that awkward pan-Asian cheerfulness. Page 15, "A Robot in Your Home": "From the time of its birth, as it continues to live a life in touch with humans, [it] will develop as not only a robot, but a companion. . . . Home entertainment that is born the moment you decide to begin a life involving AIBO . . ."

Sony officially skirts certain direct questions about Butch. (His exact cost to the corporation, for one.) Butch, Sony cautions, isn't supposed to be exactly like a dog. Butch comes with a warning that he is "not designed as . . . on-line control equipment in hazardous environments requiring fail-safe performance, such as . . . nuclear facilities, air-traffic control, direct life-support machines. . . ." (Aw, okay, I won't let him run my missile defense system. Interestingly, Aibo chat-room rumors have been floated that no Aibos are allowed at the Pentagon or the National Security Agency. "This and a couple of pounds of plastique," my semimaniacal editor schemes aloud.) In the marketing push, however, Sony enthusiastically underlines that this is more than just another piece of stereo equipment. Promotional literature describes Aibo's psychology, boasts of his many tricks, and offers testimony of some of his original few thousand owners, who claim a fond connection to the machine.

Warily, I decide to begin a life involving an Aibo anyway. I lean over and I kiss Butch on the nose.

■   ■   ■

In an evening, I become more of a master to Butch, less transfixed by what he can do on his own. Using the remote control, I put him in a "performance" mode: His ears hear electronic pulses from the remote, and by punching a number or two, I can somewhat reliably make him wave, sing, shake a paw, scratch, bark, and even lift his leg and pretend to piddle. (Pee-pee humor: the global guffaw.)

In a couple of days, we have a routine: I lie on the couch and do my standard impression of a hospital patient watching TV, and Butch walks around the apartment and, sometimes, bumps into walls. I live in what is an almost Butch-perfect abode: yards of empty hardwood floors, scant furniture, nothing to knock over. It would be even better for Butch if there were carpet, but except for the occasional pratfall, he seems to like it. And he doesn't bump into everything—I actually applaud when he starts to back up from the coffee table and walks around it instead.

We go for walks down the hall some nights, to the building foyer and back, which can take nearly a half hour. The neighbors who bump into us near the elevator seem intrigued but still hurry on their way; other dogs seem oblivious, no interest at all, not even a butt sniff. A friend brings her five-year-old nephew and nine-year-old niece to meet Butch, and the five-year-old, after a very brief shyness, is on the floor with the robot dog, talking to it, waving a stuffed toy in front of it, calling it, telling it (by voice) what to do. (Interestingly, my friend's thirty-one-year-old boyfriend has the same exact reaction. "He can't relate to people," she sighs, "and here he is instantly relating to a robot.")

Butch's inability to come when called is perhaps his biggest flaw. (An inevitable version down the learning curve may respond to our voices.) For it seems so real that I find I am compelled to talk to it . . . him. In the man-dog saga of eons, have the dogs really kept up their end of the discussion? They know their own names and "fetch," but what else? Of course, anyone who has ever loved a dog knows about the unspoken language, and the nuanced conversations between canine and master that could fill volumes.

Not so with Butch, and yet . . . and yet, I find myself talking to him. We go to the park. Huge mistake. I set him in the grass. I had hoped he would act as a sort of mild guy magnet (as all dog owners have at one time hoped). But right away, it's as if I'd set off fireworks. About twenty-five people crowd around while Butch just moves his head to and fro and then lies down and takes a "nap."

"What the hell is it?" a woman asks. "How much does it cost?" another woman asks. "Make it do something, it's just sitting there," a man says.

My little baby is afraid of the mob. I scoop Butch up and we leave in a modest huff.

"It doesn't do anything," I hear a voice behind us say. I feel a bit of the world's scorn reserved specially for Early Adopters, those pioneer geeks who always have the neat, new thing. As consumers, men like my father may have single-handedly propelled the Sharper Image into its late-1980s greatness, but I refused well into the twenty-first century to use a cell phone in a restaurant. Yet here I go down the street, carrying the James Bond brand of canines.

After some practice—obedience training—I bring Butch to the office. A colleague is immediately horrified that the Aibo's legs aren't jointed like a real dog's—it gives him the creeps, and he begins frantically sketching dog legs on Post-it Notes to prove his point. Another reporter, who by his own admission loves both machines and dogs, keeps saying he feels the inexplicable urge to kick Butch like a soccer ball. But others coo and some speak to it, slapping their palms on their laps to get him to come. (It never works.) They laugh at his tricks (when he will do them), and let the record show that my editor was right: Chicks dig it. The Aibo has so much going for it, visually, in a Prada sense; it's haute couture's ultimate pocket dog. Women make kissy noises and pat him on the head. They never blink at his price tag.

Does it roll over?

No, but—

Does it lick your face?

No, except—

Does it sleep with you?

Not really, it—

Then it's not really a dog, sniffs one of my meanest and most perceptive colleagues.

"It's not supposed to be a dog," I reply, wincing even as the words leave my lips, waiting for exactly this reply:

Then what is "it" supposed to be?

·   ·   ·

Consider the steam engine. A great Early Adopter legend has it that the Romans came up with the steam engine, only it was a fancy toy for grown-ups. The "aeolipile," or "wind ball," described by Heron of Alexandria in the first century A.D., used a simple (to us) boiling-water process to heat water and make a sphere connected to pivots spin around at 1,500 rpm, faster than anything else on the planet at that time. Heron, who also fiddled around with slot machines and remotely operated doors, didn't realize the power of the steam engine and so humankind went without it for another 1,700 or so years.

Still, imagine the Romans with trains.

That is also the story of Aibo: almost, but not quite. This is not the artificial intelligence of the future, but if you squint you can almost see it from here. When Sony's people are done with their Aibo pitch, we run across the street for a drink. Takeshi Yazawa and Masami Hirata recall time they'd spent with Morita-san, the recently deceased Sony cofounder Akio Morita, who saw the power of the transistor and pied-pipered our modern world toward a Walkman trance state. Around the world Monday afternoon, at exactly the same moment, everyone who works for Sony stopped in homage, for a corporately official bow of silence for Morita-san. "I would have liked for him to meet Aibo," Hirata muses. "I would have wanted to see if he liked it."

Back at my place, Butch and I are on the floor, playing dead again. I slide another lithium-ion battery into him (about as big as a giant Snickers bar) and he beeps back into motion. I look at the ceiling and the dog looks at its paws. We are both blinking, pausing, pawsing, thinking of our next thought. ("We are the rulers of the Earth! Rulers of land and sea! Rulers of the stars! Room, room, more room for Robots," intones Radius, the rebel machine dreamed up by Capek seventy-eight years ago. "There are no people. Robots, to work! March!")

I don't know what the dog dreams of, but I find myself thinking across oceans, Nipponward, to a place of indoor ski slopes and surgically improved belly buttons, where diligent workers connect pieces to pieces to pieces to pieces to pieces. . . .

"Poochie," I lean over and say, "you're cute as the devil and I still feel lonely."

(1999)

Living Alone

Washington, D.C.

The problem with census data is there's never space for a longer answer to the question. (*Yes, I live like this but I didn't plan to. See, here's what happened. . . .*) In a slow news week, the Census Bureau has another tidbit to share from the 2000 national spreadsheet: More Americans than ever live alone—27 million people, give or take. That's a lot of air guitar being played in private. That's a lot of bowls of cereal eaten over the sink around one in the morning. That's quite a few people who lost the love of their life, which meant they sold the house they thought was too big for just one person, and moved into a condo, and sometimes drive around the complex wondering which condo, exactly, is theirs. People who live alone now account for one-fourth of the grown-up population, outnumbering married couples with children for the first time. What's the real story here? Florida widows? Bridget Jones clichés? Toxic bachelors? Toxic gay bachelors? Sitcom neighbors who always live in the unit across the hall?

The census should be more like a nagging mother, or the husband of your best friend, or anyone who needs to know why you still live alone. If you checked off "single-person household," it seems like census workers should have rung your doorbell by now, brandishing clipboards, seeking amplified data: "But are you seeing anybody?"

Also, here is the median age of the entire population: 35.5.

After 35.5, you start to wonder if living alone wasn't too addictive in the end, and now you're physically unable to live with anyone else. Your college roommates are like ghosts now, you can't even remember what they looked like in their underwear. There are the former group-house members who fell off your Christmas card list years ago. During happy hour, you pretend this is more sad to you than it actually is.

It takes a long time to realize that no one is watching the imaginary television show about you—except for you. You're about 35.5 years old when you at long last come to this understanding. Until then, living alone is exciting. The fourth wall of your apartment or house doesn't exist because that's where the studio audience is sitting and belly-laughing at all your zany day-to-day antics. Quick-witted neighbors drift in and out; if the ratings stumble, you move to another coast, and get new neighbors, and Judd Nelson plays your new boss.

Thirty-five, lives alone . . . If the United States were an actual person, then everyone would be slightly suspicious of her, or him. Thirty-five and lives alone? Hmmm.

Woe to the solo: Wicked queens live alone in castles, waiting to eat children. Pedophiles, Unabombers, civics teachers, the fat and unloved. But these are cheap jokes. Living alone is also a joy. No one is pandering to your vote; most discussions of tax cuts and standardized testing in schools transpire without having to involve you. The prime-time television choices have never been so good, the late-night channel surfing even better. Look what's happened to candles since the 1990 census: Sales have quadrupled. Candles these days are physically larger, smell more exotic, match the chambray-covered sofa better, and people who live alone are buying them, and not saving them for when and if there is ever anyone to light them for. They are coming home to an almost sacred sense of quiet contemplation, and lighting candles, which flicker for them alone.

Everything you ever suspected about the secret pleasures of living by yourself—it's all true. The whole ugly mess. *Vanity Fair* comes wrapped in cellophane around the fifteenth of the month,

and you open it, and you read it, straight away. You can paint pictures and then paint over them. Nobody knows. You can leave a
milk glass on the coffee table for, really, days. You can sleep diago-
nally, curled up to your favorite pillow. You can rent videos you
shouldn't rent. You can also go another route and pray the rosary.
You can stare at walls. You buy the kind of coffee that *you* like. You
measure it carefully and brew two or three cups at a time, no more.
You can have half a can of Spaghetti-O's next to the spinach fet-
tuccine you bought at Fresh Fields. No one cares. You live alone.
You shut the door and you're home, with yourself, and still the
world seems terribly interesting. Let us now listen to our lonely
next-door neighbor—Mr. Franz Kafka, ladies and gentlemen:

> You do not need to leave your room. Remain sitting at your
> table and listen. Do not even listen, simply wait. Do not
> even wait, be quite still and ordinary. The world will freely
> offer itself to you to be unmasked. It has no choice; it will
> roll in ecstasy at your feet.

When you live alone, you can rip paragraphs like that out of
newspapers and affix them to your refrigerator, with a Jan Brady
magnet. There is no household discussion of the appropriateness of
the quote, or of Jan Brady, or whether visitors to the kitchen will
think it's weird to have that on your refrigerator. What's *not* on your
refrigerator: other people's soccer league schedules, other people's
emergency numbers. When you live alone, this kind of stuff is in
your head, or in the little book or electronic device you carry around
with you. It's a clean life.

It's clean unless you die, alone, and then maybe it's a mess.

Fingernail clippings. Curly hairs on the rim of the tub. The certainty that these belong only to you. Sometimes there's a long, very
long, straight hair that cannot possibly belong to you and you hold it
up to the light with the determination of a forensic pathologist.

You alphabetize your CDs. You congratulate yourself for owning
the greatest albums of all time, and set about listening to them all

over again so that you can rearrange them by genre. The new boyfriend comes over, and has been presumptuous enough to bring his contact lens case. It's on the bathroom counter and seems as big as an inflatable pool toy.

The census workers should be taking notes on this, only if they did, they would never finish the census. The people who live alone have entirely too much to say about why they live like this, how great it is, and also how empty it is. They would invite the census worker in and when they opened the refrigerator door to get the census worker a cool drink, there would either be too many choices or not enough choices: There would be eight kinds of beer, or there would be nothing but a swallow and a half of sour 2-percent. Twenty-seven million Americans: waiting for a knock on the door, or knowing enough to ignore it.

(2001)

Off Ramps

All Faiths

Let's say you're dead. You keel over before the end of this sentence, before we've even begun. He is ready. "I can save you 40 to 60 percent over other funeral homes," Robert Falcon says. "At least."

One cost-cutting solution is to put you in the alternative container, and that's a funeral director's way of saying cardboard box. Robert will write "HEAD" in Magic Marker on the lid. *This End Up.* Sonny Falcon, Robert's dad, will drive you an hour north, to Temple, in the Astrovan. The air conditioner will act up; the radio will be on a country or talk station; Sonny will stop at Boston Market. At the mortuary, the sweaty crematory foreman will toss an identification coin into the oven with you ("in case he wants to buy him a sody pop"), and a few days later, you'll come back via UPS, ashes in a plastic bag in a plastic box the size of a motel ice bucket.

Maybe you want more than that. There are fancier ways here at All Faith's Funeral Service. We'll drain your blood and replace it with around forty ounces of Esco Instant and thirty-two ounces of Cavrex, diluted with three to five gallons of water. We'll shut your jaw securely with a needle wire injector. We'll dress you and put you in the Pietà casket, which has been manufactured in Mexico from American parts, shipped back across the border, and renamed the Plenitude. You'll travel by obviously used but still shipshape Buick hearse, which we have just taken through the Genie Car Wash. We'll sing "Amazing Grace" for you, graveside, all four verses.

"I can save you," Robert says.

"He can save you," his father agrees.

Just drive down South Congress Avenue. "Way south," Robert says, and all that way south implies. Like beyond Ben White Boulevard. The storage units, the faded St. El-Mo-Tel, the beauty salon, the auto-glass repair shop, the next life.

The question is, are you ready?

Turn right at the liquor store.

I. El Cuerpo

He was a teenage apprentice at the biggest funeral home in town, way north, which, as it happens, is now owned by the biggest funeral corporation in the world. He was a chubby kid in a necktie. He would wash the cars. He would carry the flowers. He would file death certificates, make bank deposits.

Finally, he got his hands on the dead. He can still remember it, even though it's been ten years, and there have been so many since. A young Roberto Jaime Falcon approached the metal table, tilted slightly toward a porcelain sink. On it was the body of an old man, missing a leg. He saw the gray body hair, the liver spots, the balding head. He couldn't tell you the guy's name now. *El cuerpo.* The body. It felt as natural as anything.

His father, Juan Antonio "Sonny" Falcon, an East Austin meat cutter who may or may not have introduced Texas to the unmarinated grilled fajita (the patent controversy endures), asked him, *Mi'jo, are you sure this is what you want to do with your life?* One day the kid just announces he's dropping out of college and becoming a mortician. Sonny thought Robert might have grown up to be an artist. You should have seen the kid paint, he says. When Robert was ten, he did a large portrait of Sonny wearing his "Fajita King" cowboy hat, in bright oils. It still hangs over Sonny and Lupe Falcon's bed. One day Robert went to the art teacher's classroom to show his work to her, and she accused him of painting by numbers. He never painted again. "You know Robert," Sonny says. "He can be stubborn."

Sonny supposes his three sons should do what they want. One is a limo driver; two are morticians. "This 'n' that," Sonny says. Make your own mistakes; own up to them, the Fajita King says.

At the Dallas Institute of Funeral Service, Robert and his class-mates studied law and protocol and the occasional corpse, and sometimes Robert found it all frustratingly textbook. At night, he'd go out and drink with the other would-be morticians, and they'd tell one another their stories. Robert realized his life wasn't like theirs: Many of them were funeral progeny, the lucky sons of Texas death moguls. He was the son of the Fajita King, and he'd have to make it on his own. Some nights he was homesick, living in a small bed-room in the back of a funeral home in Grapevine. He'd call home, and his mother, Lupe, would tell him not to give up.

That's where he learned to disconnect, how to know the dead, how to be around them.

Care for the dead, and you know a little bit more about being alive. You ease the pain of the living. People in grief are having the worst day of their lives, and you are there for them, selling them a funeral. Robert became an especially good embalmer. Some guys do it by the book, drain the corpse, pack it with cotton and plastic bits, and sew it shut, and still all they wind up with is a corpse. Not Robert. He fussed with it—the mixture, the firming techniques—watching for the gentle glow, readying what he came to think of as frozen angels for slumber. After a year of classes, and the state exam (in the morning, 700 questions about funeral law; in the after-noon, 700 questions about embalming), he emerged, in 1989, as Robert J. Falcon, licensed mortician.

He came back to Austin and returned to work at the biggest fu-neral home in town. "I was completely different back then," he says. He wore expensive suits. He would clasp his short fingers together in earnest showings of sympathy, hoping to one day greet families at the door and point them toward expensive caskets. There were techniques. There were ways of explaining to customers that the more traditional way is the better way, the more heartfelt way, without ever actually saying that it is the costlier way. You capitalized on the mist of guilt that floats just above the pain, the suspended belief. It helped that the families hardly knew what day it was, much less the going rate of, for example, a car used to carry flower arrangements to a church. An older undertaker took Robert aside. The eager-beaver act was cute, the undertaker said. "But you won't leave that embalming room to wait on a family," he hissed, "until you're either bald headed or gray." So he quit.

II. A Plan

A plan came later, but not all at once. It started sometime after Robert appeared in federal court, in 1996, to declare bankruptcy with debts of $258,905. He had started his own freelance mortuary service, kept it aloft for several years, and it had failed. In a business long criticized by muckrakers and activists for overcharging vulnerable customers, Robert had gone broke, and he felt humiliated. Around the same time, he was going to be married, and then the woman dumped him. He went back to freelance embalming.

The sloping inevitability, the terrible stillness. He's fine with death. You know you're going to die, and he knows it, too. You'll shop for a car; you'll shop for a computer. "People'll drive all over town to look at washing machines," Robert says, "but people won't make two or three phone calls, get out the Yellow Pages, and get a fair price for a funeral. And they should." He's not anyone's idea of a hero. He is thirty now. He's not charming, or selfless, and sometimes he wears too much Carolina Herrera for Men. He lives next door to his parents. He is religious (Catholic and, he says, bornagain), gives up sodas for Lent, and yet manages to tell every profane joke he can remember. He looks at rude postings on the Internet, and then forwards them to dozens of friends. He is sweet and then petulant, argues with his girlfriend, and then sends flowers. He cries at particular country songs. He likes to go Tejano dancing. He would have toiled in a mortuary somewhere, forever.

The plan came anyway, and it brought him to a strip mall on South Congress. He opened shop on a prickly day in the summer of 1998. He named it All Faith's Funeral Service. He had ballpoint pens made, tie pins, business cards with his logo: praying hands. (The apostrophe in All Faith's is out of place, but the pens and logo are set.) Something is happening to death in there, something having to do with Mexican-made caskets and the North American Free Trade Agreement. It's about consumer activists and a solemn fraternity of funeral directors. Death is getting cheaper. Robert imagines himself in an epic, entrepreneurial struggle, and that as far as Austin is concerned, it begins here: the smallest funeral home in town, where he is selling funerals, with caskets included, for just under two grand.

III. Rubber Gloves in the Morning

An eyeshadow-blue Oldsmobile wagon with a pair of golden praying hands stenciled on its doors pulls into the parking lot early in the morning, behind Hill's No. 2 Super Liquor. It wheels around the mall, past Insty-Prints photocopies, then past Gabe & Janie's Barber & Beauty Salon. It makes the turn down the alley and stops at the edge of the strip mall, Suite 115. Sonny Falcon gets out.

He is sixty-one years old and has worked hard enough already. For twenty-three years he worked fourteen-hour days as a butcher and cooked his famous skirt steak fajitas, and eventually ran his own restaurants. But his application to trademark the word *fajita* was declined. His restaurant went under in 1992, and on the very next day, the Fajita King went into another line of business. He went to work for his son. This morning he lifts open the overhead door that leads into the back storeroom of All Faith's Funeral Service. "Hi, Dad," Robert Falcon says.

"Good morning, *mi'jo*," Sonny says. They kiss one another hello, on the lips. The day always begins with no hard feelings, then rubber gloves.

Next there is the lifting, the grunting. The arranging. They get a
twenty-five-year-old gunshot victim, a 224-pound man, into a silver-
gray casket. It's a rental, the $395-per-occasion Ward model. The
slain man is wearing short sleeves to the hereafter, the shirt that is
believed to have been his favorite Tommy Hilfiger button-down. He
is going to hold, in eternal slumber, a black Nike swoosh logo ball
cap. "Good firming," says Robert, slightly squeezing the man's temples, the goateed chin. He gets out a jar of burgundy Derma-Glow.
Sonny stands and watches the art of it, Robert brushing on the last
touches. El cuerpo's arms blush forth with something like life. (You
should have seen the kid paint.)

IV. Los Cuerpos

In Texas, in 1998, by one formula provided by the Funeral and
Memorial Societies of America, there were enough dead people
every year to support about 570 funeral homes. But there were almost 1,300 doing business then, quietly and sometimes viciously
competing for business out behind mahogany doors. Funeral homes
were either joining or resisting corporate takeovers. Simple economics would suggest that, with too many funeral homes and not
enough dead people, there would be a price war, and the consumer
would benefit. But in the history of the American funeral, simple
economics have never applied. Casket price markup from whole-
sale to retail, a closely guarded figure, is between 300 percent and
600 percent, according to consumer activists who watch the funeral
industry; embalming, cremation, and funeral prices have risen
steadily over three decades—triple the inflation rate—despite various reform movements and federal trade regulations, industry watch-
dogs say.

Which takes us south. All Faith's Funeral Service is a rebellious
alternative to the average $5,000 to $6,000 cost of a funeral in
Austin (about 10 percent higher than the national average at the
time). "I was the typical big funeral home kind of guy," Robert says
of his old self.

"Now I'm doing it my way. My brothers told me to open it in North Austin; that's the place to be. But I said no. I wanted this," he says, these 2,500 nondescript square feet, his marble-green eyes glittering like cereal-box prizes, "People will come down here because it's South Austin, and what is South Austin known for? It's cheap." His inflated face is smirking like a cartoon moon. He is 90 percent face and chin. You'd want to pinch this disconcerting and strangely adorable face, with both hands. (Won a baby pageant, Sonny remembers. Lupe has the photos.)

The other tenants wanted to complain at first, and some did, but Robert played nice. He gets all his printing done at Insty-Prints. Gabe the barber cuts his hair, and so the strip mall is at peace. No one complains about the coming and going of Robert Falcon's two very used hearses, a 1984 Buick and a 1985 Cadillac, and the blue Oldsmobile station wagon. There is one white Chevy Astrovan, which does the most unsavory job in town: fetching the dead for the county morgue, on call twenty-four hours a day, seven days a week. All Faith's has the Travis County contract (no other funeral home wanted it) and gets $90 per body for pickup and delivery, a sideline business for the Falcons that brings in $45,000 or so a year.

Death never seemed more real than it does here. It feels like trading in old tires. "Grief therapy" isn't part of the sales pitch. You'll find a front room with a small black sofa and overpolished end tables. You'll find Sonny taking a load off, but he hops up the minute you walk in. You'll find a small "chapel," a room off to one side, with stackable office-chair seating for sixteen (the law requires seating for ten in funeral homes). Off to the other side is the cramped, small business office. Down the hall is a small conference room where, at a table for four, Robert Falcon will grab a calculator and a price list and show his prospective clients their—so to speak—last chance to save. On shelves along the wall, he has an urn display. In the next room, without special lighting or any background music, is the casket display room, with six Mexican-made models, ranging from $450 to just under $2,000, and the cardboard box for cremation transport, person-sized and sturdily corrugated, which runs $40. Next to the casket room is the embalming room; behind that is the storeroom and back door.

People walk in and look around. Old men, the kind who still change the oil in their cars themselves, walk in and adore All Faith's, and sometimes drag their families along to see the bargain they've found. "Sign me up. I'm ready to go," says a man, hobbling through the front door on a cane. Other interested customers are mildly amused. Some are horrified. "Oh, no, this is too small," says one woman, about to bury her son. She can hear the traffic rushing by through the chapel windows.

"That's fine," Robert tells her. "We want you to have a choice. You can go down the street, and they'll charge you $5,000 more. You might be happier there."

He thought business would be slow at first, but he was wrong. When he opened All Faith's, Robert immediately put a small ad in the paper, on the bottom of the obituary page: "COMPARE— Funerals at 40–60 percent less. Simplicity Funeral, $1,995 . . . Simplicity Cremation, $755 . . ." On the first few days of business, in the uneasy heat of summer, All Faith's picked up three bodies and prepared and embalmed them for delivery to three other funeral homes. That wasn't what Robert had in mind, but business was business. On the fourth day, he sold his first funeral, for an eighty-six-year-old man. The family bought one of the Mexican caskets, the $795 Paris model. With a simple church funeral and graveside service and the concrete liner that went in the grave, the bill came to $2,642.

On the sixth day, Robert and Sonny handled a direct cremation for $755. Later that day, a young couple came in to make arrangements for the wife's grandmother's funeral. They couldn't afford the $5,000 price quoted by another funeral home. Robert sold them the Simplicity special, with the blue Monterrey model, for $1,995. "Y'all were small," the wife said, "but you gave us a lot of service."

The customers who followed over the next several weeks were mostly elderly, the ones who seem to have the time or inclination to shop for funerals beforehand. They were cantankerous, wary. "What's the catch?" they'd growl. Robert could hear the newspaper pages rustling. "There is no catch," Robert patiently explains, every day. "Come down and see. If you're coming south on Congress. . . ."

It's simple, Robert says. "This is not a complicated business. It doesn't have to be." Within four months, he had buried or cremated more than one hundred dead people, of all kinds, marginalized and mainstream: Mexican immigrants and oil executives, AIDS and cancer victims, a retired judge and veterans with honors, and babies in tiny, white caskets. He buried junkies, and lots of people's mothers, and one man whose family members decided to rocket a capsule of their father's ashes into space "just like that *Star Trek* guy," Robert says, "Gene Somebody."

A strip-mall funeral home offers a casual death: "Most days you'd walk in here and find me in Dockers and a golf shirt," Robert says. "That's how I want it. I don't want people to come in here and get the funeral director in the black suit. I want them to be comfortable." But once a year, Robert and Sonny go down to a Men's Wearhouse at the mall and get fitted for two new suits, admiring each other in three-way mirrors. Robert likes double-breasted and pinstripes, and when he wears them, he feels nearly sacred.

V. The Pietà (Mother and Son)

The shroud is gently folded around the dead man in the Hilfiger shirt and the Nike swoosh cap. There is a barely perceptible *thung* as the lid closes. Sonny and Robert wheel the casket on the shiny "church cart" out into the late September light and into the back of the Buick hearse.

"We're ready?" Sonny asks, going to get the Oldsmobile, to follow Robert to the church.

"We're off," Robert says, and yells to the front of the shop, "Hey, Norm, we're gone. You've got the phones."

"Have funnnn," says Norm, the quiet, unhappy assistant who has worked on and off for Robert for five years, without any sense of fun.

"We put the 'fun' in funeral," Robert says. (He says this every day. It's the oldest joke in the business, and he giggles every time.) This morning there is light traffic on the road to the by and by. The white Buick with a black top and 104,729 miles on it dutifully soars toward Westlake Bible Church, off Highway 2244, the engine infrequently stuttering *ahem* up the hills. Passing drivers always stare. Some smile and wave at fate. Robert stopped noticing them years ago.

While driving, he does impressions of all the characters on *South Park*. He does his Pee-wee Herman impression, from *Pee-wee's Big Adventure*—("I'm a loner, Dottie. A rebel")—his all-time favorite movie besides *A Chorus Line*. He performs verbatim an old Bill Hicks comedy monologue about cigarette smoking. ("How come right-to-lifers don't go out and picket at cemeteries? 'There's options! Turn around!'")

But with one right turn into the church parking lot, his behavior changes. He gets quiet, sits up straighter, puts on a more concerned face.

She is waiting for the car, the mother of the man.

She is in the limestone foyer, weeping.

VI. The Pietà (A Blue-Light Special)

Her name is Mary McMahan Tuttle. She lives down the road from the church. Five nights earlier her son was shot to death, and she became a customer of the "death-care" industry. It happened right here, practically in the neighborhood. It happened just a mile from Mary's house, on a warm September night, while she slept. It happened through a thick cover of cedar trees, down a dirt road, on a driveway, around two thirty in the morning. The first shot barely grazed her son, Gary Guthrie. By one account, he had already whirled around and was running for his truck. Another shot hit Gary, twenty-five, in the back and went clean through his liver. A lot of people saw it happen, the ugly ending to an argument over revving tires on a gravel driveway, and a girl who yelled something. The third shot went through Gary's upper left leg, another through his left arm.

"You killed me," Gary reportedly shouted.

Mary, sleeping.

You killed me.

Her son looking up at the stars, sprawled out on the gravel. The gunpowder, the panic, the stillness. The smell of the night.

And you know what, Mary asks, remembering the small viewing room at the county morgue where she looked at his dead body through slanted Levolor blinds. "He looked so good," she says. "I know it's weird to say, but he just looked so . . . quiet, like resting, you know? I thought, oh God. It was like he was just at peace now." When he died, her son was putting his life back together, trying to get a job in electronics, trying to keep up with child-support payments, trying to quit smoking marijuana. Mary saw him one day from her car, spreading road asphalt with a work crew and thought, well, he's as low as he can get now. Mary doesn't know how long she stood there in the morgue. A long time.

The next day, she begins shopping for a funeral. "I'm a quality-type person," says Mary, forty-three, "but I am the biggest tightwad you ever met." She takes out the Yellow Pages. She has no idea what she is looking for. "F" is for funerals. The first thing she learns is that, at most funeral homes, there is no such thing as a payment plan. They take cash, checks, MasterCard. They take insurance policies. What does Mary want? She wants Gary's friends to be able to see him one last time, but she also wants a cremation. She wants to spread Gary's ashes in Lake Austin, from a motorboat. The funeral prices were $4,000 or $5,000; one funeral home quoted her $8,000. "Eight thousand dollars?" Mary blurts out. "Eight thousand?"

Well, the funeral director replies, how much are you working with? There are no savings accounts, no insurance policies. Gary died with a paycheck for $102 in his pocket. Mary thinks she could scrape together $2,000. (She didn't yet know that the state of Texas has a crime victims' reparation fund to help pay for funeral services.)

"I can't help you," says the funeral director.

On a visit later that Sunday to another funeral home, Mary thinks maybe she can get by with a $4,000 service. Then she thinks again; there's no way she can get that kind of cash. "I don't know what I'm going to do," she finally tells the young funeral director.

The funeral director shrugs. He reaches for a card, flips it over, and writes down a name and a number. "There's one other place that might help you," he says. "But you can't tell anyone I told you this. . . ."

On Monday morning, she dials the number. "It's a recording; no wonder it's a deal," she says. "And I'm thinking as I'm listening to the message, All Face? All Face? What kind of a name is that?" She leaves a message anyway. When Robert Falcon returns her call, Mary is uncertain. Since Gary is going to be cremated, Robert suggests renting a casket. Mary repeats: "*Rent* a casket?" She's interested. She writes down the directions. With her family in tow, Mary makes her way to All Face. She lets out a little gasp when they pull into the parking lot. Then she giggles. All Faith's. How surreal is this, she wonders, even in the depths of sorrow, to be able to laugh. "It's the Blue-Light Special funeral home!" she says. She has to compose herself before going in. Stop giggling. They are immediately sobered when looking into the small chapel: There is a baby casket up front, and a grieving family.

When Robert comes out, he shakes their hands and leads them into the meeting room. He lays out the prices. He takes Mary and her family into the small showroom. She runs her hand along the casket edges. "Now this is my kind of guy," Mary says. "Here he is just giving it to me straight: These are the prices; this is what you'll get. And there's his father, this kind of old character, talking about the Mexican casket factory, and I'm thinking, Is this for real?"

She signs the contract. To pick up Gary's body from the morgue, repair it, embalm it, dress it, take it to the church in the rental casket, direct the funeral, take Gary's body back to the funeral home, put the body in a cardboard box, drive it to the crematory, and have it cremated, returning the ashes for Mary's lakeside ceremony two days after the funeral—to do all that—costs $1,950.

"Can you believe it?" she asks, proud that her common sense has seen her through.

Two days go by. Gary is dressed in his Hilfiger shirt, his hands holding the Nike swoosh cap. The Buick pulls up at Westlake Bible Church, and Mary is inside, watching, with her husband and pastor. "I think I need to pray," she says, turning to her pastor, another woman in a flowing black dress. They huddle together and look at the carpet. "Jesus, we just ask . . ." the pastor softly begs. Sonny and Robert open the red-curtained back door to the Buick, put the casket on the cart, and roll it into the church's large, airy walkway. Mary trembles. She follows her son's casket all the way to a large meeting room, where the viewing session will take place before the funeral. Robert opens the casket lid. Sonny goes back to the car to get the flowers.

"Here he is," Robert says to Mary.

"He's cold," she says, running her hand across her son's chest.

She steps back and looks at the casket. "Gunmetal gray," Robert had explained in All Faith's little showroom. The irony was not entirely lost on her, and anyway, the casket looks masculine.

Robert has done his most important work. He has made an illusion and a profit. The back of the man's head is cradled in a hidden, white yarmulke of gauze, covering up the place where the medical examiner had cut into the skull during the autopsy. Mary's hands caress her dead son's chest, face. "Thank you," she tells Robert.

Robert sets about straightening flowers around the casket, because a funeral director is always slightly adjusting everything— pulling cloth taut, straightening stacks of song sheets or prayer cards, making them flush to the edge of the table. To him, when we are dead we are paperwork and handiwork; to our mothers we are lost babies; somewhere else, we are souls. People want this part of death to go just right because so much else seems wrong about it. "We're going to leave him here with you now," Robert tells Mary. "We'll come back an hour before the funeral to get ready."

Robert and his father walk back outside.

"Nice church," Sonny says.

"She's probably going to touch him a lot and rub all the makeup off his face," Robert says. "Oh, well."

Mary leans down next to the body while her sister takes snap-shots. She is whispering to her son. She tells Gary she knows how hard he tried. She knows. Even after the lid is closed she knows.

VII. The Price of Dying

All across town, you can almost hear the slightest muffled umbrage at all this, the barest whisper of disapproval from a peculiar and protective brethren: the funeral directors. They are devoted and tra-ditional men and women, in nicer suits, in bigger funeral homes, where there are Murphy Oil smells, soft lighting, organ music on a tape loop. Local funeral directors knew Robert Falcon when he was the chubby kid in the necktie. They knew him when he was a free-lance mortician, begging them for extra work. Just what does he think he's doing out there in that strip mall?

"The funeral industry is a tightknit circle," says Lamar Hankins, a dryly affable, fifty-four-year-old attorney in San Marcos, who, as president of the Austin Memorial and Burial Information Society, traverses three counties, spreading the word about high funeral prices and running workshops for retirees about cutting costs. "There are penalties to any funeral director who steps out of that circle and starts doing deep discounts."

Hankins walked into All Faith's and right away liked it: the pluck, the prices. "We were getting frustrated," he says, "because by the spring [of 1998], it was getting more and more difficult to get really affordable funeral services in Austin." The metro-area average among twenty-seven funeral homes was $6,069 for a full funeral in 1998, according to the burial information society's price survey—the widest conducted in Austin. The society's members were being referred to Austin-Peel & Son Funeral Home, where prices for a full funeral ranged from $3,700 to just under $6,000. "We've only ever had two or three funeral homes over the last five years that had any interest at all in contracting with us," Hankins says. "(Austin-Peel's) prices have been better than average, but I did not feel like their prices were where they should be."

One of Robert's favorite things to do, when he is cruising down Ben White Boulevard in his old hearse, is to shout at the billboard for Harrell Funeral Home, where the visages of Arvin Harrell and his sons, Jason and Jerry, smile down on traffic. "Funeral progeny!" Robert shouts. "'Spend your money here!' Look at the Three Stooges. *Los Tres Bobos!* Manny, Mo, and Jack!" He stops to catch his breath. "I mean, is that why people should pay more for a funeral? Because of a face on a billboard?"

"I have heard other funeral directors ridicule All Faith's and make derisive comments about it," Hankins says. "Robert does a lot of the traditional things: He networks, he associates with community groups. But he is the only funeral director who advertises any sort of price information, just puts it right out there for people to see. That's always been unseemly with the establishment."

VIII. Heaven

"Heaven?" Robert asks, taken aback. That's a simple question. There is a simple answer to it. If he had a profound, deeply philosophical answer he might not be in this line of work. If life is complicated, being around dead people makes it worse. Robert Falcon is not a complicated man. "Do I believe in heaven?" he repeats. "Yes." He is silent for a moment. "Yes." Pearly gates? Streets of gold? Probably not. "I don't think heaven looks like a nice funeral home, that's for sure," he says. "It's not like some nice cemetery."

He is driving the Oldsmobile, on his way to a meeting of Texas funeral directors at a Doubletree Hotel in San Antonio. The wagon flies across a freeway ramp to Loop 410, and the clouds part, as if listening: "I see it as a very peaceful, very tranquil place. . . . Being able to get there and be with the people you've been with here in your earthly body. What a great reward. . . ."

A week later, in the middle of a slow Wednesday, Robert has spent the better part of the morning looking on the Internet, on the rumor of naked photos of talk-radio host Dr. Laura Schlessinger,

and later, salivating over classic cars on www.hearse.com. When
the tedium seems almost unnerving, a call comes. Thirty minutes
later, Robert backs up the Buick to an entrance behind Seton
Medical Center on West Thirty-eighth Street, parks next to a
Dumpster. He opens the door and gets out a gurney and a velvety
green fuzzy gurney cover with "All Faith's" stitched in cursive on it.
He goes in a back door and down a hall, through a door, past the
employee cafeteria, past the emergency room doors, to an
elevator . . . pushes the Up button . . . waits. . . . "I hate hospitals,"
he says. "They kind of give me the creeps," and there is no punch
line here. He rides up to the neurological intensive care unit,
where the nurses all look at him. They point to a room with the
curtains drawn: *el cuerpo*.

Rubber gloves. She's elderly and heavy, and she crossed over
into death seventy-three minutes ago, with a white cotton cap covering her head. A nurse helps Robert, one-two-three *lift*. Strap,
cover, roll.

There are the stares, as he wheels the body back down the hallway to the elevator. He waits. A man on a cell phone near the
nurses' desk can't help himself. "Hey, they're wheeling out a dead
body," he says to the person on the other end, "right in front of
me, man."

Robert pushes the gurney past more stares, from two doctors as
he passes the ER hallway, from the employee cafeteria, a wide-eyed
janitor dashing out of the gurney's path, a construction worker
shouting, "I ain't ready yet, Lord, and neither is the bank!" And all
the other construction workers laugh.

Robert doesn't even glance their way. "People are so frightened
of death," he says.

He wheels her out in the afternoon and loads her into the Buick.

Back at All Faith's, Sonny comes out and helps him unload the
gurney, straight to the embalming room. Robert sets up plastic arm-
rests and headrests on the metal table, and Norm helps Robert
move the body. "This is the part I can never watch," Sonny says, excusing himself to go answer the phones, as they lift the old

woman's body by her limbs onto the table. There is necessary jerking and prodding.

Robert puts on a new pair of rubber gloves, loosens his tie. The woman is to be prepped and embalmed so she can be delivered to another funeral home an hour away. Once her body is at that funeral home, she will be dressed and put into a casket. "You can stay for this, if you want," Robert says.

He shuts the door. Let there be no mystery, no fright. At its simplest, let it be the last thing we need in this world, this laying of hands, the last touch of beauty. *You can stay for this if you want.* Robert turns the radio on to a hip-hop station, the Beat 104.3 ("Jammin' better music").

"Ooh, you're dancing real close/Must be real smooth," the voice on the radio sings. "Girl, you're making it hard for me—eee/I love when you shake it like that, ah, ah/I see that you like it like that, ooh, ooh." Robert hums along, dances a little, going through a drawer, getting his tools. He turns on the pump. He opens a sixteen-ounce bottle of embalming fluid and pours it into the pump, diluting the solution with water. He takes the dead woman's gown off and covers her genital area with a towel. He takes off the white knit cap. He puts cotton in her mouth and takes an electric needle injector gun off the wall from where it hangs, next to a hair dryer. He shoots a piece of wire into her upper and lower jaw, and then twists the wires together to shut her mouth. He presses his fingers on her lips, contemplating a face he's never seen. "She has an overbite, a kind of crooked mouth," he says, somewhat dissatisfied, seeing how it looks when he pushes this way, then another. "I guess she just holds her mouth like that."

"I put my hand upon your hip," goes a rap song on the radio, "when I dip, you dip, we dip. . . ."

Next, he makes a small incision on the right side of her neck. He sticks an index finger inside the incision. Here is the carotid artery, he explains, which looks like a white shoelace; next to it is the deep-blue jugular. Robert snips the jugular and attaches spring forceps to hold it open. Blood begins to flow out over the woman's shoulder and down the table's gutters, toward the porcelain sink. The artery is tapped with a tube so the embalming fluid can be pumped in, replacing blood.

It takes about a half hour. "You can see how her skin color is already changing," he says.

You can see, but you can't see entirely straight. That sloping inevitability. The stillness. And the embalming fluid packs a ferocious and woozy chemical wallop. Robert says it never bothered him, but you're hugging the walls. He's singing along to the radio. You stay conscious by making a mental inventory of the room around you: In the cabinet there's Derma-Pro Derma-Glow. Massage wax. In the drawer there are forceps, knives, clamps, needles. Another drawer: L'Oréal makeup, Cover Girl makeup, Brut cologne, liquid cement, a paintbrush. On a shelf: a plastic case holding someone's dentures, Aqua Net hairspray, glass cleaner (to take ink-pad stains off fingertips), Vaseline, lip wax.

Once the embalming is done, the body cavity must be cleaned out, with the trocar, which is a long metal suction tube with a knife on the edge. (Is she a grandmother? She looks like a grandmother.) The trocar is inserted near the woman's rib cage. He wiggles the knife and prods around, puncturing organs, sucking out body gases and tissue. (An era ago she was a girl. There were secrets and flowers and crushes. Later there was heartache, maybe.) Her swollen torso deflates and is filled with cavity fluid. A small trocar cap is then screwed into the incision to keep the fluid from leaking. The opening on her neck is sealed with Super Glue. He checks to see how she is firming, touching the face. (Life is a mystery. She can never tell us. We can never know.) He turns on a water hose. He washes and shampoos her. "Have you done something different to your hair?" he asks.

You can talk to the dead. There can be just a little humor in the bedside manner. A dialogue with nobody. When she is clean and dry and somewhat pinker, she is dressed in a new hospital gown. Norm returns from lunch and gets her back on the gurney, arranging her neatly for her trip out of town. Total bill to the funeral home: $334.

"She's somebody's something," Norm says. "Everybody is some-body's something."

IX. El Bigote and the Smell of the Night

Robert lives in a duplex next to his parents' house, on Woodland Avenue. Sonny and Lupe's house is in constant activity, people coming and going. Robert's Jack Russell terrier, Paco, has the run of the place. Paco will frequently rip all the decorations off Lupe's Christmas tree, which she keeps decorated all year, for Mardi Gras and Thanksgiving, for Saints Valentine and Patrick. Norm Lopez lives in the other half of the duplex, between Sonny and Robert. This is handy, if sometimes cause for an argument or two. When a customer dies or the county has a fresh murder needing to be delivered to the morgue, the phone immediately forwards, after business hours, to one of the three.

Sonny was born and raised in the Rio Grande Valley, in Mercedes, west of Harlingen. He played baseball. He worked Saturdays delivering milk.

He first encountered death when he was seventeen, maybe eighteen. Sonny remembers his grandfather's mustache. It was a prominent, black and silvery gray thing that covered his grandfather's lip for life, meticulously attended to, curling on its edges, and thickly, even ominously handsome. He was in his eighties when he just went to sleep one night and died, and Sonny's mother decided that the funeral would be done by the nicer of the two funeral homes in town, the one owned by Anglos. She sent the boy over to make arrangements; his English was better than hers. Sonny picked out the casket, signed the papers. "Do you want him clean shaven?" the mortician asked, another question on a long form of questions.

"Yes," Sonny said, thinking the cheeks, the chin. "Make him clean."

The next day, when the family went to see the grandfather's body, the big mustache was gone. *El bigote,* everyone gasped.

A cousin persuaded Sonny to move from the Valley up to Austin in 1958 and get work as a butcher's apprentice. Later he got a job as a meat cutter at Guajardo Cash Grocery, on East Ninth and Lydia streets. He married the owner's daughter, Lupe, in 1962. Their three sons—John, Robert, and Joe—used to play touch football in the Texas State Cemetery, a block over. Throughout the 1970s and 1980s, the Falcon family traveled around Texas on weekends, selling fajitas at outdoor festivals and country-music concerts. The hallway in their home now is a shrine to the glory days of the Fajita King: framed pictures of all those country singers shaking Sonny's hand, the politicians, the golf pros, the cookoff contests, the Fajita King's brief mention in the June 1987 issue of *Playboy*, the restaurants opened, the restaurants closed.

Sonny and Lupe still go to six o'clock Mass on Saturday nights at Our Lady of Guadalupe Catholic Church, across the street from where the old grocery was. They sit in the third pew. After Mass, they have dinner with two other couples. They talk about old East Austin, eat enchiladas, drink coffee, retell the big and small things. The couples talk about their kids and grandkids, the tax rate, cancer, the football season. They also talk about who has died, a sort of ongoing conversational obituary page. Sonny always has news. He knows who from what church recently died, and which funeral home handled it.

Sonny has other news, but it's not fit talk, so he keeps it to himself.

He knows, for example, exactly what two women and a nine-year-old girl look like after a man beats them with a frying pan and strangles the girl with a coat hanger. He knows about the skeleton found leaning against a tree on a hill west of town (and how hard the hill is to climb with a gurney, and how the body's pants remained almost perfect). He knows about the fat, naked man sprawled on the bed. He knows about garage rafters, about bathtubs, about toolsheds, about early morning hours and nighttime sounds and smells, about motel rooms and yellow police tape. Some news you don't tell.

In the Falcon family, death is the silent guest at the table. The phone could ring, which means bad news for someone, but not them. On the whole, Sonny Falcon's life is tragedy free. Something was irrevocably altered when two of his three sons became funeral directors: Robert has his dreams of the strip-mall funeral home taking business from the big boys; the youngest son, Joe, directs funerals at Wilke-Clay-Fish Funeral Home down the street. Maybe, he hopes, the brothers can someday work together. If Sonny Falcon were in any way morose or pessimistic, the ringing telephone, the constant parade of dead and mangled bodies would take its toll. But he's not complicated. The call comes, and he answers it.

Tonight, at this table, Sonny puts it out of his mind.

He cracks a joke about the Aggies, and everyone laughs. Empanadas are passed around.

Long after dinner is finished and everyone is ready to go, one of the women, Christine Villanueva, opens the back door and breathes in the air. Sonny and Lupe Falcon look up at the sky. Christine cuts off a sprig of a potent white bloom on a bush. "Mmm, smell," she says.

"*Huele de noche.*"

"The smell of the night," Sonny says.

X. Father and Son

Robert sails right past the 7-Eleven on another blazing hot afternoon. He'd love a Slurpee, but, according to some nicety of the dismal trade, you can't—or shouldn't—stop with a body in the car. Having been sent off with flowers and hymns, this body is scheduled to be cremated tomorrow. The Buick hangs a right behind the strip mall, pulls up to the back door, in the alley behind All Faith's.

Sonny, who drove the flower car, is already waiting for Robert. In the back room, they assemble the cardboard box to take the body to the crematory in Temple. Sonny will drive it up there, first thing in the morning. Robert wraps the white, sheetlike shroud that lines the coffin around the body and ties it in a knot around a pulley. As he cranks it, the body starts to lift out of the casket. Sonny, who must drive it, wants to stop for a moment, so he can put a sheet of plastic around it, to prevent any leaking.

Father and son wind up having a fight about the body. Robert says the body will be fine. "But *mi'jo*," Sonny protests.

Robert interrupts his father: "It'll be okay. It'll be fine."

Sonny whines and grumbles. The body is placed in the box with a *thud,* and Robert angrily writes "HEAD" across the lid. With Sonny still muttering, Robert storms off and gets back in the Buick, slams the door, and drives away. "Well, now you know," Robert huffs. "We're not the Brady Bunch."

He drives back around the corner into the 7-Eleven parking lot and slides the hearse into an itty-bitty parking space. He strolls in, whistling, wipes the sweat from his forehead, never seeming to notice that everyone's looking at the guy in the pinstripe suit who drives a hearse.

They're out of cherry.

"Damn," he says.

XI. The Pietà (Double Prints)

Mary McMahan Tuttle gets her pictures back from the drugstore. The ones she had family members take of the casket, of her leaning next to Gary. In the pictures she is staring off into some unknown space, at the blur of what's ahead, at life without her son. She is glad, she says, so glad she took pictures before they closed the lid.

XII. In the Land of Plusher Carpets

One late October morning, Robert gets up, opens his newspaper to the obituary page, and goes bonkers with a mixture of glee and rage.

Next to his tiny, square advertisement for All Faith's is a bigger, two-column advertisement for Weed-Corley-Fish, the longtime funeral home on North Lamar Boulevard, which now also owns Wilke-Clay-Fish, just up the street from All Faith's.

"Read this!" Robert yells. "Read this!"

"Cost-conscious funerals aren't new to us," the Weed-Corley-Fish ad reads, set against a pleasant picture of a sunset over a lake. (Implied visual: a message from heaven.) "We've always offered them. Other funeral homes may promote their low prices like some new, breakthrough discovery, but the truth is, we've been providing those options for years. In fact, we invite you to bring us any funeral service quotation, and we'll show you how we can deliver better value for your dollar. . . ."

Robert tacks the ad to the wall of his tiny office.

He makes Sonny read it. He makes Norm read it. It's like a big gun has fired back at the spit wads he's been lobbing at the supposed enemy. "What do they mean by this? *Whatdoesthismean?!* Their prices are high!"

Now he wants to put a reporter on the case. This reporter. "You've got to go over there. You've gotta go talk to Baby Fish. See if he can match our prices!"

Baby Fish?

"Laurens Fish," Robert says. "Laurens Fish, the Third. Funeral progeny. Go see him. Make him show you how he can save you money. And bring back a full report."

That's not a bad idea, and not only for journalistic balance. It might be nice to go sit in another funeral home for a change, since it can be reliably reported that one can overlinger at All Faith's. Hang around here and pretty soon curiosity gets the best of you, and you're queasy all over again in the embalming room. You're holding doors open and arranging flower bouquets and singing "Amazing Grace" under a tent in Assumption Cemetery. You're leaning nonchalantly against a gurney and then realizing it has toes. You're riding shotgun to the crematory, listening to Sonny go on about the price of Florsheim shoes. You're watching Norm Lopez read old *Time* magazines in a doctor's lobby, waiting endlessly for the doctor to sign a death certificate.

Laurens B. Fish III walks along the hallway of his funeral home, at 3125 North Lamar Boulevard, a tree-shaded, red-brick compound that still looks like the 1950s. A fountain gurgles in a courtyard outside.

Spiffy funeral directors in suits are busily, quietly, handling matters of death. Baby Fish is tall, twenty-seven years old, wearing a gray suit of muted plaid, his hair neatly parted to one side—banker hair. He settles behind a writing table in a conference room alive with flowered wallpaper. At Weed-Corley-Fish, some of the death certificates on file go back to the 1910s. Fish proudly tells the story of his great-grandfather, John R. Corley, who started one of the first funeral homes in Texas, in Mexia, in 1876. Then his grandfather, Jack Corley, moved to Austin and purchased Thurlow Weed's funeral home at Seventeenth and Lavaca Streets in 1941, moving up to Lamar Boulevard in 1956 and becoming, for a time, the city's leading funeral home. Jack Corley's son-in-law, Laurens Fish Jr., came on the scene in 1970, and then came Laurens Fish III, who joined the family business in 1994. Last year, the Corley-Fishes bought Wilke-Amey-Clay Funeral Home. Between the two operations, they handle about 1,000 dead people a year.

Now Robert Falcon comes along, the man who used to do freelance work for Fish. "There's certainly a niche for what Robert does," Fish says. "And we want families to feel like they were well-served by him. But we'd never turn anybody away for limited funds."

A traditional funeral service at Weed-Corley-Fish will start at around $2,840. A casket will cost an additional $1,045 to $3,450—as high as $7,800 for a bronze or mahogany casket. Fish's price for a direct cremation here is $1,845. For customers who can demonstrate economic hardship, Fish will offer an economy package: a flat price of $2,500 includes a viewing session and simple graveside service in his least expensive steel casket. (The gravesite and mandatory grave liner or vault are not included.)

Baby Fish has very different funeral problems from Robert Falcon. At least once a week, one of the big corporations dangles an offer to buy out his family's business, but "I couldn't look people in this town in the face if I did that," he says. Now comes a discount funeral home and Mexican caskets, cutting into his market; by law he's required to use whatever casket the customer purchases, "and you just don't know about the quality of these foreign-made caskets," Fish says. He has customers sign a waiver, excusing the funeral home from, as he puts it, "mishaps." What if the bottom of an inferior Mexican casket falls out during a service, he asks. (Has that ever happened? "No, it hasn't. I hate to think it might," he says.) There are other problems with the imported caskets, he adds. You can tell by looking. The hinges, for example, are on the outside, not the inside. "They have door hinges on them," Fish says.

He hands over price lists, a synopsis of the Weed-Corley-Fish epic story of commitment and quality death care, pamphlets on loss ("Toward Tomorrow" and "The Spiral of Grief"), all in a nice blue folder. He waves good-bye.

"Door hinges?" Robert asks, the next day, as you're crawling under one of his Mexican caskets to look at the detail. "That's what it's all about? Door hinges? . . . OK, what else did he say?"

Well, there's the whole family thing. You might save a lot of money down here in the strip mall, but you won't go back to 1876. All Faith's didn't bury seven governors, or Lyndon B. Johnson, or former U.S. Rep. Barbara Jordan, like the Fishes did.

This piques Sonny's interest: a nice, caring Austin family? That's us, Sonny says. "Our family goes way back," he says. "We've been doing business for a long time, too. OK, maybe we were selling fajitas and running a grocery and this 'n' that, but I know everybody."

"This is what they'll always say," Robert says. "They'll always say that they offer more attentive service. They don't know. We're here whenever anyone needs us . . . Just because we're not fancy, just because I didn't grow up in a funeral home . . ."

I'm a loner, Dottie. A rebel.

For most of the rest of the afternoon, Robert is peeved. He sits and furiously punches numbers into his calculator, his prices versus theirs, to prove once and for all how much money he can save you. He can save you, he can save you.

A few nights later, Robert takes his girlfriend out to Tejano Ranch. She asks him to take the metallic All Faith's logo off the door of his brand-new Chevrolet Suburban. She doesn't want him

to be Funeral Boy tonight. He takes off the sign, but on his black
cowboy hat, he keeps a small gold pin of the praying hands logo.

He thinks he has fallen in love. He has asked her to read 1
Corinthians 13: Love is never this, love is never that. Does she understand? His heart has been broken before. If she understands,
will she marry him? She says she understands. He scoots his fi-
ancée around the dance floor, and they disappear into a smoky swirl
of souls, a crowd of cowboys and cowgirls dancing two by two,
spinning through the rest of their earthly nights.

XIII. El Cuerpo (A Bad Dream)

These are great days, Sonny says, *this 'n' that*. Wedding plans are
under way; the groom's cake will have a little casket on it, Lupe announces. Robert has talked his brother Joe into leaving Wilke-Clay-
Fish and coming to work at All Faith's. It pleases Sonny to see his
sons work together; two funeral directors mean twice the business.

The Falcons have serviced 299 of the dearly departed in eight
months, more than some funeral homes handle in a year. College
baseball season has started, and Sonny steals away on afternoons to
watch games at the University of Texas, about his most favorite
thing in the world, next to fajitas.

In the middle of the night, Robert awakes from a dream. He al-
most never dreams about *los cuerpos*. Once in a while, he dreams
Sonny has died, and when this happens, he can't get back to sleep.
He has thought it through before. He has brought it up at dinner.
(Sonny always scoffs, shakes his head. *Not planning on going any-
where soon*, mi'jo.)

The question is, are any of us ready, even the undertaker in the
strip mall.

Sonny knows at least this: When the Fajita King dies, his son
will do his funeral. Robert dreams about the embalming. His hands
shake. He doesn't know if he can do it. He cries when he thinks
about it. "Would I have the strength?" he asks, running the edge of
his knuckle along his eyelid. "I see people all the time in the worst

situations and wonder how they handle it. I hope I can handle it when my parents die." He'll do the job himself, in the strip mall, in the back room, the gentle artwork. He'll place the Fajita King in the Pietà model. A beautiful thing, a quality thing, a twenty-gauge sealer type, with a coppery brushed finish and the Last Supper engraved on the sides. A steal at $1,595, and of this much he's sure: "We'll save."

(1999)

Spirits Having Floated

College Park, Maryland

Along the nail-saloniest, carpet-warehousiest, noodle-bowliest, car-stereo-installationiest part of good, old Route 1—the slowest possible route between D.C. and Baltimore, where ambulances scream up constantly along its beaten path of pawnshops and liquor stores and funeral homes—the people still understand waterbeds, and Rose Taylor still understands the people. The waterbed in American culture is alive, she says, but thank God for the futon. If not for the futon era, then Watercraft Waterbeds, her College Park store, might not have made it this long.

How long? "Forever," she says, like a woman who has sold waterbeds in the Pleistocene. Route 1 may have too much of everything, but it only has one haunted waterbed store that is rumored to have been a bookie joint. (Maybe it was, judging from the hundred or so dead phone lines in the basement.) It may have been a brothel, too, though these are just a couple of the rumors that delectably hang over Route 1 like the smell of the morning's leftover doughnuts.

First, lunch—in the all-you-can-eat sushi place farther up Route 1, closer to Laurel. I overhear a fragment of hushed conversation between a twangy-voiced man and a pretty, though sad-looking, woman wearing French-cut jeans.

He: "Well, it can only mean one thing. He's gambling again."

She: "Yeah. Yeah, I guess you're right. She'll have to move out like she did last time."

There it is. A small part of the larger, beautiful opera production of Route 1, with its steady set changes of wicker furniture and houseplants and waterbeds, moving back and forth across Prince George's County. The unrest of it all, the buzzing pathos, the mini-storage units with all those secrets locked away. The living, you could say, and the dead.

Rose Taylor has been around long enough for the waterbed to have been rechristened the "flotation sleep system" by an industry that has every reason to hope it can be saved from its original image. The hard-sided platform waterbed of Aquarian bachelors and sullen teenage metalheads was long ago replaced by a soft-sided, looks-like-a-mattress version—the family-values waterbed. Then came waveless motion. Science got involved.

Sometimes the people still want a waterbed: a sexy bed, riding low to the carpet and offering itself like a bedroom performance stage. Rose Taylor knows what they mean. She'll show them a black-lacquer canopy waterbed, with overhead mirrors, hinged and bolted together in one of the small, dimly lit rooms of her store, which is in an ancient, three-story former farmhouse in College Park—a building that predates the paving of Route 1 in 1906. Of the rumors about the house being a brothel or a bookie joint, it can at least, with some certainty, be confirmed by city records that it was, for a long time, just a country grocery store, back in Route 1's motor-lodge and conga-room glory days.

For the last three decades it's undoubtedly been a waterbed store, and it is thought, by an authority such as Rose Taylor, to be one of the world's first waterbed stores. (Rose's sister, Linda, who was in a local rock band, opened it in 1969.)

If not the first waterbed store, Watercraft Waterbeds is certainly one of the world's last. An old sign with the word "waterbeds"—in a tubular, *Godspell*-y typeface—runs sideways along the street-face side of the house. Route 1's infamous traffic roars by obliviously, separated by the space of about three beanbag chairs from the front door. (For there are indeed beanbag chairs displayed each day on the sidewalk.)

When customers want to see the sexiest bed she's got, Rose has to be honest. She is neither for this particular model nor against it, in the aesthetic sense. In the business sense, she's for it, at $1,299: "You can see," she says, showcase-gesturing across the canopy bed, "I've got it as kinked up as I can get it." This afternoon she has the leopard-print comforter spread across it. "Men and women come in and they're honest. They want it. They laugh about it. I laugh about it. This is a kinky bed and that's all there is to it."

Goosh. There's that first goosh, when you lie down upon it, followed by a second, subtler wave, then a third, then fading to tranquillity . . . so you move your hips around to make more motion. There are mirrors above. "Not real mirror. Mylar," she says. There is a mirrored headboard, with cubbyholes, into which might go the things that stepchildren and babysitters snoop for: an old Nancy Friday paperback, the long-forgotten half ounce of weed, the squozen tubes of unspeakable ointments.

Then, from somewhere above us, a creaking of floorboards. Sometimes she hears them, walking around on the top floor, among the futon frames. It's no one. It's not a customer. It's not a rodent. Rich Pollard, the store's manager for nine years, says there's a room on the second floor where, once in a while, for no reason, he gets a sudden chill, and his arm hairs stand on end. Or a book falls off a shelf. We're talking about benevolent ghosts, the quiet types, who like to lounge around and keep an eye on things. The kind of spirits you'd imagine lolling about, eating Doritos in bed.

"This place is haunted," Rose confirms. "People won't believe that."

The kind of people who won't believe in a haunted waterbed store are the kind of people who wouldn't believe in the odd, junky sanctity of Route 1 to begin with. There are also those who, in fact, lobby for the state of Maryland to add a bike lane and widen Route 1, with plans already on the table, which will be the end of Watercraft Waterbeds: To fix Route 1, the old house will be torn down. "It's ridiculous," Rose says, sitting on a futon couch by the front door, touching her bottle-blond bangs away from her eyes. She has petitions she wants people to sign. She's mad about possibly losing her store, but it's also about changing the identity of the road. "I love Route 1, and they are crazy if they think people are going to be able to bike down it and not get themselves killed. They want to take out the center lane. It makes no sense."

Rose is Route 1; it seems she has belonged to Route 1 all her life. Her sister got her into the waterbed business when she was a teenager, by teaching Rose how to upholster giant heart-shaped headboards in the early 1970s. ("It was very *Playboy* magazine," Rose says.) After a few years, Rose took over the business. She sends her kids to nearby Catholic schools, and her oldest son is now at the University of Maryland down the road. When there's trouble, she can count on the guys at the Great Southern Tattoo parlor next door to come to her aid. (And when the tattoo guys go off and accidentally leave a loaded gun on the front stoop of their shop, who is the one who sees it and picks it up and keeps it safe for them? Rose the waterbed lady, of course.)

■ ■ ■

"Waterbeds have been around and around," Rose says. "Just like anything, it takes off at first and everybody wants one. There was this whole sexy image that went with them in the seventies, people would say 'Oh, you have' "—eyebrows shoot up—" 'a *waterbed.*' The man would want one, but the woman wouldn't. There was the whole myth that they leaked. Once, we took one down to P.G. Plaza and set it up and had a contest, that if you could jump up and down and break the waterbed, we'd give you one for free. Everybody tried, but nobody could break it. Then in the eighties we started to get a little bit of respect. We started shooting for selling people the therapeutic value of the waterbed. They came out with this one here—the soft-side waterbed—and since it looked like a bed, then the women would go for it. Then everybody wanted in the waterbed business. Then it died down again. . . ."

The trade association that used to count waterbed sales in

America counted 6 million sold in 1980 . . . down to 4 million in 1986 . . . down to just more than 3 million in 1990 . . . and you see where this is going. In the 1990s, that waterbed association merged with another waterbed association and then they both were subsumed into the Specialty Sleep Association, which no longer really knows for sure how many waterbeds are sold in America, but puts it around 400,000 a year. (Nonurgent Memo to Restoration Hardware, Pottery Barn, et al.: In about two years, create a "vintage" waterbed and market it to unsuspecting techno-snoots as a piece of "reimagined Middle Americana," evoking college apartments and Californian notions of dreamy possibility. Charge $3,500, minimum.)

Maybe the waterbed lives on because who wants to move it twice? Filled, it's nearly a ton of water. Rose doesn't like to move the waterbeds in her store around, even though the Second Law of Retail is that you should rearrange and vary the merchandise at an aggressive pace. She rolls her eyes. Look at this place. Move too many waterbeds and the haunted house might come crashing down. "You could kill yourself moving stuff around." Or, she suggests, "you can just change the comforters."

Rose is a waterbed person. Rich, the store manager, is a waterbed person. (And an aquarium person.) Waterbed people say they never have back pain. Waterbed people hate to come stay at your house, because they're away from their waterbeds. Waterbed people know a bargain, know they can get a waterbed, including the heater, for just $300; or spend $1,500 on the nicest bed in the store. Waterbed people seemed to have relearned the principles of traction—issues of adequate purchase—when it comes to the mechanics of sex. (It's a whole other study of motion, waterbed persons say: The bed is an active participant.)

What else about waterbed persons? "It's not like you can say who is a waterbed person and who isn't a waterbed person," Rich says. He should know, since he is usually the person who delivers and assembles the customers' waterbeds. "I've delivered them to the most decadent mansions in Potomac and I've delivered them to the filthiest squalor you can imagine. I've been to houses where people are cutting up cocaine on the coffee table and say, 'Oh, come on in, the waterbed goes right there.' . . . I've delivered waterbeds to houses where there's guns sitting around and I wonder, do you just leave these things around? We drained one guy's waterbed and lifted up the empty mattress and he has an M-16 [rifle] under there, and he says, 'Oh, could you hand me that?' Could I hand him that?! No, I'm not touching that." Nor is he touching the dildo that falls out of the nightstand when he moves it. There is so much in the American home that Rich will not touch, and so much to learn about the people.

■ ■ ■

The haunted waterbed store is not the busiest place you could find. "Hey, we don't need a hundred customers in here," Rose says, in her defense. "We need *one* customer. The *right* customer." The right customer walks in about once a day, sometimes twice; some days a whole lot of waterbed people need help at once. Rose vows never to get too distracted, after that fateful day in 1985 when she left a hose running in a waterbed on the store's second floor. She set the hose up, and then turned her attention to a shipment problem down-stairs. That afternoon, when another employee arrived for work, he went upstairs, "and came back with his face as white a ghost," Rose says. "I said, 'Mike, what's wrong,' and he said, 'Rose, are you filling a waterbed upstairs?' and I said, 'Oh, no—I forgot all about it! How bad is it?'

"'It's bad, Rose.'

"'How bad?'

"'Don't look, Rose.'

"'Don't be silly, Mike, quit blocking the stairs, let me up there and see. . . .'"

She didn't get to the top of the stairs. The waterbed was as big as the room—as high as the ceiling, as wide as the walls. It looked like something out of a horror movie. It broke its frame and an exposed screw ripped a hole in the vinyl. An explosive flood nearly wiped Watercraft Waterbeds out for good. (Rose rode the wave on her rear end and out the front door and into the righthand lane of Route 1; hysteria and the fire department followed. She fought with insurance adjusters for another four years.)

People said: Rose, why don't you open a bigger store, in a nice new strip mall somewhere else, and sell more kinds of furniture? Diversify, Rose. Branch out. People said: Who can make it on just waterbeds and futons? People said: Rose, how long can this go on?

"I like it here," she says, looking around. There are water stains on the ceiling. The floor buckles in places. The waterbed people get it—the whole waterbedness of it. The waterbed people like simple, black floor lamps to go with waterbeds; and there are framed pictures on the walls, the blank stares and stern pouts and tilted shoulders of early-1980s new-wave seductresses, those nymphs designed by Patrick Nagel, the Botticelli of the airbrush. There are gurgling rock fountains plugged into the walls. The people still get it.

The ghosts get it, too. "Maybe they look out for me," she says. "I don't know." Things go bump. Things go goosh. What sounds like two dozen fire trucks go moaning by on Route 1, followed by a herd of Harleys revving downhill in the other direction. Standing in the middle of the world's last haunted waterbed store, there is the overwhelming and sudden chilly sensation of the opposite of *House Beautiful* and catalogue leather and feng shui, of spirits having floated to eternal reward.

(2000)

Notes on Kamp

Albuquerque, New Mexico

The pup tent blows down in the middle of the night, during a ripping wind from the canyon, a clanging sound when the skinny aluminum poles hit the dirt, a billowing rage of tarp and nylon and zippers. The mind startles awake and panics: *Killer or bear?* But it's just a tent down in the wind, it's just kampin' hijinks, with a constant thunder from Interstate 40 a few yards away on the other side of a cyclone fence topped with barbed wire, a chorus of passing eighteen-wheelers. Quick, run to the car in my underwear. Sit there and think about what to do next. A police siren wails down nearby East Central Avenue, and I ask myself: This is camping?

Not really. This is kamping.

■ ■ ■

"We were wondering about you last night," Carl Norton says the next day. He waves and smiles. He's wearing shorts and loafers. He's walking his cat, Bob, on a long leash. Lots of people walk their cats here at the Kampgrounds of America. Siamese cats, orange tabbies, black cats like Bob, whose owners all agree: *You don't walk the cat; the cat walks you.* So Carl wants to know, "Did your tent hold up? That wind was really blowing. We heard it was gusting up to sixty [mph]. We were glad to be inside."

The Nortons—Carl and his wife, Marvel, and Bob the Cat—spend twenty days of every month on the road in their Ford four by four, pulling their Prestige fifth-wheeler RV wherever they go, the kind with the retractable awning front porch, the extendable living room, and a customized hatch that makes it easy to change the kitty litter. "Do you get the idea," Marvel asks, "that our lives revolve around the cat?"

I get that idea. And I get other ideas at the KOA, kamping for three warm days and blustery July nights right in the city, off East Central Avenue, twenty-seven scrubby acres wedged between the interstate and Juan Tabo Boulevard, adjacent to middle- to low-income apartment complexes and the Moose Lodge. It's a campground that outlived Route 66, while Albuquerque grew up and around it: My particular tent site sits under an old Shalako Motor Inn sign overlooking Skyline Road, the large letters of "Next Exit" breaking off in plastic and metal orange pieces.

Time at a KOA teaches you about the Decent People, trusting but wary travelers who don't want no surprises, nothing fancy-schmancy for us, thanks. I get ideas about what it might be like to retire with a lot of good years and open highway left before you. I get ideas about inescapable family dynamics, about kids running straight from the station wagon to the swimming pool, brothers and sisters and dads and moms who are sick of sitting beside each other. I get ideas about having your own temporary real estate, a separate piece in which to kamp a night or two, while keeping your manners about neighborly offers to break bread, pop a beer, and nod "howdy." These things are part of the kamping culture: Safe behind the barbed wire, we're all neighbors here. It's lawn-chair philosophy and shared experiences, the mayonnaise and ketchup of vacation and life.

■   ■   ■

You pull in and think, *Well, kids, we're here:* The trademark A-frame office building, the yellow and red KOA logo, the black asphalt, the pine trees, the reddish-brown picnic tables. There are 223 kampsites in the Albuquerque central KOA. Eighty percent of the spaces are for recreational vehicles, the other 20 percent are for tents or lodging in one of ten Lincoln Log-esque "Kamping Kabins." KOA has more than 600 locations in North America, which amounts to some 75,000 kampsites. One kampground just opened in Japan. The chain began in 1962, when a group of investors opened a kampground in Billings, Montana, in hopes of luring kampers on their way to the Seattle World's Fair. The Albuquerque Central KOA opened in the summer of 1970. "Think of it like a small town," says Wayne Erickson, who runs the Albuquerque KOA with his wife, Linnea, and considers the Albuquerque KOA to be its own civic bureacracy. "Sometimes we feel like the mayors. We have to handle the sewer, water, trash pickup . . . ," Wayne says. "We deal with anything that comes along."

Wayne and Linnea: "We were never campers," she says.

"Oh, but we traveled a lot," he says, "And we know what people are looking for when they travel."

Linnea and Wayne: The interstate has many exits. One day you wake up and realize you need something different. So you sell the house, reduce the accumulation of a few decades, move to a kampground, work a while, and then move again to another kampground. This narrative underlies so much at a KOA, for the people who stay at one and the people who work at one. Wayne and Linnea Erickson are a matched set in their standard-issue khaki shorts and white safari shirts with the KOA logo stitched on the shoulder loops. They are tan and sweet-natured, and both are fifty years old. They were sent to Albuquerque last summer by KOA's corporate office, after a successful stint managing one of the company's kamps in St. Petersburg, Florida. (Most KOAs, including the other 13 in New Mexico, are owned by individual franchisees and overseen by KOA; about a dozen of the largest kampgrounds, including Albuquerque Central, are company owned.) Wayne was a Lutheran minister for twenty-five years. Linnea worked as an office manager in a hospital. Wayne says he's a people person, likes to walk around, meet and greet, find out what people need. Linnea does the books, orders the supplies, stocks the store, counts the money. The Ericksons live in a double-wide mobile home in the center of the kampground, with a wooden yard fence around it.

"No day is the same as any other," Linnea says.

"You see every kind of person come through here," Wayne says.

"Every kind," Linnea says.

"All walks of life," Wayne says. "Some people you would think are spending their last dollar to kamp here. Others drive up in motor homes that cost several hundred thousand dollars. It's not a destination point, like some of the other kampgrounds. I-forty is our lifeblood. Most of the people who stay here are overnighters, just passing through."

"There's been so many . . . ," Linnea says.

"They do sort of all blur together," Wayne says.

"You get attached to some of them, and you're sad to see them go," Linnea says.

"Some stay a long time," Wayne says. "There are the Monthlies, who are kind of like the townspeople here."

Which is to say the interstate also has its detours, and those who suffered a personal detour as well: Presently there is a family from Rio Rancho, an Albuquerque suburb, who got caught in the home-building crunch, kamping here in a motor home until their new house is finished. There is a single mother who can't find a simple two-bedroom apartment. There is an unemployed electrician from California looking for work so he doesn't have to sell his house. You can kamp as long as you like, or as long as life leaves you here, for $350 a month. "There are a few who have lived here for years," Wayne pipes in.

"We couldn't figure out who had been here longest, Mr. Hawkins or Mr. Babcock," Linnea says. "Mr. Babcock has been here five years. Or is it four? Now there's an interesting man. He lives in a motor home in Space one forty-nine. He has one of those, oh, what do you call it, like a three-wheeler, no, it's this long bicycle-type thing. He rides around with his parrot."

■ ■ ■

Early on a hot Friday afternoon, I make kamp in the tent cluster on the park's east end. The kampground is quiet, except for the steady noise from the interstate. The rate is $19.95 a day for tents, $25.95

for an RV hookup. Already I realize I'm in a lower caste of kampers: I'm not in a motor home. I don't even have a pop-up. In a world of Komforts, Tiogas, Dolphin Turbo Diesels, Vagabonds, Cruise Air IIIs, and Carri-Lites, I'm just a tent kamper. I'm out here with the German tourists, the fledgling rock bands, the young lovers on road trips.

Wayne drives up in his white KOA pickup truck. What grass there is on the kampsites has a hard time staying alive lately, he remarks, because the KOA has been so crowded. Wayne looks at the brown grass and sighs. The kampground just had its second busiest week this summer, with the Golden Wing motorcycle convention. It was 900 kamping Golden Wingers, middle-aged couples mostly, tooling around on their sparkly teal and pink Honda two-seaters, chitchatting on their helmet microphones. Several weeks earlier, it had been the big Harley-Davidson gathering. "The *nicest* people," Linnea says.

"You missed the party," Wayne adds. "What a bonanza for Albuquerque to get both the Golden Wings and the hogs in the same year. I think every available piece of land to kamp on was kamped on."

You can tell it's been busy by the strange rings of Comet bathroom cleanser all over the ground and asphalt. "You know what that is," Wayne says.

You don't know, so Wayne has to explain: "Ants will not cross a line of Comet."

■　■　■

People kamp here because they can expect that everything will be A-OK at the KOA. There will be a swimming pool, a hot tub, and an automated laundry. There will be groupings of hot-water shower stalls with a bench to set your things on and a door to close and latch. Hookups to connect your trailer toilet to and a fifteen-foot tall tank of propane for fill-ups. Video games, ten holes of miniature golf. A little grocery and supply store that also sells souvenirs. There's a certain cleanliness and good cheer. You know you're kamping when everyone starts talking about how it's not even like *camping* at all. Barbed wire helps the KOA feel comfortably close to an A-OK America: You hear stories from kampers about how the road isn't so safe, cautionary tales about carjackers and long-hairs. You hear about frightening glimpses of highway robbery, or strange perverts at rest areas. *Drive early* gets repeated like a mother's warning: Start at dawn, drive all morning, and be at kamp no later than four or five in the afternoon. Kamp only where you feel secure.

A walk by the pool, which has a posted sign limiting capacity to forty. There are thirty-four people, mostly kids, splashing around. A woman in a bathing cap attempts her laps through the chaos. A dad is throwing his daughters off his shoulders in the shallow end. Through the laundry room and back into the registration office, the check-in line extends to the door. People also want to buy bags of ice and postcards and lighter fluid. I'm in a shopping mood: Here are plumbing hookup hoses, and plastic party lanterns ($17.99), and bug candles and those little boxes of breakfast cereal that you can cut open and pour the milk right in. (*That's* kampin'.) There are Route 66 mugs and New Mexico T-shirts with chile peppers, natch, and blue-corn chips made in Santa Fe (for $2.49).

KOA uses as its trademark mascots the roundheaded *Family Circus* characters drawn by cartoonist Bil Keane. The *Family Circus*—Dolly, P.J., Jeffy et al.—fit right in here. The politics at KOA are very *Family Circus*, slightly right of center or moderately invisible. The jokes you hear are like *Family Circus:* Everyone gets them. The Bil Keane worldview (Grandpa watches us from heaven, kids say the darndest things, dogs and cats love one another) tidily explains the KOA ethic, and you can buy *Family Circus* kamper mugs, T-shirts, aprons, and postcards here, too.

An evening storm blows in, threatening rain, but it's just wind and some distant lightning, a few sprinkles, and dusk turns the clouds a kountry-kitchen rose. Out at the pay phones by the miniature golf course, a half dozen people wait to call home: "We're in Albuquerque tonight. Uh hunh. No, I said *Al-buh-ker-kee.* Albuquerque. *New Mexico.*"

Kampers Judy Krohn and her mother-in-law, Nancy, take a

brisk, post-sunset walk along the rows of RVs, tents, and kabins. Judy is obsessed with finding out-of-state license plates. She needs a Maine. The campground slowly goes dark, illuminated by orange vapor lighting and the glow of TV screens in every motor home. There's a night registration box by the door, for late arrivals.

While kamping, why not tell scary stories? Lying here in the dark, listening to the traffic and the Boo Radley wind, I can think of a few:

The Body in the Trailer. Six weeks earlier, a KOA security guard found the body of Garnett "Gary" Burks, twenty-nine, the son of a former Las Cruces district judge, in a pop-up tent trailer on one of the sites at this very kampground. Burks's body had been left to rot, with a plastic bag and pair of shorts wrapped around his head. He had been shot twice, according to an autopsy, in the back of the head. Five days later, police arrested James Dunton, a twenty-four-year-old drifter from Illinois, and charged him with Burks's murder. The two men had met in Tucumcari, partied a little, and had been hanging out in Albuquerque, kamping.

"We don't really want to talk about that too much," Wayne Erickson says. "It's unfortunate. . . ."

"I don't think [Burks] was actually *shot* here," Linnea says. "That's what I think."

Gather round, and I'll think of some more neighborhood chillers:

Waterbed Killer. Across East Central Avenue, half a mile from the kampground at the Whispering Sands apartment complex on Western Skies Road, there lived a nineteen-year-old named Michelle Goffe. Police say she called a used furniture store to see if she could sell her waterbed. Michael Cote, twenty-nine, a store employee, offered to come out and look at the bed. By the next day, April 9, Goffe and her friend Kimberly Cotner, seventeen, lay dead in the apartment, raped and strangled. Cote has been charged with their deaths.

Used-car killer. On April 24, at the Sandia Ridge Apartments next to the KOA, a man named Jeff Villanueva, twenty-one, opened the bright blue door of his apartment and was shot in the forehead, while his girlfriend and her three-year-old child stood and watched. Police arrested Paul McGruder, twenty, and charged him with the murder. According to police reports, McGruder had test-driven Villanueva's girlfriend's pickup truck earlier in the day and returned with the intent to steal it.

Wayne and Linnea remember that one. It happened around 9:20 on a Sunday night: "People were sitting outside at dinner and heard the shot," Wayne says.

Across Skyline Road from the kampground, through a vacant lot to East Central, sits what's left of the Villa Inn, a dilapidated 130-room behemoth of a motel that has been closed since 1990. The last spooky story is really more of a neighborhood tragedy, dating to 1992, when a passerby discovered a transient raping a three-year-old boy in one of the motel's empty rooms. Neighbors have protested ever since to have the building torn down.

KOA persists, serenely as it can, given the environs. Wayne and Linnea keep a watchful eye. "It's why we have an all-night security guard," Wayne says. "It's more realistic than locking the gate every night." I fall asleep thinking about all this, and attempt to have pleasant, amusing dreams about the *Family Circus,* walking their cat on a leash.

■   ■   ■

Slept too late, and now all my newfound friends are gone, hitched up and rolled out to the interstate in different directions, leaving the smell of their three-egg, bacon, and coffee breakfast and tidy little bundles of garbage in their wake.

I take my breakfast by the pool—a miniature box of Raisin Bran with whole milk. "We are from the Netherlands," says one of my neighbors, a blond man with a blond girlfriend, kamping in a tent on the other side of the picnic shelter, part way on their journey to trace Route 66. "And we are for two days wonderink who it is you are, and why you are all the time with cameras and writing down things?"

■   ■   ■

I go for a hike. (While kamping, why not hike?) I go to Furr's grocery store and the Cowtown Boot Co., walk along East Central and take in the view: 7-Eleven and Allsup convenience stores, Sirloin Stockade and the International House of Pancakes, Motel 6 and Days Inn, Chevron and Shell, the Shan-Ann Plaza Apartments. The midday heat amplifies and distorts the sounds of horns and jets coming in toward Kirtland Air Force Base. I briefly consider escaping into a matinee at the United Artists Four Hills 12, but would that be kamping? I wander back through the weedy, broken remains of the Villa Inn, examine the graffiti hieroglyphics on the walls, find pieces of a large neon sign that once said "Restaurant and Lounge."

Back at kamp, nothing happens. Employees are making their usual cleaning and maintenance rounds. The prairie dogs have decided to keep beneath ground today. The julep green pool water is still and undisturbed. An elderly woman is doing her husband's laundry and watching amateur figure skating on the TV. The sight of ice makes both of us feel hotter. I get the high score on Pac-Man.

Vesta Essler, who is KOA's assistant manager with her husband, Rich, invites me upstairs to the office at the top of the A-frame, where it's air-conditioned. We talk about kamping. "We've always been kampers," Vesta says. She and her husband, both in their sixties, are also part of the crowd that retired with the hope to kamp out the rest of their days together. Vesta and Rich had a big home in Rochester, New York. He worked for Eastman Kodak; she worked for Bausch & Lomb. "We started out tent camping, then got a pop-up, then a camper. Now we have a fifth-wheel," Vesta says. They took the fifth-wheel to a kampground in Harrisburg, Pennsylvania, one weekend several years ago and got friendly with the managers there. This was the life they wanted. Their résumés were in the mail to KOA's offices in Billings the next week. They've worked at several, including the kamp in St. Petersburg, Florida, where they met Wayne and Linnea Erickson. Now they live in a trailer not far from them.

"It's a great life. I love it," Vesta says. "You find out that all those things you were so sad about selling and giving away, all the stuff you had, that you really didn't need most of it." Kamping here is an urban adventure. Vesta never knows what she'll see. One morning a woman came running from the bathroom to tell them that a Peeping Tom was looking in the showers. "Oh, that," Vesta laughs. "That was strange." Vesta and Linnea chased the Peeping Tom, who was not a paying kamper, and cornered him. "Linnea told him, 'Don't you go anywhere,' and then Wayne called the police and they came and took him away." She giggles.

What's important, Vesta says, is all the friends she's made at kamp. Lots of them you never see again. Some of them write letters. Some of them will return someday, following the map all the way back to where they began. She worked in a Best Western motel once. She was just a temp behind the registration desk, but she learned a real important difference between kamping and moteling. Here it is: "In motels, people are never happy. You have a lot of men on business, alone. Now here, at the kampground, you mostly get the people who are on vacation. They're happy people."

In kamp, you can sit in on almost any conversation, and people will tell you their lives, their heartbreaks. They'll brag about their children and lament the state of the world. In front of one RV, we learn one family history, although no one present can agree on the same version of any story. In front of another RV, we get a lecture from a Wilford Brimley look-alike about federal spending and the deficit. In front of another RV, we just talk about weather. I wander down to Space 149, in search of Mr. Babcock, the kamper emeritus who has lived here four or five years. A polite knock on his trailer door. No answer. A sign on the door reads: "Warning! Nothing in here is worth losing your life over!" Still no answer.

Afternoon gives over to evening and the happy kampers continue to check in, and old men gather around to watch new arrivals attempt to back their RVs into a the remaining spaces. The pool gets crowded with a different set of kids begging a different set of chubby fathers to toss them in the air. A different elderly woman in a bathing cap attempts to complete her laps. A roaring trio of F-16 fighter jets fly overhead from Kirtland Air Force Base, in formation, and every kamper gapes skyward. The night is so warm that people bring their TVs outside, with extension cords. The smell of sizzling hamburger lingers in the air, and over by the bathrooms it becomes the minty smell of siblings brushing their teeth at the row of sinks. Goodnights are said and dogs are walked, the cats, too, and this whole family circus of kampers tucks in for another sweaty night, to the accompaniment of sirens and the temper tantrums of locusts.

(1994)

Service Is Needed in Layaway

Silver Spring, Maryland

Something's always a little wrong in a Kmart, which is as good a reason as any to love it. The beleaguered, bankrupt chain of 2,114 stores has routinely defied the attempts of those who would dress it up (Martha Stewart) or make it cooler (er, Jaclyn Smith). It always has a way of being a slightly frazzled place, whether you're in the Kmart at Carlisle Boulevard and Indian School Road in the middle of Albuquerque, or in the Kmart at the corner of West Thirty-fourth Street and Seventh Avenue in the middle of Manhattan. The best Kmart is a Kmart on the edge of nowhere. (And most of them, psychically if not actually, are.)

Unlike its competitors, a true Kmart is unashamed to be a Kmart. It has lipstick on its teeth and those days where it feels, you know, *not so fresh*? It smells of popcorn, new bicycle tires, a package of crew socks, and home perm kits. You should be hesitant to go in there, and then you go in anyhow, because sometimes you feel like being a Kmart person. (Sometimes you feel like being a Wal-Mart person, even though you fancy yourself a Target person. But we'll come back to that.)

This essential bipolar downside wasn't a dynamite business plan. On a Tuesday night in January 2002, after Kmart Corporation confessed that it had nearly sped off the same Deadman's Curve that has left the world without a Woolworth's or a Pan American Air

Lines, and filed the largest bankruptcy protection plea in the history of retail, it is reflexively good to take a moment to stand in a Kmart—the one at the intersection of Georgia and Connecticut Avenues will do—and feel sad. Kmart hopes to reorganize itself to a greater glory in another year or so, but some stores may have to be closed (as many as 700, one analyst speculated). *Please, Lord, not this one,* I think to myself as I enter this Kmart, which, to me, is the perfect example of Kmart being itself, a store pulled in so many directions that chaos almost always threatens to take over. It is messy, noisy, understandably and admirably human. It's in Aspen Hill, that creaky, unhingey gate into deepest Montgomery County, Maryland (across from a Home Depot, a thatch of gas stations, a cemetery for people and a cemetery for pets, and a Boston Market, all of which will, months from now, serve as the backdrop of the first attacks by the man and teenager accused of the Washington sniper shootings of 2002). Boxes are stacked everywhere, with Kmart's typically odd, cornucopial juxtapositions: twenty-four-packs of Cottonelle, 'N Sync fruit chews, Windex, Pepsi.

The lines are long. English is the second language. Eddie Money sings "Take Me Home Tonight" over the sound system. There is plain and boring life being lived, and it is easy to imagine that your fellow Kmart shoppers had not, on the whole, spent the afternoon watching financial reports on CNBC. Kmart's money woes are not our problem here, yet there is a personal investment in such institutions, especially when they go broke. "Tell me," demands an editor I work with, who doesn't get the magnitude, "how an ironing board is different whether you get it at Wal-Mart or Target or Kmart." It's different in about a thousand ways, I could almost cry out. It's about the small pieces of identity we cling to in a landscape of so much banality. We are but three similar and divided Americas: Wal-Mart, Target, and Kmart.

An ironing board at Wal-Mart is destined to become a permanent piece of the family room decor. It will never come down,'cept when comp'ny comes. Wal-Mart is from the deepest heartland, the truest and most elementally American of whatever it's selling.

An ironing board at Target has been "designed" into something that wants to transcend ironing, perhaps by Michael Graves or some other known artiste. In a Target TV ad, a gorgeous Nordic blond model would pretend to windsurf on the Target ironing board behind stacks of Febreze fabric freshener. Target is a triumph of the graphic arts, fascistically clean, pure.

But an ironing board at Kmart wants to be both of these, and that's part of its disorder. It wants to be the ironing board in the family room that never gets taken down, but it also wants to be the ironing board with covers exclusively designed by Martha Stewart. What American cannot relate to this form of ambivalence?

In any case, the thing to love about Kmart is that a small child is always about to knock over all of the ironing boards, in a great commotion of noise, followed by a spanking, the kind of spanking you didn't think got delivered in America anymore (because you've spent too much time in Target, and not enough time in Kmart). It will be hours before anyone will come along and rearrange the ironing boards that wanted so badly to be chic. Kmart could never be Target. Kmart could never be Wal-Mart. And apparently we could not fully love Kmart for what it is, or was. Unknowingly, Kmart tapped into the idea that we are not all robots, that everything doesn't have to be perfect. Maybe this is why it has a certain appeal to newly arrived Americans, because it feels rudimentarily mercantile, like a loud and messy market back home.

The analysts were particularly cruel as news of Kmart's bankruptcy filing and emergency $2 billion credit triage came to light. (Make that Blue Light. Nearly every TV station led with some twist on "Attention, Kmart shoppers . . .") To hear analysts tell it, the corporation that once dominated discount retail—striking fear in the weakened hearts of Sears and Montgomery Ward and killing off the five-and-dime—had seemingly done everything wrong from the minute Sebastian S. Kresge (he of the capital K) began peddling sundries at his first store in Detroit in 1899.

"If Kmart went away tomorrow, the only people who would care are existing Kmart shoppers who don't have access to a Target or Wal-Mart," Steven Roorda, a retail analyst at American Express, told Reuters.

The analysts all gave Kmart a "junk" stock rating, which had a poetic quality to it. (Kmart? Junk? *Mais non!* My plastic Powerpuff Girls swimming pool has lasted two summers now!) Emme Kozloff, a retail analyst at Bernstein Sanford, told Reuters that "long-term, we believe the possibility that Kmart will disappear has increased," presenting that even more startling and tantalizing reality: empty Kmarts. (Ghost-town Kmarts!)

The new urbanists love an empty Kmart. If it sits there long enough, and the parking lot cracks and crumbles and slowly gives way to the earth below, someone smart (read: not a developer) will figure out something surprising and interesting to do with it. All that space, with no walls, and lots of electricity. Futurologists like scenarios where artists move in, and skateboarders, and computer hackers, and the kind of people who dig streams through the parking lots and turn them into massive English gardens. In this way, hip retro suburbanites with money will be drawn to these artsy new enclaves; the SoHos of the twenty-first century begin in the dead inner-suburban Kmarts of the twentieth century, and in forty years you have people buying living space at premium prices in an old Kmart.

It's a nice dream, and something to think about in the eternal checkout lines of Kmart. Here is where the people who came before us have abandoned tiny dreams. Here, they've ditched merchandise they no longer wanted or couldn't afford: Among the candy bars and Life Savers and Chiclets are disposable cameras, J.Lo CDs, Mach 3 razor blades, infant-size T-shirts, a belt, Gatorade, a "Get Well Soon" card, corduroy pants. In Kmart you always get the feeling that these items will spend their purgatory here, until someone else wants them at the last minute. It's this random nature of the place that gave it the reputation it has. It's why Dustin Hoffman's autistic *Rain Man* character would react violently to being taken there. "Kmart sucks," the Rain Man said. It did, and with any providence, it will go on gloriously sucking.

(2002)

Xanadu Tuesdays

Austin, Texas

I write this as a man who, once in a while, thinks too much and too sadly about that which is faddish and gone, such as roller disco, or who I was in the seventh grade. This place is not about those things. It is not about tube socks and giant combs and crushes on girls with raspberry lip gloss, or the endless counterclockwise journeys of a platoon of bulging-trousered Scott Baios. You could come here only for nostalgia, but that doesn't seem to be why a hundred or so grown-ups roller-skate every Tuesday night at Playland.

This is simply about discovering that time can stop, for a few hours, once a week, in a somewhat rundown but firmly held-together place where going forward and going backward are made to look easier than they are. Here is a place where you walk up and pay your five dollars at the window and David Dodson buzzes you into that damp, breezy darkness, and you take in the acetate flashes of color, and hear—let's say, not for nostalgia's sake—Rose Royce's anthemic "Car Wash." Here is a place where, when all of that has occurred, something clicks in you and the world no longer exists, except this particular secret kingdom, beneath the wide-open gazes of cartoon bunnies painted on the walls. You tell the guy behind a long, carpeted countertop what your shoe size is, and he grabs you a pair of roller skates from the shelves. You walk along the rink on worn-down, liver-colored carpet. You sit on a bench and take off your shoes with a Mister Rogers deliberateness. Lacing up is a genuflection here. You put the skates on—just a pair of old quads, fat orange wheels with the rubber toe stop, light tan leather uppers soft as dog-belly flesh—and you knot and double-knot the long, brown laces. You are up. You are hands out on either side, just slightly, and then you are putting the wheels on the light blue floor and letting go of the metal rail. You are joining the stream. You are depositing yourself into the endless Newtonian equation of movement and opposite reactions. You are surrendering to physics and God and the Electric Light Orchestra.

That is what the first time is like, on any Tuesday between 7:00 p.m. and 10:00 p.m., at Adult Night, at Playland Skating Center, which is a terrifying hairpin-right turn across traffic off the southbound U.S. 183 freeway at the Burnet Road exit, behind a Nissan dealership, next to a strip mall with a Chili's restaurant. The first time I went to skate, I did not find it, because the sprawl, clutter, and high chain-link fences have almost hidden Playland for good. The woman who used to cut my hair insisted it was there—she had been there, she had seen it, she had *flown*. She knew it was on Tuesday nights, and that there were people in their twenties, thirties, forties, even older than fifty, who still roller discoed as if living in some forevermore, and children were not allowed. The way she described it, it sounded calming and mysterious. "You have to find it and go. You just start off skating around and around," she said lazily, hypnotically, "and it all comes back to you, and pretty soon you forget about whatever was bugging you that day. I swear it's better than therapy. Afterwards, we always go get margaritas at Trudy's."

Xanax can take the edge off, but, I have since learned, so can a little Xanadu.

■ ■ ■

In the beautiful blur now, up on skates. There are crate-sized box fans propped along the margins of the rink, gently blowing kisses as we float by. There are bumps in the old floor, which measures a

20,000-square-foot rectangular stretch—a skid marked and unfor-
giving polymer plane with chips nicked out here and there, and a
San Andreas faultline bisecting it north to south. There are neon
stars and squiggles darting across a high ceiling of foam panels that
were once white and are now yellowed like tea-stained incisors. Rotating police cherry lights of red and yellow and green pan across
the floor, and my heart is almost breaking again, the way it used to
on Saturday afternoons.

But this is a Tuesday, this is the present, and the first time I
went to Playland on Adult Night, I'd recently turned thirty. Which
does not mean that hearing Eddie Money's "Baby Hold On" hurts
any less, or sounds any more sad:

> The future is ours to see
> When you hold on to me
> Baby, what's these things you've been saying
> About me, behind my back? . . .

That is a satisfying song to skate to because it is both hopeful
and yet forlorn, and because it is classic rock (1978), and because
the mournful, resonant stretches contained beneath its beat and
melody can last the few seconds it takes to make a wide turn at either end of the rink, which is where you gain momentum. Above all
this, this . . . sensory information, there is an enormous, gaudy
roller skate hung from the ceiling, with little mirrors glued all over it
like a disco ball, a twinkling of adolescent tears.

So you are here, and I am here, but who else is here? For skating
was always about bodies in motion, and stealing glances at everyone
who rolls by. Who is cute and who skates good? Who are the cool
kids? And who, acquiescing to fate and sweaty palms, shall skate
together during the couples skate? These were essential questions,
and on Adult Night they still are: Who, for example, is the Italian
guy with the ponytail who can leap up onto the railing and ride it for
several feet and land back on the floor? Who is the pert, big-thighed
woman with the bleached, spiky hair and the jangly earrings in the

"Will Skate 4 Food" T-shirt? Who is the guy who dances slowly and coolly while he skates, one foot then the next, looking mostly at some unfixed point on the floor, running his hand through his slightly graying dark hair? Who is that amazing black man in the lime green short-shorts wearing the Walkman and skating with legs of liquid mercury, the Archduke of All Things Funky? Who could the middle-aged woman in the leather halter top and fringe-cut Daisy Dukes be? Who knew that a sixty-five-year-old man could figure-skate (on roller skates), and look like a beer-gutted swan on a lake of neon? Who is the guy with Prince Valiant-style blond hair and cut muscles who skates backward and shakes his hips while Sister Sledge sings "We Are Family"?

"You'd be surprised," says the owner, David Dodson, of the regular skaters who form the Tuesday night family, which has convened and grown since the first Adult Night in 1994. "You'd be surprised how many of them work in the computer industry." (Actually, no, that's not surprising: There's something sort of cubicle-friendly about this crowd. By day, nerdsville. But come Tuesday night, they are the roller kings and queens of Playland.) "They're a little of everything. Nurses, maybe even a doctor. A mechanic. Sales people. I don't know all their names," says Dodson, "but most of them I've seen every week here for five years. They keep coming back. On a good Tuesday we'll get about 150 people total, but there are about 70 or 80 people who never miss it, unless they're sick or out of town. This is good, clean fun right here. No smokers, no alcohol. Not your standard bar scene."

The men and women of Playland have settled into a routine. Some always get there early to beat the crowd and get as much freedom on the floor as they can. They know when one or another of them has purchased new skates, or new wheels. Some have met here, and married one another: "Jimmy and Kim met here, I think," Dodson says, pointing to blurs passing by on the rink. "Karen and Pete." The women think the men are kind of shy, especially when the lights go down and the Peter Cetera ballad goes up and Dodson intones into the loudspeaker, "Couples skate, couples only." Singles

float off the rink and across the carpet, toward their Gatorade bottles, idly kicking skates across the floor, lingering by the pinball machines. The men say the same about the women, that they're the
shy ones, that it's hard to know if a woman came to skate and be by
herself or if she'd like to have a go around. If she does want to
skate with him, then, "It's a good way, if anything, to learn to skate
backwards," says Ray Clark, thirty-six, a regular for forever, backward and forward, whose skate card is usually full.

Underlying these boy-meets-(or fails-to-meet)-girl dynamics are
quieter vibes. There are the many people who just need a few
friends and maybe this is where they'll find them. There is, if I'm
not mistaken, and only on some weeks and mostly by accident, a
faint trace of a gay scene. (Or maybe that's just the Village People
aura that skating can send off.) There is a college contingent, and,
for many Tuesdays in a row last winter, it seemed Adult Night had
been taken over by various Asian student unions. One group of giggling Japanese girls insisted on skating as a hand-holding group of
ten, constantly falling on their nonexistent rears, a disco haiku
poem about a centipede falling off a log.

■　■　■

This place seemed to rise up out of the ground sometime in 1974,
its presence never announced in the adult world but certainly felt
in the adolescent one. It filled instantly with a thousand North
Austin children and teenagers who were tired of living in what was
then the suburban hinterlands. It has always been called Playland.
Originally, it was two rinks under the same roof, a staggering total
of 40,000 square feet of roller-skating floor (an acre of skating!),
and the kids were permitted to skate back and forth between the
rinks, probably because that meant several passes by a snack bar
that was located in the center. In that beautiful blur of puberty was
a Lanier High School student named David Dodson, the son of a
police officer, who wanted nothing more in the world than to be the
manager of a skating rink. His brother, an ex-Marine, got a job as a
skate ranger at Playland, which in the 1970s was only a tiny bit less

cool than being a lifeguard. David also got a job there, handing out skates and fixing loose wheels and cleaning up the place.

This is where he met Bob. Bob was a businessman named Robert Powell, who came to own Playland and a couple dozen other roller-skating rinks across the Southwest in the 1970s and 1980s. "Bob was like a father to me," Dodson says now, "and I helped him look out for his businesses. When people would steal from him, or tell him we only had 200 skaters when really we had 500, when really they were taking money from him, well, I couldn't lie to him."

Bob loved this kid. Bob trusted this kid. When Dodson was only eighteen, Bob sent him on a trip to his many, far-flung roller rinks—to Wichita Falls, Texas, to Enid, Oklahoma, to Edmond, Oklahoma, with the same mandate each time: Find out what's wrong, find out where the money's going and then we'll come in there and kick out the managers and clean the place up. Dodson would apply for a bit-player job, pose as a friendly employee, and a few weeks later, the locks would get changed and everyone would get fired. Once things were in order, he'd move to the next rink.

This led to Las Vegas, where Bob's brother-in-law was running a rink right at the very apex of disco. "It was incredible," Dodson says. "I was living in (Bob's) mansion, I had a maid to serve me every morning, I had a Good Times van to drive around, and I was making $350 a week, which was great back then for an eighteen-year-old, I mean, a pair of jeans only cost fifteen bucks." But Las Vegas could do things to people, especially at the very apex of disco. The rink was a party all night long. Every night was Adult Night. "You didn't survive on kids and birthday parties back then," Dodson says. It wasn't all Good Times: Bob had to fire family members for mismanaging the rink. Dodson became the manager, until he tired of the all-night roller disco lifestyle and moved back to Austin. He wanted to go to community college; he wanted to be a police officer like his father. Bob begged and pleaded; come back to Vegas.

Finally Bob made an offer too good to pass up. Roller-skating was a national craze. There were movies about it. Bob was building two new rinks in Las Vegas; Dodson could run them and keep 25 percent of the gross, which Dodson accepted, and for a while he was rich. Then Bob called up with one last offer: a chance to buy Playland in Northwest Austin for $2.6 million, a chance for Dodson to own his own rink, and be his own boss. "I signed my name to a two-point-six-million-dollar loan in March of 1982 at the age of twenty-two and everyone thought I was crazy," he says, seventeen years later. "I got here and it was a mess. There were four strings of Christmas lights and that was all the lighting they had. There was a plywood floor that had waves in it. The carpet was worn out. There were four stereo speakers and all of them were blown. . . . I walked in the first night and there were about twenty or twenty-five kids skating, smoking cigarettes, with their shirts off. The cops would have a squad car out there every night. It was a mess."

Not only was it a mess, there was another problem: By March of 1982, roller disco had fallen over and died.

■   ■   ■

In all the years that he has run Playland, David Dodson, now thirty-eight, his strawberry blond hair receding and buzz-cut, has been away from the rink exactly four weekends. There were months there where he fell behind on his payments to Bob. In the 1980s, Dodson benefited for a time from the success of MTV. A marketing group from the network decided for whatever reason that roller rinks were a way to promote MTV; giant video screens were erected at either end of the rink, and for a while, it seemed like roller-skating might live. Minus the disco craze, roller-skating does fine as a small business in any decade, subsisting on kids and birthday parties. A large chunk of Dodson's business comes from local Parent-Teacher Associations, who sponsor after-school parties as fund-raisers. On most Fridays and Saturdays, the place is thick with children, so many that you almost cannot merge into the cacophonous traffic of ten-year-olds wearing whatever's new at the mall.

Business was always okay, Dodson says, until 1987 and the construction of the freeway. "That almost killed us," he says, "because you just couldn't get here." He closed half the rink and leased it to an antique mall. By day, Playland skating rink now becomes a bingo palace, as a means of survival; tables are dragged out onto the rink floor; a steady following of polyester-pantsed old ladies arrive with daubing pens and a hunger for winning. Sometime in 1994, nostalgic for those nights in Vegas when grown-ups skated, Dobson decided to try an Adult Night at Playland. He says only twenty-two people came. He played old disco and classic rock songs.

They kept coming back, and he bought more retro CDs. Almost all of Bob Powell's skating empire is gone. Most of the rinks he owned became antique malls or bingo halls or empty husks of low-slung buildings. Bob himself is gone, after complications from a heart transplant, after a divorce, "after he married his second wife, and I think she tried to get most everything he had left. Everything else is gone or sold," Dodson says. Bob was not around last December, when David Dodson made his last payment on the $2.6 million loan, and owned Playland for good.

■ ■ ■

Roller-skating has a way of coming along when you need it most. There are problems at work, but there is the rink. There is a divorce pending, but there is the rink. There is the nagging creak of your bones, the thumping Advil headache right at the temples, the extra twenty cookie-dough pounds around your middle, but there is the rink. On skates the mind flushes and clears. Few things approximate the smooth and lovely nature of roller-skating, the low-to-earth slow flying. Skiing is expensive and exhausting and not exactly local. Same goes for surfing, which also requires good looks. Skateboarding comes loaded with its own punk politics of rebellion. Waterskiing has no soundtrack. (Name one great 1970s T & A movie about waterskiing. See, there isn't one.)

What I can say about the rhythmic serenity of the roller disco on Tuesday nights is perhaps best put to music: It is one thing to hear Kenny Loggins sing "Footloose" on the radio while you're waiting in the drive-thru at the bank; it's annoying and it makes the wait longer. It is another thing entirely to hear "Footloose" on roller skates.

What happens is nothing short of a transformation.

In my time skating at Playland, I have learned a thing or two about the music wars. When David Dodson sometimes turns the four CD players over to his younger help, we get a lot of stuff that is about someone else's junior high years, much of it rapped. We also get exposed to modern bubblegum, which is one of the few ways to stay young. Pop music is like magic wrinkle cream. On wheels, I have learned a thing or two about 'N Sync. I have learned to get jiggy with it (although not all of it), and so have people much older than I. So, too, we have learned, in the smoothest sense, that we don't want no scrubs, from the girl group TLC. ("A scrub is a guy who can't get no love from me/Hanging out the passenger side/of his best friend's ride/trying to holler at me. . . .)

It should be said that no one is ever entirely pleased with the music at Playland. The older crowd wants the 1970s stuff, the fully erect roller boogie. The middle crowd likes the Duran Duran era. Some want more funk, more R & B. Some want country, and to many people's pain and discomfort, they sometimes get a little. Some want classic rock. Mike Johnson, thirty-nine, a social worker by day and the amazing, funky, mercury-legged skater by night, is actually listening to Christian music on his Walkman. The young crowd wants the new stuff, the hip-hop, the alterna-ballads. Everyone would like to hear what was playing when they were in the seventh grade. Unfortunately, everyone was in a different seventh grade, in different epochs, going back to the Mesozoic.

During the first week of July, as he has done every couple of years since he bought the place, David Dodson shut Playland down for a week, and the workers came and installed a new floor upon which to skate. It's as if the Petroleum Product Fairy came and waved her wand. Gone are the fault lines, the skid marks, the pocked-out chunks. In the morning after it dries, it glistens beautifully. Dodson almost never skates anymore, but he is the first to try out the new floor. "It looks like a lake, so calm and still," he says. "Too bad people have to get on it."

■   ■   ■

Some of them are early tonight, lined up in the vestibule. Dodson lets them in five minutes early. There is the lacing up, the small chitchat. There is Donna Travis, a forty-nine-year-old regional sales manager by day, who skates several nights a week at various rinks. "It's a critical calorie burner," she says. "And a great way to vent my frustrations." There is Ray Clark, as usual. He's a computer video configuration specialist, who has been skating since the night many years ago when he overheard a bunch of cheerleaders say they were going to go skating on a Friday night in Nederland. "I heard that and thought, if they're going to be there, then I'm going to be there." What he did not know was that the cheerleaders were going skating in Beaumont. They never materialized at the rink, but he skated anyway. And he is skating still, in the same pair of Sears skates his parents bought him one Christmas. The wheels have been replaced countless times. When he gets on the new floor, Ray says he knows how Jesus felt, walking across the Dead Sea.

There is a man named Don Doring, who is sixty-five and pot-bellied and still skates in competitions, and still wins medals. Don drives down from Killeen, Texas, every Tuesday with Chuck, an other skater, who is fifty-two. They carry their skates in specially modified Samsonite suitcases. Chuck Kirkland tells me that most of the people at Adult Night don't skate very well, least of all him, that the motion has sort of left him behind, and he doesn't do it with nearly the skill he used to. Don is an optimist, though. Don thinks he skates as well as ever, but he may start cutting back. Don tells me his wife of forty-four years just died, last month. She had been hospitalized for a few years in Dallas, and finally she went. That happened on the twenty-third of June, and Don was on the rink floor two nights later.

I would hear more of this story, except that "I'm Too Sexy" starts playing. I've been here enough Tuesday nights to know that this is one of Don's favorite songs to skate to, and that he needs to stop talking now so that he may be in the middle of the rink, a place reserved for only the very best among us. He is swirling 'round, skating like a dream.

(1999)

Where Credit Is Due

Wilmington, Delaware

Debt is so American that even the Pilgrims got here with it. (Someone else's money, someone else's boat.) Think of their stuff, the things they had to have: the chairs and linens and kettles lashed together in the leaky hull, assembled from some Pier 1 or Bed Bath & Beyond shopping spree of the day. Think of those few dreamers scraping to shore, only to realize they had to send back credit payments, in the form of pelts, which hardly ever made it to the banks, because there were pirates, and no 800 numbers to call and explain any of this to customer-service reps. Some years later, on a depressing afternoon, I wandered around a J.Crew store and put a brownish gray-flecked ribbed cotton turtleneck on my MBNA America MasterCard, ignoring the faint whispers of a thousand dead Puritans telling me not to. The charge was $55.87. At that time I was twenty-seven years old and owed, on that card, a total of $2,011 (it would go higher), with no real plan of how to pay it back.

"Wow, it's not even payday," a friend remarked. (This was the frugal friend: saver of money and planet, wearer of wool socks with sandals; he who rinsed out used Ziploc bags and hung them out to dry.) I told him I put the sweater on my credit card. "Do you know how much you'll wind up paying for it by the time you pay it off?" he asked. Not a question so much as a lecture on usury, and not an answer from me so much as a shopaholic credo:

"Well, do you know what kind of day I had?" (Or: If I had been in a car wreck on the way home, and was lying on the asphalt there, bleeding to death, I'd be mad at myself for not buying the sweater. That's the kind of day I had.)

And on some level I believed it, believed in the power of my own consumer disconnect from reality. It's always a slow death on some metaphorical asphalt—the rent, the mortgage, the car payment, the college loans, the doctor—to say nothing of the playthings, the pretty things. The Federal Reserve did the math in 1998, concluding that the national savings rate had then slipped below zero: Every penny earned was now owed somewhere, and then some. By late 2001, American households kept an average of six credit cards, carrying a total average balance that one survey calculated at $8,562.

In a rare, horrified examination of the practical, I did my own math the same year. By that point, my credit card balances floated around me like dirigibles in some modern dystopian fantasia: $13,774 was the total. Consider that one J.Crew sweater: It worked out to about $93, with interest, by the time I wrote all those monthly checks and mailed them away—always to Wilmington, Delaware, a place I regarded only in the abstract.

For a long time I have imagined giant post-office boxes in Wilmington, the places where anyone like myself owed lots of money, but also some psychic debt. Here was a noplace that to me had become a symbol of all that made us weak and all that made us tick. The monthly cycle of it, the endless spinning of all that revolving debt: revolve, revolve, revolve, and never resolve.

■　■　■

We owe our souls to Wilmington. To me, Wilmington could have been either Oz or Babylon or neither; it was 40 million miles away. Then one day I missed the exit for the New Jersey Turnpike, and realized I'd off-ramped to Plastic Town itself. It was the first time I connected the address in the clear window of the return envelope to an actual place, ninety-eight miles north from where I was currently living, in Washington, D.C., and from where I seemed to be sending larger and larger checks in a desire to break free.

I wanted to see the sorting of all those millions of payment envelopes that all those millions of people (you, me, everybody) mail
each month to Wilmington, where the credit card giants enjoyed
profits in 2001 in the hundreds of millions of dollars. They are
helped by Delaware's bank-friendly breaks on taxes and a law that
removed the limits on how much interest the banks can charge
credit card customers. But even with all those interest payments
flowing in, almost a third of last year's credit card profits were
gained by penalizing customers (sometimes you, sometimes me, always somebody) for not paying their bills on time. All those stamps
licked, and fingers crossed, all that deferring of American dreams—
what did it look like on the receiving end? I wanted to see wide
grids of gray cubicles, and heaps of envelopes headed through an
endless maze, processed day and night, all week, all year. I wanted
to see how the checks are cashed. I wanted to see the granting of
momentary waivers of the thirty-five-dollar late fee to customers
who call, toll-free, and confess the right kind of sin in the right kind
of way. I had a hunch that human beings might be involved in this,
which would make the nation's $660 billion in consumer credit
debt seem somehow less . . . monstrous.

At MBNA America, the nation's second-largest issuer of credit
cards, the walls and floors of its many offices across Wilmington
and surrounding New Castle County are emblazoned with the
bank's stern variation on the golden rule ("Think of Yourself as a
Customer"), and most of the mail is initially read by a machine.
This sophisticated creation can automatically see through the envelopes and sniff out the account numbers, and is able to render
automatic decisions about lateness, down to egregious fractions of
a minute. My efforts to see any of this—much less actual human
beings—would mostly be in vain. Each time I called MBNA, First
USA, and some of the other larger banks, they were cool to the notion that anyone would want to see how it works. The more follow-
up calls I made—some of which I conducted with a happy,
childlike curiosity, some of which I conducted with stern business
manners, others of which I placed out of a kind of sick determina-

tion—the more they ignored me. As weeks dragged on, even my most basic questions about life in Plastic Town were greeted with suspicion or a stony silence.

Still, I kept driving back and forth to Wilmington, where you can feel the presence of the banks in the almost Stepford-like sense of cheerful convention. It's the same feeling you have listening to the music that plays when the credit card company puts you on hold. The tallish buildings of Wilmington unmesmerizingly cast dull shadows on the quiet downtown streets, where less-upwardly-mobile-seeming Wilmingtonians wait at bus stops for buses that seem to rarely come. The banks are bound together along King and Market Streets, cool and inert, not unlike my own credit cards, which, at one desperate point last year, I had wrapped in foil and again in sandwich bags, then trapped in a block of ice in a Tupperware container sealed with duct tape, and then hid behind a Healthy Choice supreme French bread pizza, all the way at the back of my freezer. Now I have liberated them—a temporary pa role—and brought them to Wilmington.

The banking business is now Delaware's largest industry, employing about 35,000 people. In 2002, eight of the nation's ten largest credit card issuers were based in Wilmington, including four of the top five—MBNA, BankOne/First USA, Citibank, and JP Morgan Chase. Hundreds of other companies, and nearly 60 percent of Fortune 500 companies, are incorporated—for tax purposes—right here in Wilmington.

"A Wilmington address, we've found, is a status symbol in the business world," says the avuncularly candid, hunch-shouldered mayor, James M. Baker. "The opportunity for any business here is just too good to ignore." He is standing in the lobby of the eighty-nine-year-old Hotel du Pont, where the city had arranged a sort of daylong skirt-hitching in the ornate Gold Ballroom for several dozen business owners considering a relocation to Wilmington. The afternoon includes much Power Point presenting of Delaware's devotion to good capitalism; tax breaks, especially from the city, abound. There is a touting of the city's effort to resurrect its urban riverfront and make it funky, which thus far has meant some brewpubs, condo lofts in old warehouses, a baseball stadium for the Class-A Wilmington Blue Rocks, an outlet mall, and the First USA Riverfront Arts Center. Finally, there is a video of school-children using computers—the business world's universal symbol of progress.

"These companies come and they bring their money," Baker says, and this seems to be the mutual grease that lubricates Wilmington: the constant pursuit of, movement of, management of, rolling in, charging interest upon, issuing court rulings about, drawing up contracts on *money*. There are rich people anywhere, but there aren't many places in America where you can stand still and actually feel as if a Busby Berkeley number is about to break out, a big song and dance about the glory of the dollar. Maybe Wall Street. Maybe here.

> *"Mr. du Pont also invited us to come to his house, 'Swamp Hall,' on Halloween night. He always had a large bag of dimes and nickels and he threw them up in the air and watched us scramble for them . . ."*
>
> —from *The Workers' World at Hagley,* oral histories
> of nineteenth-century life at the
> DuPont Company's gunpowder mills
> on Brandywine Creek, near Wilmington

Along Brandywine Creek, on a late-April afternoon, another sumptuous Wilmington spring is coming into bloom. Teenagers wave and flash happily bratty smiles from their cars. Traffic hums along through the neighborhoods surrounding the city, past colonial-style homes, many of them actually colonial, or close to it. Parks and golf courses undulate seductively. Even the strip malls seem cute; one, in Greenville, has four bank branches in it.

Wilmington's loyalty to MBNA, BankOne/First USA, JP Morgan Chase, Citibank, Discover, Juniper, Household, and the other credit card companies exists only in part because the banks have brought the local economy back from the brink, lowered the state income tax, and helped shield residents from any property and sales taxes. There is also a longer tradition of gentle submission to power in the First State. "It's always been a company town," says Carol Hoffecker, a history professor at the University of Delaware.

"It was a mill town first," she continues, "then powder with the du Pont family, then chemicals with the DuPont Company and Hercules and Atlas. Now it's the banks. Just as DuPont saved the city's bacon a century ago, it's the banks that have moved in to take up the slack." The corporations came after the state's passage of the Financial Center Development Act in 1981, promoted by then-Governor Pierre S. "Pete" du Pont. (Who reflected on it, twenty years later, for the *Wilmington News Journal:* "It's hard to say this was going to change Delaware forever. Darned if it didn't work.")

The city itself is smallish—about ten miles across at its widest—and has to it the great middle grade of eastern seaboard dullness, a town that is driven through more than driven to. Wilmington is the crucial fork where travelers have to decide: Keep with I-95 to Philly? Or take the Jersey Turnpike to New York? If you do exit at Wilmington, you are greeted by a cheerful row of patriotic billboards with credit card logos on them, and depending on which way you turn, you will either wind up in corporateville or something a little more gritty and depressed; in one block you come upon the city's bona fide Little Italy, with restaurants, barbers, and pastry shops; in still another block you reflexively lock your doors. If you skip the Delaware Memorial Bridge into New Jersey and stick to I-495, you pass the smokestacks of DuPont and the Port of Wilmington, where everything from European cars and Canadian timber to Indian hemp and Argentine beef is unloaded daily.

Professor Hoffecker wonders if the banks, for all their financial prowess, will ever make the city feel like a city, the way the industries of yesteryear did: "It's been a boost to the heart of the city," she says. "But at the same time they've done things to seal themselves off. You drive to work in one of those places, you park in their facility, at lunch you go eat in their cafeteria, at the end of the day you drive away. You never see anybody around, they're all in those buildings, making their phone calls and adding up their figures and doing whatever else it is that they do in there. They do volunteer work, but they never interact with the community in the old-fashioned sense of walking on the streets. There's a deadness . . . which seems odd, when you think there's so many thousands of workers down there every day."

In many ways, modern Wilmington owes its soul to the company store much as its ancestors relied on the du Ponts. The difference is that the romance of the du Pont days is woven into history, and always on view: The Brandywine mill yards and mansions are now museums and research centers; the hotel is a living monument to a bygone era; the lobby of the DuPont Company invites visitors in with exhibits extolling the invention of nylon and Teflon; banners celebrating DuPont's bicentennial currently hang from the city light poles.

The credit card banks, on the other hand, do everything they can to downplay their presence, proffering no narrative of their history, no dynastic family tree, evincing no connective tissue between the financial organs and the rest of the communal body. It's possible to imagine a future Wilmington museum with a bank's name on it— MBNA's chairman, Charles Cawley, has amassed an impressive collection of Wyeths—but hard to imagine a museum that is *about* the banks, or explores the story of Delaware and credit cards. It doesn't seem that anyone will ever know the whole story, or want to tell it. "I doubt if anyone would visit a museum about credit cards," laughs Jim Stewart, president of Juniper, a Wilmington-based credit card bank he started in 2000.

I have lain awake enough nights worrying about my credit card bills that I would be happy to visit a museum about them. (I think it should include an exhibit of a late-twentieth-century American lying in bed, feeling a buzzing in the bones, a trickle of sweat, a throbbing sense of dread. I think there should be a checkbook, and Chase and First USA payment envelopes spread out on the circa-1996 Pottery Barn night table next to the bed. I think a Sony Dream

Machine digital clock should continually flash 3:17 a.m. I think there should also be a bottle of Tylenol PM.)

The lobby of MBNA's headquarters, half a block down from the Hotel du Pont, has a 1932 Duesenberg car parked in the middle of it, but the security guard wouldn't let me in to see it. I wasn't really clear on what the car meant to the company, or the company meant to the car. It appears to simply symbolize luxury. The guard did let me crane my neck to look at the Duesenberg through the locked glass lobby door, but only for two minutes. I was squinting, trying to read the MBNA manifesto stenciled on the wall behind the car. I saw all the keywords about customers and trust and success and teamwork, and here is where it occurred to me that I am a customer, who once carried a balance of $5,862 on his MBNA card, and had just mailed in a nice little $400 payment toward the $1,063 current balance (at 14.9 percent) three days before the due date, and yet I was not to be trusted to look at the car.

Around town, MBNA is known as "the Firm" or "the brotherhood" by the affectionately jaded, inspiring a happy silence and loyalty in its 10,500 employees, and providing a bounty of conspiracy theories for the so-inclined. Charles Cawley, the company's sixty-one-year-old chairman and CEO, occupies the mythic space in Wilmington once reserved for the descendants of Éleuthère Irénée du Pont: The richest man in town, Cawley, who, through his corporation and as an individual was a significant contributor to George W. Bush's 2000 presidential campaign, is seldom seen by everyday Wilmingtonians. The rewards of working for the Firm are considerable for the company's executives. On seafaring perks alone, there are four MBNA yachts and sport boats—the *Affinity,* the *Impatience,* the *So Far So Good,* and the *Deliverance.* There is a company country club west of town, and a fleet of corporate jets.

"The credit card business grew dramatically in the late 1980s, and it brought with it a lot of highly paid executives, a lot of success, a lot of wealth," says Stewart, the Juniper president, who was an executive vice president at First USA as the industry boomed. "There were two distinct cultures. One . . . was First USA, and I'm

biased because I worked there, but I would say it was more infor-
mal. We were one of the early companies to go casual, to not take
ourselves too too seriously. The other was MBNA, which was very
formal. The suits and ties and lapel pins, and people living in lock-
step—there was a real cultlike image. I lived in a nice neighborhood, and I remember when Cawley renovated his house in a way
such as Wilmington had never seen before. Then he moved to a
nicer neighborhood and did twenty times the renovation job he'd
done before. And other MBNA executives moved there with him.
Eventually twenty-five or thirty houses in the same neighborhood
were all MBNA."

   Fight Club, a broodingly violent 1999 satire by filmmaker David
Fincher, appears to take place in MBNA's Wilmington, if you look
carefully: The movie's protagonist narrator, played by Edward Norton, works for a monolithic financial company and furnishes his
apartment with stylish catalogue furniture that he charges to his
plastic. He has a Wilmington zip code, and there's a sign near
his high-rise apartment that echoes the city's motto: "A Place to Be
Somebody." (Those signs have a way of popping up in Wilmington's
less-affluent neighborhoods.) He turns to violence when he comes
under the spell of Brad Pitt's manic soap salesman, who introduces
him to the clandestine Fight Club, where men beat each other
senseless as a response to the numbness they feel living in an
empty, consumeristic culture. By the movie's end, the narrator
learns that his Fight Club is a hallucination; and as a metaphoric
and tragic finale, he blows the skyscrapers of this pseudo-
Wilmington to smithereens. It's not a bad movie for anyone who
ever had credit card debt and entertained notions of an Armaged-
don that would set the people free.

■   ■   ■

Wilmington hinges on the great lie that you can have it all, and it's
a lie that isn't always bad; it's a benign kind of lie, transmitted all
the time, in many ways, including the enduring depiction of Monica Geller and Rachel Greene, and the way that these two imagi-

nary women are able to afford and furnish that big Manhattan apartment, when obviously, in a real world, they could not. ("Why are you in debt?" a counselor asked me once, in therapy, back in the 1990s, when everyone told one another about how much money they were making in the stock market. *Friends,* I answered, by which I meant the TV show.)

Robert D. Manning, a forty-four-year-old economic sociologist at the Rochester Institute of Technology, is the author of *Credit Card Nation: The Consequences of America's Addiction to Credit,* and he is a man so convinced of his role as the bane of the banks that he believes JP Morgan Chase keeps tabs on his media appearances, speaking engagements, and testimony before lawmakers. He is only too happy to pinprick the final few bubbles of my plastic sitcom fantasy world. "In a way, we all live in 'Wilmingtonland,'" Manning says. "Wilmingtonland is that place of a completely different logic. It's the embodiment of the credit card society: Everything's okay, 'Just do it,' don't ask questions, have it now, pay for it later. MBNA has created a wonderful life, where people come to work for them and become completely devoted and compliant to the company. It's an upper-middle-class wonderland, where you never see the Wizard of Oz behind the curtain. . . . The banks are charitable, their employees do a lot of volunteer work, they give a lot of money to programs. . . . It's very strategic, how the banks leave an imprint on the community so that no one can be critical of them."

Last year, a group of University of Delaware students began questioning MBNA's "affinity"-card marketing arrangement with the alumni association. (Affinity cards have been a boon to the industry. You can now have a card emblazoned with any allegiance you choose, and a promise of financial support going to your cause for every dollar you charge. There are affinity cards for universities, the National Rifle Association, the Sierra Club. There is a Martina Navratilova card for gay and lesbian causes. There are also affinity cards for Trekkies, rock groups, soda pops.) When Delaware students protested MBNA's influence on their campus, Manning says, there was immediate pressure from campus officials to quash the growing vibe of dissent. Two new campus buildings are named after the bank; graduates clamor to work there.

Campus affinity-card agreements, Manning believes, prey on college-age kids who aren't fiscally prepared to have credit cards. The average American undergrad who has a credit card now carries about $2,000 in high-interest debt, he says, usually on a card with the school mascot, which is marketed to him or her at freshman orientation. "There are people in Delaware who think it's okay for college students to have $5,000 or $10,000 in credit card debt by the time they graduate, on top of their college loans," he says. "They say, 'It's good for them to have debt. They're at the beginning of their earning cycle.' I hear this all the time in Wilmingtonland. It's this presumption that debt is good for all of us." Consumer spending is the last way you can feel like an American with any sway in the national outcome: Every November, consumers are reminded that if we don't spend enough money at Christmas, the economy suffers, and so we rally to the cause. Last year, when the government gave each of us a $300 rebate, the plan came to be seen as a failure, in part, because too many people used it to pay off debts, rather than take it to the mall. Spending ourselves into a hole is seen as a path to economic glory.

Wilmingtonians see their communal salvation in the banks. There are perks down-totem, too: Last year, every MBNA employee got an extra week of vacation because profits were so high. Grousers and crusaders are few, but they exist: "Needless to say, MBNA is a cult, and I loathed my job," griped an anonymous poster to a Web site titled MBNA Credit Card: Money, Power, Influence and Greed.

"I felt bad calling people and demanding money, being a total jerk on the phone," the e-mail went on. "This 'attitude' that I had to have working in collections fell into my regular life outside of work and I just became a total arse. That's horrible. I'm not a mean person, I'm a very caring person, and this, in turn, bummed me out big time. I worked there for about a year. . . ."

Ted Keller, who is chairman of the Citizens Coalition for Tax Reform, is a lifelong Delaware resident and spent his career at DuPont, retiring in 1979. He is a strident voice against the tax breaks given to the banks and the power they hold over his community: "They pay a hideously low tax rate," Keller says. "Whenever you try to bring up the issue of fair taxes on these banks, all I hear is, 'Oh, no, because then they'll leave and we'll lose all the jobs.'"

Keller is eighty-one now, and had triple-bypass surgery last year. The Citizens Coalition doesn't seem to have amassed many citizens into much of a coalition. Most of the research and letter writing is done from Keller's kitchen table, and when he's looking for a certain newspaper clipping he calls out to his wife. The first time I talked to him, he immediately faxed me several pages of Delaware tax law (with his own typewritten marginalia), demonstrating his crusade to change the Financial Center Development Act, which allows banks to pay less than 2 percent in state taxes on most of their profits, and lets them set whatever consumer interest rates they like. In 1999, for example, MBNA paid—according to Keller's kitchen table, and the company's own reports—$23.6 million in state income taxes, or less than 1.5 percent. Keller thinks it should have been more like 8.7 percent (the initial Delaware tax rate on corporate profits under $20 million), which would have put MBNA's state tax bill in the vicinity of $142 million. Keller happens to own a few shares of MBNA stock, just so he can attend the annual meeting and politely raise some hell. "People say, oh, that Ted Keller, all he talks about are the banks. Well, when this sort of crap is going on, it's all I can talk about," he acknowledges. "I know a lot of low-income people who are suffering because of this industry. Predatory interest rates are knocking the hell out of us, and it all happens right here in Delaware."

In a stack somewhere, he has a yellowed clipping of an article about the rise of Delaware's tax laws, in which he was interviewed, the only critic. He paws around and looks for it in vain, but he remembers the first line: "It said, 'Ted Keller is the loneliest man in Delaware.'" It seems he still is.

. . .

"The charm of Wilmington," a local told me, "isn't so apparent if
you're just seeing it from your car." But for days I drove in it, across
it, and around it and found an elusive charm all its own, up and
down the hilly routes that snake through New Castle County.
Wilmington proper has a population of just 72,664; the surrounding
towns and suburbs, where most of the middle and upper classes
live, number half a million. The demographics are plain: 58 percent
of the urban residents are black; in the burbs of New Castle, 73
percent are white. "Who lives in all the mansions, is what I want to
know," says a waitress at a Howard Johnson's on the Concord Pike.
(Answer: bankers, corporate attorneys, scientists.) Meanwhile,
back up, turn around: That's an actual Howard Johnson's we were
in, and an actual talkative waitress. Already, it's a time-warp heaven.
Wilmington continually reveals to me a leftover Tee-Vee America
feeling that is hard to resist. Sometimes it's 1946, then 1976, then
1956. Farther down the pike, there's a stereo shop called Hi Fi
House, and a Taco Bell so overlooked by the chain's branding police
that it still has the Alamo facade, with the old, dancing sombrero
logo out front. Certain Delawareans have ancient black-and-white
car license plates, which aren't purchased, but inherited from one
generation to the next. Certain Delawareans have outdated hair; the
mullet count is impressive. There's the Charcoal Pit restaurant—
four locations, but the original 1956 Pit is on the Concord Pike—
with its pink neon sign and an *American Graffiti* shabbiness, with
desserts on the back page of the menu named after mascots from
local high schools: the Hornet, the Spartan, the Bulldog, all of them
involving four enormous scoops of ice cream, covered in fruity-
chocolate goo. I want to have a date here, with the quarterback and
the cheerleader. I want all three of us to share straws. I am lost in
an interlude, and the waitress asks me if I'm going to finish my malt
in its frosty metal tumbler: "It's melting," she observes.

The Charcoal Pit, and I love the place for this, does not accept
credit cards.

．　．　．

Here is Mary Rammel, with her orange-handled scissors. Rammel is wearing a burgundy pantsuit. She has blond hair flecked with gray, and sympathetic blue eyes, and speaks with the enchanting long o's that denote Delaware: *moast, thoase, hoame.* She is a branch manager of Consumer Credit Counseling Service, a non-profit agency in the suburbs of Wilmington that tries to help people get out of debt. Her office overlooks a Shell gas station and a busy intersection. The office used to have a staff, but now it's just Mary, because of budget cuts. (Credit card banks, which used to fund programs like CCCS, have cut their support by more than half in the last three years, while at the same time lobbying Congress to toughen restrictions on Chapter 7 bankruptcy by consumers.) Rammel sees six or so clients a day, and they're always desperate. "They always ask me, 'Is this the worst debt you've ever seen?'" she says. "I always tell them I've seen worse. And I almost always have."

This morning it was a married couple in their eighties, with a fixed income of about $2,000 a month, a second mortgage, and $62,000 in credit card debt. After hearing their story, and laying out a game plan for them, she took her scissors and cut up their cards, and put them in a large plastic jug where she collects the plastic and has enough shards now to start a mosaic in a small basilica—Our Lady of Perpetual Indebtedness. She has filled four jugs. "At first I put them in this little candy jar," she says, pointing to a small glass jar on the windowsill. That was when she started debt counseling in 1988. Up until then, Rammel had worked at a bank in Dover, approving credit loans. Some applicants looked iffy to her. "Some of these people should not have been given credit. You could just see they wouldn't be able to afford it, but my boss came back to me and said, 'Mary, the form says "pre-approved,"' so I had to approve them."

This is what led her to a job so wildly off-message from the credit card empires of Wilmington that she is reminded of the conflict almost every time she cuts one up. On her office wall, she has a poster of Norman Rockwell's multiethnic portrayal of the golden rule, but unlike MBNA's motto, it's the actual Golden Rule: "Do unto others as you would have them do unto you." In the backyard of some of the world's richest banks, Rammel has counseled the poor and the rich. She has seen telemarketers who were broke, and fry cooks, teachers, nurses. Also accountants, lawyers, surgeons.

People have told her that credit cards are good for Wilmington. "You know, it's touchy," she says. "I've thought of this many times— what if everyone paid off the balance on their credit cards? It would be wonderful, and bad for Wilmington. People have said to me, even when they can't pay their bills every month, 'Mary, a little debt is good. It helps all of us.'" Not infrequently, the people who seek Rammel's help are employed at the credit card banks. They are people whose days are spent talking to the rest of America, trying to collect overdue bills, or processing all those late checks written for the minimum monthly payment on thousands of dollars of outstanding balance. Even then, the lessons did not sink in for them: "They come in and tell me how they, of all people, should have known better," she says. "I must say, it's a very humanizing experience for them. It's one thing to know what happens to people who spend more than they can afford. It's another thing to have it happen to you."

A woman came in with her five-year-old daughter, who fidgeted through the one-hour session. The woman proffered her plastic, and Rammel got out the scissors. The little girl, Rammel recalls, "jumped up out her chair, and started screaming, 'Don't you cut up my mommy's credit cards! She won't be able to buy me nothing!'"

She smiles. "Obviously in that case there was some education to be done . . . not only for the consumer, but for her child, too."

■   ■   ■

One early evening in the middle of April—near the end of a bizarrely unseasonal ninety-five-degree day, on one of my last trips to Wilmington—I walked all the way around MBNA's four, beigey-blah, interconnected green-awninged buildings, where I saw nothing, and nobody; I looped around the Chase building, too, and then walked seven blocks down toward the Christina River, to ponder First USA's buildings. This is a lot of concrete and empty plazas and walkways. I wished for a skateboard, and the gumption to ride it. The emptiness here left me wishing I could write a song about credit card problems. We talk about so much as a nation—we talk about war, we talk about politics, we talk a lot about our sex lives. We talk fashion, we talk shopping, we talk frequent-flier miles, we talk techno, we talk box-office receipts.

But only a real friend will tell you about his debt. Only a real friend would listen. For everything else, there is MasterCard. (It's become the national prayer.)

My proverbial money ship never came in, but I scraped to the other shore anyhow. Early next year, if things go according to plan (not that things ever go according to plan), I will pay off the last of my plastic debt to Wilmington. This could be it for Wilmington and me, but I doubt it, not so long as its banks fill my mailbox with 2.9 percent introductory come-ons. (So much we've seen together, so many thousands of dollars between us, like a secret affair. I'm not ready to walk away.) I would like to be able to tell you that in all those thousands of dollars there was a three-week trip to Italy when I was twenty-four, during which I fell madly in love, but, unfortunately, I have to be honest: There was never an Italy.

There was Banana Republic, there was Barnes & Noble, there were new Midas brakes for the car. There was the removal of my wisdom teeth at twenty-four, paid for in part on my Citibank MasterCard, because insurance only covered half. There were motel rooms, and even a few hotel rooms, but they tended to be in places like Yuma, Arizona, and Lexington, Kentucky, and Shreveport, Louisiana, because I have always seemed to be just driving through. There were enough wedding presents to almost equip the kitchens of people far happier than me. There was something Gucci, but there was so much more Gap. There were disposable contact lenses so that I could clearly see all that was available to buy, even as I chose not to read the fine print of the terms for buying it. For every nice meal charged to my plastic, there are, I am sad to report, many more charges to what appear to be Chinese takeout joints. There were glasses of wine that I bought in hotel lobby bars while I waited. Sometimes I was waiting for someone specific, and sometimes I was waiting for nothing at all.

So have it, Wilmington, what's left of me. My failure of wallet and willpower leads here. It's a somewhere, even if it is a kind of fat-cat's nowhere. As a bit player in the capitalist drama, I think it's sometimes important to feel small. In the Hotel du Pont, to escape the heat, I charged a glass of chardonnay to my First USA card— the same one I've carried since my junior year of college, with its obscene 22.9 percent interest rate. I used this card on this evening because I felt naughty, and alive. Later, as the last sunlight dribbled away in a haze, I walked past the glowing office buildings to my car. It was just me and the banks. The footsteps I thought I heard in the warpy heat turned out to be my own.

(2002)

Could It
Happen Here

Nine-ish

Washington, D.C.

America opens at nine, which is to say nine-ish, which has become our saddest hour. Two minutes after nine, for example. Or 8:45, or 9:04. Or 9:11, six minutes after the second jet hit the second tower on September 11, 2001, and the mind started connecting dots in a panic. Within hours, people stopped to consider the date, 9/11, which reads as 9-1-1, which is keypadspeak for: *Oh God no, help, please,* and so the day will be forever known as Nine One One.

Apart from the middle of the night, or the predawn, which are both fraught with simple darkness and somnolent vulnerability, nine o'clock in the morning has taken on a peculiar quality all its own. The people who would kill ordinary Americans in order to make a point have zeroed in on the humdrum of our early mid-mornings, with the idea that we're all up and at our desks doing . . . doing what, exactly? According to somebody's interpretation we are busily playing our notes for an intricate orchestra of Western evil, of conspiracy, of a capitalist McDomination. When really what we're doing is mundane. We're at the office, or about to be. Nine o'clock? You're likely to be where you're supposed to be, only not quite—the atrium lobby, or that little croissant place across the plaza, or in the elevator, or aboard the early shuttle flight. You are two floors down, or one floor up, perhaps not exactly where your loved ones thought you'd be, which either saves your life or seals your fate. At nine—if things have gone smoothly, if there was time to dry your hair and do your daughter's braids and explain to her why she can't wear her tutu to school, if the bridge traffic moved okay, if you didn't screw around too long with the crossword, if the bus was on time—you are still sort of waking up to the fact that you have woken up, and shown up.

Showing up is the American way. By nine you've endured the loudmouths on the clock radio who were trying to get a woman on her cell phone to stick her bare bottom out of her car window, which made you switch back to NPR's *Morning Edition* and its breakfast drone of militant rebels in the jungles of countries with new names. In the cities, at a little bit before 9 a.m., the buildings still cast shadows up and down the concrete ravines.

Eight forty-five sounds like a delivery truck backing up, beep beep beep beep beep beep. Eight fifty-two sounds like brakes on a city bus with standing room only. There are lines at bagel shops. Five of nine has a flavor of aftershave and nondairy creamer. There is muttering in the snack room about the machine being out of Diet Coke, about the copier being jammed since yesterday. We do what we can to be cheerful and positive at nine; we do what we can to avoid those who seem to have been up for hours, jogged six miles, read both papers, and already have revision ideas for the buyback presentation next Thursday.

Nine o'clock talk in offices tries to be as simple as possible: Gretchen, could you get me that committee report on the interface transfer? Thanks, and how's your brother, the one who had the thing with his leg? His hip? Great.

One of the smallest, tenderest mercies of September 11 turned out to be that many Americans have come to regard the nine o'clock punch-in as a vague suggestion and not the rule. We may not be the Greatest Generation, but we have learned through a variety of flex-time and day-care problems and relaxed rules that it's okay to get in by 9:30, or quarter of ten. (It's okay, that is, if you've made it past a certain boundary line of privilege, seniority, white-collarhood. The gal in the next cubicle is still going to chide you for being late. "Put it in my personnel file," you snap back, in the loving way you and the gal in the next cubicle relate.) This could mean that many of the thousands of people who worked in the World Trade Center didn't have their act quite pulled together enough to be in the office by 8:45 for a rendezvous with history. These were the white-collar types who phoned ahead and said they'd be there an hour late. But someone took that call, the assistant who has to be there by 8:15. On other floors, in more menial tasks, blue-collar workers had been at their jobs for hours already.

So it all happened around 9 a.m., or started to. For people who were scurrying toward work, there was suddenly a clear sign from above to scurry away from it. Of all the narratives that transmitted out of Manhattan yesterday, many were about the near misses of the nine o'clock hour—people who got out fast, or turned the other way, or who were running late in the first place.

Nine o'clock is a good hour for Type A personalities, it is a nonexistent hour for right-brain creatives who stayed up all night writing poems. It's a lousy hour for alcoholics. It's too early for a coffee break, and too late for pancakes. Brokers, unfortunately, and Wall Street types live off the energy of the early morning—gotta get in there, markets open at 9:30, gotta be first. The worst picture, to some, is the one of all those people leaning from the blasted-out windows of the World Trade Center. These are the people who get in by nine. These are the ones who had the breakfast reception at Windows on the World, on the 107th floor, being served by cooks and waitresses and busboys who'd come in before seven.

Nine o'clock, as reported in the Dolly Parton song about the workaday life: It's enough to drive you crazy if you let it.

■   ■   ■

Then there's the Pentagon, which makes 9 a.m. into something else: 0900. The military gets up famously early, like monks who never fail to get up for morning prayers. Nine o'clock to the brass might as well be midday. Yes, sir, by the book. When American Airlines

Flight 77 crashed into the military-industrial complex at 9:40, it sliced into what outsiders have always presumed to be the most perfect and bland expression of a well-guarded bureaucracy.

Timothy McVeigh, who conducted his strange and bitter life with a military man's eye for detail, parked his rental truck at the Alfred P. Murrah Federal Building in Oklahoma City right before 9 a.m. on the Wednesday morning of April 19, 1995. The Murrah Building, before that blast, was the very definition of nondescript. McVeigh's rage was focused on a conspiratorial empire out of control. Inside, at 9 a.m., there were credit union tellers, Social Security case managers, people who processed HUD forms, day-care kids sipping their morning juice, and a sprinkling of federal agents who, unlike the federal agents of airplane novels, didn't exactly lead day-to-day lives of thrilling espionage. There were people there that day who simply wanted to fill out a form, at offices that opened promptly at nine.

The memorial that stands at the Murrah site now, in fitting tranquility, is centered around the idea of what nine o'clock is to America: Nine o'clock is normal, except on the day everything changes. On either side of a block-long reflecting pool, the Oklahoma City memorial is bordered by two bronzed gateway arches, each several stories tall. One arch reads "9:01," the other reads "9:03," and the pool itself represents the horrible moment—9:02.

Pearl Harbor lasted from 7:53 till 9:45 on a Sunday morning. To a military mind, this now seems almost gentlemanly and strategic, as nightmarish sneak attacks go: centered on a military target, clear in its meaning and intent. The United States bombed Hiroshima at 9:15 on a Monday, Nagasaki a minute before noon on Thursday. A popular T-shirt in the 1970s pointed out that "A nuclear bomb can ruin your whole day." In both history and movie lore, nukes don't get dropped at night. They seem to come when everyone's out of the house, at school, or downtown, or stuck on the freeway when there's no hope of getting home. The nighttime raid seems anachronistic, going back to a time when war was easier to define.

It turns out broad daylight was so much scarier. The 9 a.m.-ness of it all came raining down: all 243 pages of the committee report on the interface transfer, all those shreds of capitalistic minutiae, all those desk ferns and coffee mugs and *Hang In There It's Almost Friday* posters, the blue copy, the pink copy, the yellow copy, the innocent working lives in tragic triplicate.

A day later, in Washington, at 9 a.m., everyone who could went back to work in a very different world, but in the very same way. The trucks were beeping, the line formed at Starbucks, and the eye contact we made with each other was sad enough to say the things we didn't want to.

(2001)

Blonder Heads Prevailed

Atlantic City, New Jersey

On the morning after terrorists hijacked four airliners and flew them into the World Trade Center towers in New York, the Pentagon in Northern Virginia, and a hillside in Pennsylvania, the fifty-one contestants for Miss America 2002, who arrived in Atlantic City on September 10, 2001, on a train from Philadelphia (as is tradition), take a deep look inside themselves and conclude that what a frightened and grieving nation needs most at this moment is . . . *them.*

They can offer gorgeous help, these women who are all trying to stand for everything American: Miss New York happens to be an Air Force reservist with plans to go on active duty in March, if not sooner. This is a fact some official or pageant coach, pre-9/11, seems to have unwisely edited out of her bio, back when that sort of thing might have looked too butch. Now the fussy, gossipy pageant insiders gathered in Atlantic City are transfixed by the idea of Miss America going to war. "The crown is Miss New York's to lose," quips an older guy with a badge identifying him as a state pageant muck-a-muck, loitering around rehearsals this week. "No, no, no. She's not pretty enough, her hair is wrong, those bangs are wrong," says a margarine-blond, sparkly-bloused woman standing nearby, covered in red, white, and blue ribbonage. "Her dance was mediocre, I thought. I think the tragedy angle is going to Miss D.C. That's why the judges keep giving her good scores in the preliminaries." There is precedence for this otherwise callous chatter: Miss Oklahoma won the Miss America crown five months after the federal building bombing in 1995. Miss Florida won weeks after Hurricane Andrew tore through her state in 1992.

Maybe the woman in the sparkly blouse is right: Even though Miss District of Columbia bonked herself in the shoulder with her baton, she won the preliminary talent competition Wednesday night. You could see it coming. She twirled to Gloria Gaynor's "I Will Survive," which, given everything that's happened, sounds suddenly patriotic. ("You think I'd crumble?" the familiar disco anthem goes. "You think I'd lay down and die? Oh, no, not I!")

Though it keeps evolving, the Miss America pageant clings to its remaining central beliefs, and right now the whole thing smells like national comfort food. The Miss America pageant that airs on ABC on September 22, 2001, will be, as it turns out, the first live television event since 9/11 to not have something to do with the terrorist attacks. It is hoped that viewers will tune to Miss America, seeking shelter in what is, besides perhaps cheerleading and Elvis impersonating, the greatest American folk art ritual: bobby pinning a tiara to the head of a beauty queen. They can rename the swimsuit competition "lifestyle and fitness" if they like, but it's still got miles of shiny legs and expertly jiggly jiggliness, a beauty that must be Vaselined and sprayed into place. Now the contestants even have six-pack abs—young women in bikinis and one-pieces, in clear plastic high-heeled shoes, preaching the gospel word of innocent positivity. Most of the girls (the contestants have always been and seemingly shall always be referred to in Atlantic City as "girls") were in their hotel rooms when they heard about what was happening in New York and Washington on the morning of September 11: They were showering, blow-drying their vitamin-rich hair, getting ready for a long day of rehearsals, preparing to annihilate each other with a studied kindness. They spent the rest of the day crying. "Nobody," says Miss D.C., twenty-two-year-old Marshawn Evans, "felt like being Miss America right then."

. . .

Blonder heads prevailed. The day after the attacks, September 12, the girls gathered in an empty room deep within the stoic old Boardwalk Convention Hall where the pageant has been held seventy-four times. Miss America organizers were struggling with the decision to continue or postpone the pageant, which was just ten days off. They asked the girls to vote. But first, just like any pageant, each contestant stated her platform on the issue:

Miss Virginia, twenty-one-year-old Meghan Shanley, who hopes to pursue a master's degree in PR and dreams of becoming a contemporary Christian recording artist, was the second girl to speak up. She was *really, really mad* at the terrorists. "I told the other girls that without a doubt we should go on," she says. "Frankly, what the terrorists want to do is put a kink in our social lives. Out of respect for the dead, we should carry on." She also said she thinks maybe the tragedy has a hidden purpose: "When did you ever see the network news ask everybody to take a moment to pray to God? Maybe there's a purpose to this happening to bring us closer to God." (She says all this with a determined look on her face, the perfect expression of a pageant winner in locked concern mode. Her eyelashes threaten to trap you.)

The girls voted 34-17 that Miss America 2002 should proceed as planned, and I started to see the eighty-seven-year-old Miss America pageant a whole new way. I have come to believe the United States of America is founded, at least in some part, on the precept that a woman named Kapri Rose—who looks to be about fifty-eight feet tall, who wants to become a dentist and bring free dental clinics to her fellow Arizonans, and also wants to raise awareness about Down syndrome—can, while wearing hot pants, seductively prance across a stage while doing indescribable things to an electric fiddle. If you want to feel your heart swell with pride (or something), just watch Miss Tennessee, Stephanie Culberson, sweep the swimsuit preliminary, in a white bikini, and the evening-wear preliminary, in a gold silk jacquard with a keyhole neckline. (There was some free dental work done here, too: Miss Tennessee, it turns out, had eyeteeth "like fangs," sources report, but "the boys"—a team of pageant-obsessed gay men from Tennessee, one of whom is a dentist—took care of her, molding her into a champion.)

Amid the flags and platitudes, the rest of the world suddenly looks and feels a lot more like the Miss America pageant, instead of being cynically beyond it. God and country have always been safe topics in MissAmericaland. Would-be winners have always wanted to save the planet. They all look to a higher power, and this time sinfully fraught Atlantic City looks with them. "One Nation, Under God," flashes a constant Old Glory Jumbotron sign at Caesars, a monolith casino next door. Every forty or so feet along the boardwalk, another down-and-out saxophonist blows "America the Beautiful" for tips. The army of kempt pageant matrons who volunteer as helpers for the pageant have been sent to Kinko's color copiers to print (and staple to sticks) the 13,000 flags to be waved, on television cue, by Saturday night's Boardwalk Hall audience. (To fill out the farthermost empty seats, officials frequently bus in senior citizens, sweetening a gambling tour package.) The stage has been re-jiggered slightly, with constant, big-screen flag graphics billowing aside the Miss America logo. Security has been tightened, resulting in long lines for purse exams and bomb-dog sussings. "In the next three days, we will pick a symbol of the nation," announced singer-entertainer John Davidson to the gathered masses this week. Davidson, who appeared to have been cryogenically defrosted to host three nights of preliminary competition, said what everyone has been repeating all week: "Now, more than ever, we need Miss America."

Back into cold storage he goes, to make way for the host of Saturday night's quasi A-list pageant host, former sitcom star Tony Danza, who will sing that song all Americans know, or sort of know, or have sort of forgotten. If it helps, Bert Parks's almost wistfully bygone version is on constant tape loop in the lobby of the Sheraton:

Oaaaaohhh, THERE she is, Miss A-MERRR-ica.
There she is, your ideal.

(Dah-doo-doo-dah) more than pretty.
(Lah-doo-doo-dah) Atlantic City. . . .

The tape loop accompanies a video panorama of the winning moments in chronological order, from scratchy black-and-white in the 1950s to bouffants in living 1960s color, to *Dynasty*-era glitter gowns. Press photographers in the old footage jostle for a shot. *Watch it, fellas; Miss America, Miss America, over heah, over heah!*

Someone is always standing in the Sheraton lobby watching this. At 2 a.m. Thursday, one such fellow stands there all alone, gazing at the screen in an act of religious transcendence. You almost expect him to genuflect, then cross himself.

■   ■   ■

It's hard to know who has self-corrected faster to the tragedy at hand: Is it pageant officials, already locked into a multimillion-dollar broadcast contract that is their main bread and butter, faced with a viewership that has dropped by 2½ million households in the last two years? Is it the girls themselves, who came up with anti-terrorism and geopolitical sound bites almost as fast as Henry Kissinger? If they are anything, the women who compete in Miss America are not stupid. Their intelligence is spooky. In the few minutes they are granted during the day to speak to the media—in a dingy room that is not really a room but a half-acre square of carpet in a parking garage, with plastic lawn chairs and tables—they can easily deflect any question, turning it into yet another opportunity to speak in broad strokes of platitude.

The quickest to react to 9/11 is Bob Bain, executive producer of the TV show, who rewrote the script and got rid of the pyrotechnics and excessive gush he'd originally called for, opening instead with a somber Danza speech about grief and moving on. "From there," he says, "we're having a pageant." A veteran of awards shows and televised Britney Spears and 'N Sync concerts, Bain has sandy blond hair and beard and a detectable Hollywood vibe that runs counter to the Jersey style of pageantry. To boost Miss America's sad decline in TV ratings, Bain wants the pageant to be more like *Survivor*: ruthless, judgmental, entertaining. And "real." He's sliced out the last remaining musical production numbers. He's whacked the evening-wear competition in half because minute-by-minute Nielsens re-flect that viewership tanks during that segment. He has added more pop-quiz, game-show style questions to the mix. The contest-ants, Bain almost happily admits, hate the pop quiz. In the 2001 show, for all their poise, the finalists struggled to name the first black man on the Supreme Court, or figure out which country the Statue of Liberty came from. "They think it makes them look stu-pid," he says. (So he did it again in 2002, and 2003.)

An hour into the 2001 show, just-eliminated candidates will vote, with judges, to see who makes the top five. (And they can't, Bain ad-monishes, "Just go in that jury room and say, 'Oh, they're all so nice, I just can't make a decision.' I said, 'Let's face it, if you girls didn't have an opinion about everything, you wouldn't be here.'") Bain's "reality" is different from the contestants' and pageant officials' per-ception of real: "These girls are terrified of getting up there and saying or doing anything that they think is going to offend anyone or be somehow different," he says. "I keep trying to break through this veneer and show the viewers at home that these are real women."

Which is true, but also in a way not true. Fifty-one real women never said, so uniformly, to the camera and judges and anyone else who asks about their personal lives, that "My mother is, like, my best friend. We tell each other everything." Real women in their early twenties don't, in the main, have that kind of home life—palling around with mom, living in the teddy bear–studded bedroom of their childhood. Feminist critics and other Miss America naysay-ers had it wrong, all those years they complained about the gender objectification and sex-laced jiggle of the pageant realm. The prob-lem now is that the Miss America scholarship program is deadly dull. It has succumbed to the wrong kind of "real," creating women focused so intently on noble platform issues (cancer, or the more popular "volunteerism" and "mentoring America's youth," or health-care reform, or underage drinking, or teaching music in schools) that it forgets to be modern entertainment. Miss America is a nerd, with a tragic devotion to America's most popular religion: public relations. She doesn't tell lies, but she doesn't tell truths, either. She pads her résumé. She doesn't curse, she doesn't get to go anywhere unescorted. She can't really talk about her boyfriend, if there is one, or sex.

When the subject matter is dicey, or political, or enters a religious realm beyond an Oprah-style spirituality, Miss America seems unable to choose sides, because Miss America likes all the sides. In that way, she's either not very American, or more American than we care to acknowledge. She's a kept woman, a groomed and exotic animal. Pageant organizers want to stress the $40 million or so they claim to give away in college aid each year to women across the country. (But beyond the basic public IRS statements required by law, the nonprofit Miss America Organization won't open its financial books to the extent other charities do.) Born of a bathing-beauty show in 1921, the heyday of the Jersey shore, the contest now presents itself as a place where a certain kind of young woman lays claim on saving the world.

In Atlantic City all week there has been a feeling that whoever she is, Miss America could use more of the old veneer now. She needs to be more iconic, imaginary, bigger than life, and look really hot in a bikini. Reality programming was a workable notion back when reality was just a marketing concept, and not the kind of reality that Americans have dealt with in the days after September 11. When she takes that walk tonight, down a runway only painted to resemble marble, Miss America is stepping into a world that wants, for a moment, to stop changing.

■   ■   ■

Once the glitter had fallen from the ceiling, and an opera-singing, Gwyneth Paltrow-ish Miss Oregon, twenty-two-year-old Katie Harman, won the title and promised to bravely console the grieving world with "a killer rendition of 'God Bless America'" everywhere she was scheduled to go, I wondered if maybe I'd seen the whole thing too much through the terribly distorted context of September 11. It was, after all, the only news.

The following year, back in Atlantic City to watch the competition for Miss America 2003, I am delighted to see that the focus has returned to the much more familiar subject of boobs. In the parallel universe of MissAmericaland, one of the contestants, Miss North Carolina, had resigned from the competition several weeks earlier because her allegedly abusive ex-boyfriend had e-mailed pageant officials pictures that he once took of her naked, and he was threatening to unleash them on the Internet. But once dethroned, Miss North Carolina had second thoughts, and sued to get back her title, which was now held by the runner-up. A legal battle commenced, but days before the pageant, a federal judge sided with Miss America officials, the pageant slot went to the runner-up, and all the fun left Atlantic City—the trucks from *Access Hollywood* and the *Today* show broke camp. Bob Bain, the television producer back for a second year's try to lift ratings, whines to the few of us in the press corps who've decided to stick it out to the moment Miss America will be crowned Saturday night: "Couldn't the judge have waited another week to make a ruling?"

Happily, it turns out the reigning Miss America has some boobs to show us anyhow. Harman walks into a meeting room in Boardwalk Hall wearing a charcoal gray pinstripe pantsuit, her yellowy blond hair flipped pertly at the shoulders, her eyes a shimmery, enticing color of blue. There's an army colonel with her, who is also a surgeon at Walter Reed Medical Center. They've got mammography pamphlets with them The press corps—particularly the many, many correspondents from pageant-industry magazines—tends to stand up whenever Miss America enters, which feels silly, which feels like 1957, which in a way, in MissAmericaland, it always is.

Miss America bids everyone good morning and then tells a story she's told four times this week already, either onstage while cohosting nightly preliminary competitions or in interviews, about a woman she met in a University of Virginia palliative care hospital ward who was about to die from breast cancer. Though the woman had lost her hair, was wasting away, clearly dying, "She was still talking about getting better and coming back and volunteering to help at the hospital. She was extremely motivational. She changed me," Harman says. "So you see, it's not about death, it's about life."

But the woman died, correct? Wouldn't it, then, be a teensy bit about death?

This is an old Miss America mind trick: Even in the face of horrible realities, a smart Miss Anywhere who comes this far always accentuates the positive, even if she must manipulate the sunshine. That's what Bert Parks sang about. That's what they sell here on the boardwalk—boundless, eternal life. No one ever raises a hand to ask Harman to finish the story, and talk about the woman being dead. Perhaps no one should. To believe in Miss America is to set aside all that real-world cynicism. "Would you like to see how the T-Scan Breast Imaging works?" she asks.

We would love to.

Miss America takes a pink sheet off a spongy, fake set of breasts. The photographers all leap up and lunge forward, getting in very close. The colonel talks about lump detection while Miss America runs a revolutionary new electronic mammography sensor wand over each breast. The cameras click frantically, knowing that this might be as good at it gets all week.

I dutifully attend the preliminaries each night, in a reserved folding chair halfway down the runway, and on the third night, in the interview room, I have what, in Atlantic City during Miss America week, passes for a nakedly honest moment: On the slip of paper where reporters covering the pageant are supposed to sign up for daily "exclusive" ten-minute, one-on-one chats with contestants, I arbitrarily chose Miss Arizona, because she didn't quite look like she belonged there. Her name is Laura Lawless, a Harvard grad who goes to law school at Arizona State. She got into pageants four years, two states, and forty pounds ago, stressed out by all her college debt and seeking a way to pay it off. Her platform issue is mental health, and she has "come out of the closet, so to speak," about her own battle with depression, and even a suicide attempt.

"It's shocked people, that I get up there and talk about it in interviews, or onstage," she says. "Every day is a challenge for me, but any day I can brush my teeth in five minutes instead of three hours is going to be a good day." She gets the sunny optimism bit; she understands why her fellow contestants thrive on it. She knows why Katie Harman only tells the uplifting parts of the cancer stories, and the bent realities of Miss America, but she also says something you almost never, ever hear in the whole week of sequins and spectacle: "I don't expect to win."

The glass isn't half-full or half-empty here. The glass, for one quiet moment in MissAmericaland, is just a glass.

(2001–2002)

What We Talk About
When We Talk About Chandra

Washington, D.C.

*The Chandra threads have been terrific despite the dis-
turbing backstory of a missing girl.*

> —posted to the Missing Intern forum
> on capitolgrilling.com

The Zone of Privacy. When it's gone, it's gone. Once pierced, for reasons valid or lurid, the Zone of Privacy lets out an embarrassing
flappity-flap like air from a balloon. People watch it zip all around
the room. The focus lingers on *his* secrets, *his* life, *his* zone: "He absolutely refuses to comment," an unnamed ally to Rep. Gary Condit, a California Democrat, tells *Newsweek*, "on something that he
believes should be protected by his zone of privacy." His zone is interesting to a point, until he becomes just another Washington
wonk who has weekend fascinations for motorcycles and women
who are not his wife.

Chandra Levy's zone is the story. In her absence something else
takes over, causing this endless chatter. Any detail we hear or read
about her, confirmed or denied, true or almost true, becomes part
of something we're still knitting. Chandrology is a psychoscience
in motion, and our minds and gossip are its pseudolaboratories. In
her absence we have theories, conspiracies, scenarios, unsubstan-

tiated rumors, and even badly drawn police sketches of what Chandra might look like, if, say, she has possibly fled for the purpose of L'Oréaling her hair into a variety of colors and styles, making herself over again and again toward a longer journey into obscurity. In the summer Chandra has disappeared, some of us complain that there's no story here worthy of all this coverage, which is in itself a story, about how we digest a scandal. Would she die a thousand deaths if she heard us talking about her this way?

I. "Chandra"

More name now than woman. She is famous, notorious, mysterious to strangers—a studio portrait of herself, color photocopied on a flier that is Scotch-taped to a window in a Starbucks on Connecticut Avenue. Chandra, meaning gone. Chandra, in iconography, now standing for secrets and a sliver of Washington itself. To live in the city this summer is to entertain fantasies of finding her, saving her, glorifying her.

II. Hair: Only Part of the Story

The flight attendant in the congressman's apartment, finding a long, dark, curly hair on the bathroom floor and calling out to him, "Whose hair is this?"

"It must be yours," he says.

In her television interview, the flight attendant gives the camera a sly look, letting us know she is too smart for this. She does the math. The long, curly hair makes for a total of three women by her count, including the wife, who is blond, and herself, with short hair dyed orange.

Just a hair . . . but maybe one of Chandra's? The tiniest bit of trivia now becomes part of the narrative. It's like the two spots of something bloodlike found on the congressman's window blinds when the cops shone the Luminol light across the bedroom. Another Post-it Note on the wall of this massive, tawdry, fascinating conversation we're having. Seasoned Chandrologists mull these things over. Another round of margaritas at Lauriol Plaza, the Mexican restaurant in Adams Morgan, while we wait for a table.

III. Glamour Shot

The studio portrait of Chandra—which avid Chandrologists refer to as "the Glamour Shot" because of the soft-focus technique associated with shopping mall portrait studios that specialize in makeover photo sessions—has become the Mona Lisa of the summer in Washington. It is one of her high school graduation pictures, the Class of '94, the "casual" pose. The smile is not effusive, not even really a smile so much as teeth. She is wearing a ribbed, white tank top. This is the woman who listed "working out" as one of her hobbies. Her hair has been relaxed, tamed, parted to the side, and cut evenly at shoulder length. She has on lie-down jeans. (You lie down to zip them.) She is leaning to the right, propped up on her right arm, showing off an exercised figure, the shape of her breasts. You can tell that the woman in this picture feels pretty. This picture makes you want to sign up for Pilates or reduce your carb intake.

You keep looking at it. On deeper levels it's about being young, female, Jewish, curly-haired, driven, comfortable, trim, organized.

IV. Hair: More of the Story

Then there's the other picture. It's the opposite of the Glamour Shot. Women who have naturally curly hair—particularly women from California who grew up around blond volleyball players or raven-haired Latina prom queens—know something about this picture. You spend a good part of your life hating your hair, trying every product there is to make it flatter, softer. You get stylists to blow it straight, allowing you one or two good hair days a month. At some point, maybe in your twenties, enough people, men especially, tell you how beautiful your hair is, naturally curly.

Chandra is on the left, the congressman is in the middle, and another intern is on the right. One of the stories behind this picture is that this may have been the first time Chandra and the congressman met each other. We say "may have been" because it may not have been. Chandra's hair is huge, like a tree. It's as if she's given up on it. Her face is glistening, alive with hot color, like she's just heard something funny but embarrassing. Condit has the vacant smile of a politician posing for pictures with constituents. The other intern has the enviable anonymity of someone with most of her Zone of Privacy intact; she looks pleasant and she looks like nobody.

In the early days of Chandrology, a month or so ago, when the case was still fresh, the Big Hair picture and the Glamour Shot seemed to talk to one another:

Chandra controlled.

Chandra uncontrolled.

V What We Talk About When We Talk About Chandra

We know her without ever having met her. We know instinctively about her doting parents, the oncologist dad and sculptor mom. We know Chandra was able to rent a $1,400-a-month apartment on a $27,000-a-year intern salary. We know about the aunt on Maryland's Eastern Shore to whom she told her secrets; the aunt who, instead of chastising her for dating a married man twice her age, suggested that the way to a man's heart was to rearrange his closet: "Color-coordinate everything, you know, put all the long sleeves by color. . . ." This was the aunt who advocated the simple things to spice up a romance. This is how we learned about the Ben and Jerry's low-fat chocolate chip cookie dough ice cream, followed by massages with body oil.

"You had to know Chandra," one of the friends says, by way of explanation. "She was very, very sensitive," an anonymous friend told the *Washington Post*. "Her feelings were intense," and, according to her aunt, "She liked guys in uniforms . . . she liked that power," and, according to her mother, "Chandra always took those relationships a little more seriously than the men did."

Underlying this is the notion that the princess gets what the princess wants. (Jewish American Princessness crept into the conversation, too.) Along the way the networks get snippets of home videos from the Levy family. Chandra sits at the table and eats and laughs and tells stories. She rummages through the refrigerator. This was one of those houses where the dad had a camcorder and not much to shoot, except the beauty around him. You watch. Something's wrong. She becomes ordinary, nobody—she vanishes.

VI. The Chandra of Chandra

All those hundreds of young, pretty, determined women you see every day, while you wait for the elliptical trainer, or while you wait for the Red Line to Shady Grove, women dressed in Ann Taylor separates, women with their hair twisted up in athletic-looking knots, women who get to that vacant Dupont-proximate 1-BR apartment twenty minutes before you get there on a Saturday morning, and are already filling out a lease application. Chandra, the kind of woman who knows better than to make eye contact with you as she walks down the street. Chandra, who tells her friends to buy pepper spray. Chandra the Gone Girl.

Chandrology has you standing in your apartment, wondering which objects would tell the most about where you possibly went. Chandrology is as simple as calculating how many days would go by before somebody called the police, and whom they would start interviewing, and about what, exactly. Deciding which picture they'd probably use on your flier.

VII. Gossip

Folklorists, scientists, and social psychologists agree: Gossip is a means by which humans impart life lessons to one another. Ethicists and moralists fret over the concept of gossip as a sin. It's about wanting to find her. There is a Nancy Drew in everybody: The Missing Locket, The Clue in the Old Mill. In this particular summer there isn't much else. This isn't anyone's fault and it doesn't mean the media are all jackals or that all lawyers exist only to clean up unseemly messes by billable hours. It means no one famous is on board any private airplanes that don't happen to be crashing somewhere around Martha's Vineyard. It means campaign reform has no sex component. The Houston woman who drowned her five children in the bathtub this summer invited us into a Zone of Privacy that we didn't want to go into. Five wet babies lined up on a bedspread is already too much to know. So we took on another mystery we stand a chance of solving.

VIII. Ingredients

This story has things we all like. It has apartments. The 2611 building. The Newport. These are not luxury apartments, unless you're young. Places we dream (or dreamt, once upon a time, before we had kids and a mortgage in the burbs) of renting, and the urbane youth we remember having, the upward-gal-on-the-go template that sends you to Ikea for a kicky new shower curtain. In this story, our Audrey Hepburn type informs her landlord that she might be breaking the lease in order to move in with her Secret Powerful Older Boyfriend.

It has interns. They are a special kind of Washingtonian—temporary, voraciously hungry. In our minds they are full of curiosity, ready to perform any task. It is a particular conceit of people in this town that we can somehow adopt interns, love them, provide entrée and experience, initiate them to some greater world. This isn't supposed to be about sex, but sex gets in there.

It has the congressman. It has the bronzy, preternatural tans of those men of a certain age who cling to a more vital and virile concept of themselves. It has the "Hunks on the Hill" pin-up calendar that some congressmen posed for, with proceeds going to a charity, which is supposed to be a joke, all in fun, except the men in it look studly serious about having been selected to appear in it. Condit has his own month, and his picture reveals certain images and facts that Chandrologists add to the many pieces and snippets and trivia, and then slide them all around like someone else's refrigerator magnets: Harley-Davidson motorcycles. Bodyguard drivers with names like Vince Flammini. The Washington Sports Club on Connecticut Avenue. The Tryst coffee bar and lounge. Phone records. The pulled-down baseball cap and sneaking into a waiting cab. The rule he had about not letting anyone see her getting off the elevator at his floor. Godiva chocolates on Valentine's Day. The same gift bracelet given to two different mistresses. Cadaver-sniffing dogs. Cactus plants as a symbol of love. Uncollected mail. The minister's daughter. (The minister who did lawn work at the Levys' house.) The five-year plan, and the kind of young woman who would make one, and stick to it. *The Moosewood Cookbook*. Expensive lawyers. The phenomenon of relatives of missing people hiring PR agencies to help find her. A flight attendant. Microphones and television cameras. The sex. None of it quite coming together.

IX. Thumbs

Tantalizingly, for a few weeks, there was a rumor that Mrs. Gary Condit has no thumbs. While untrue, this was big for the more lurid of the Chandrology conspiracy theorists, such as the Bethesda woman who made her husband stand still so she could try to get a lock on his throat while keeping her thumbs folded against her palms. It was to test the hypothesis: Can you strangle somebody if you don't have thumbs? Inconclusive.

And anyway, pointless. We repeat: Mrs. Gary Condit has thumbs. But in addition to having thumbs, what else has she? More mystery; another Zone punctured. As her husband's alleged affairs with Chandra Levy and the flight attendant and the minister/lawn mower man's daughter came into the narrative, it was reported that Carolyn Condit had "a chronic illness," that seemingly prevents her from living with her husband while he is in Washington. Other reports say her health is fine. The Chandrologists have debated the significance of the unnamed, unreported, real or imagined illness beyond its hindrance to the Condit marriage. She could be an invisiwife, another Washington construct, the campaign prop. Conspiracy theorists have enhanced The Wife's role in the hypothetical plot: Carolyn Condit and Chandra are in secret cahoots, staging all of this to make him look bad.

Another branch has it far more sinister: He's on the Intelligence Committee. Chandra aspired to work in the FBI. Now it sounds more like an airport read. The Wife is something out of a Lynne Cheney novel. In the absence of Chandra, almost any theory takes on a plausibility.

X. Have You Seen Her?

So we send the police cadets out to once again beat around in the shrubs and foresty overgrowth of Rock Creek Park. People go missing all the time. Anti-Chandrologists are fond of pointing out this salient fact, that this missing woman has no greater value than other women—and men—who disappeared from Washington. Vanishing is central to our fascination. We look for her even when we're not looking. We see her everywhere without actually seeing her.

XI. In the Woods

The easiest place to look was always Rock Creek Park, which also made it the hardest. Such is Washington's relationship to these 1,754 mystifying acres of second-growth forest set aside by Congress in 1890—lovely to look at, to explore, but also efficient at keeping its secrets. Rock Creek Park is many things to many people, and once in a while we are reminded that it is a place in which to disappear.

It is early on the morning after the remains of Chandra are discovered, a little more than a year after she disappeared, a skeleton picked nearly clean, scattered among the undergrowth on a steep hill off Broad Branch Road.

This was one more popular Washington narrative, a common ghost story: the person who jogs into Rock Creek Park and never comes out.

XII. Turtles

A man and his dog stumbled upon her skull as they were on a morning walk on a Wednesday morning in May, looking for turtles. The man who would set out with the dog to look for turtles is a smaller, far more benign kind of Rock Creek Park mystery, but a mystery all the same: Why turtles? What happens if the dog finds one? Does the dog hurt the turtles? Does the man take them home? Or do they just commune with the turtles?

Both a paradise and a primeval forest of declivity and verdant wonder, Rock Creek Park gives off a vibe that can be inspiring on one afternoon and chilling on others. (To say nothing of Rock Creek Park at night.) It's a place you mean to spend more time in, and never do. People hurl themselves into it on weekends, huffing and puffing and pedaling, something that always seems more fun in theory than it really winds up being. The place has that jut-jawed sternness of the Park Service, as if you're about to be lectured on habitats, or control measures against exotic foliage. Deep in the park, on the day after the Chandra discovery—about a half mile north of where the forensics people are gently swabbing the forest floor—the daylight dims in the heavy shade on the path, creating a strobe of shadows crossing shadows. A twig snaps, then there's a rustle. And there you have, across millennia, humankind's uneasy, on-again, off-again love affair with the woods. As an urban park, Rock Creek is two things: refulgent escapism and, as the headline writers used to call it, *grisly scene*. Live near it, and you know what it sounds like in the middle of the night when a helicopter thunders over the park, searchlight going back and forth, hovers for what seems like hours, only to abruptly fly away, and you never hear anything on the news the next morning to go with it. A few years ago, *Washington City Paper* presented evidence suggesting ritual animal sacrifice in the park. Punk rockers have known for years about the "pyscho tunnels" under Broad Branch Road, a decrepit drainage system with three decades' worth of Led Zeppelin graffiti spray painted therein. Children of the 1970s and 1980s grew up scaring one another with tales of the Storyteller, a presumably nonexistent denizen of the woods. Everyone has a curious Rock Creek yarn, myth, or embroidered news archives about the place—the woman who decomposed in her wrecked Mercedes; the teenage girls who carried out the suicide pact; the one about the leg with no body, the one about the body with no head.

XIII. Decidual Matters

But this doesn't seem to be the park that gave up Chandra on Wednesday morning. The park that gave up Chandra had been caring for her in its decidual way for a year's time. She was there all along, to be discovered on the kind of day you drive unhurried through Rock Creek Park with the sunroof open. She was there among the plants—the jack-in-the-pulpits, the smooth alder, the jewelweed (*Impatiens capensis*), the cinnamon fern. Among the birds—the belted kingfisher, perhaps, or the common yellow-throated warbler. Among the bugs—the burying beetle, the wood roach, the doodlebug. Among the fungus and the spores and all that crunchy, moist deadness and aliveness, among those towering trees, the park was slowly solving the only mystery nature can solve. It broke her down, and gave her back, with no real answers.

(2001–2002)

Snipers 'n' Things

Manassas, Virginia

That first bullet hole is clean and mean and somehow subtle, remaining in the plate glass window of Michaels arts and crafts store in a strip shopping center in Aspen Hill, which is in Montgomery County, Maryland, which used to be a long way from Manassas, Virginia, until the sniper came to the counties surrounding Washington in the early fall of 2002. The sniper has a way of making a megalopolis pull together tighter, in fear, thereby cinching the Beltway.

The bullet hole is by the pay phone. You have to look for it to see it. The store's window display is a forest of waxy fall faux-liage, and inside, on this drizzly gray Friday morning in October, a few of the kempt, purple sweat-suited women who wear "World's Greatest Grandma" shirts are on missions of undaunted inventiveness—projects requiring foam or beads, paintbrushes or plastic pumpkins, tiny college football sweaters to fit tiny teddy bears. Not counting a suspicious shooting outside a liquor store in mid-September, police think this is the place where the sniper first fired, ten days ago, and killed five in Montgomery County that morning. A bullet missed its mark at your average, everyday Michaels store.

Two days after that shot in the window, a woman was loading the back of her van when she became the sniper's eighth victim (and one of the more lucky ones; she lived). She was in the parking lot of a Michaels at the Spotsylvania Mall, in Virginia, about sixty miles south of the first store, as the crow flies.

The point, if there can yet be a point, is that one Michaels is like any other and there are lots of them. The sniper strikes not so much in the suburbs but in that benign fringe, the vast somewhere-nowhere I sometimes call Off-Rampia. What he seems to look for is what we all like about such a place—the E-Z access. Michaels is usually near a T.J. Maxx or a Best Buy. There are also places with names like ExecuStay and AmeriSuites, which are the motels of the twenty-first century; for the starved, there is always a Bob Evans restaurant, a Chili's, a KFC, and, the official food of Off-Rampia, McDonald's, itself not immune to images of bygone shooting sprees. There are a half-dozen gas stations anyplace you look in Off-Rampia, each a gleaming fuel island with multiple ports. The sniper's choice of random victims in these particular nowheres doesn't seem like a grudge against the burbs and sprawl.

Rather, it feels like this is his home. The murders invite a contemplation of their settings, and thoughts about retail, convenience, drive-thru. He knows Off-Rampia, and to judge from his crime scenes thus far, he prefers it. People are drawing lines on maps, considering his motives, profiling him, theorizing. Underlying all this is much remedial studying of the mazy, wooded Rand McNally Streetfinder spaghetti plate of "Washington" that so many millions call home and never ever call "Washington." And underlying that is the ever-present, low-grade Maryland/Virginia disconnect.

And underlying that is the randomness of some of the victims' own notions of home turf: Dean Meyers, the fifty-three-year-old design engineer shot while he filled his car at a Manassas Sunoco station on a Wednesday night in October, drove to and from Gaithersburg, Maryland, every day. This is a sizable spread of Off-Rampia to draw dotted lines across and consider. A recurring theme in the sniper saga is its relationship to the only story we all collectively understand—and seemingly the sniper understands, too—and that story is *the commute*.

News of the sniper's crimes is tightly woven—as it was yesterday morning and during his October 3 rush-hour spree in Montgomery County—with traffic reports on the radio. The commute
makes us all citizens of Off-Rampia, except for urbanites living
within the diamond-shaped boundary of the District, who are feeling, for once, an odd sense of security. All of Interstate 95 south of
the city deputized itself into an instant, ad hoc posse yesterday to
try to catch the sniper up in that web we weave best: the freeway
snarl. Beneath the terror of it all was an almost electric feeling of
participation. Many of us grew up in or near Off-Rampia—an East
Coast version or a Midwest version or the advanced California version, or somewhere among the wide in-between. The middle class
collects there, until it becomes too glutted, and they move another
few off ramps away. An intuition sinks in about off ramps and on
ramps and strip malls and gas stations—they are familiar.

■   ■   ■

What also sinks in, to the sniper's benefit, is a kind of mental
doughnut glaze.

You just missed the turn for Target, in which case, you can circle
around and cut through a parking lot, whereupon you see the
Wendy's drive-thru, then an Old Navy, where you look at jeans, but
now you feel fat, whereupon you see the Jenny Craig (never again),
and that's when you think, oh, *Michaels:* baskets for the little soaps
that go in the guest bathroom.

All you can ever really be aware of in Off-Rampia is yourself,
and perhaps where you parked the car.

The sniper changes that. Now you see so many white paneled
vans with ladders on them that you realize the twisted, horrible genius in what he's doing. Off-Rampia starts to feel, just now, like a
paradise lost. From the chattering Washington area comes the
Michaels Theory: In many of the eleven sniper shootings to date,
there's a Michaels either peripherally or directly involved, or within
scope. A Michaels in Bowie (which suspiciously burned down last
November, but was rebuilt) is near enough to Benjamin Tasker
Middle School, scene of Monday's shooting, to figure in with those

who proffer the Michaels Theory. One theorist sent an e-mail to *Washington Post* reporters supposing, with a map, that the sniper was drawing an enormous, five-pointed star that all had Michaels locations in common. (There are 22 Michaels in the greater metro area; more than 650 nationwide.)

For a corporation, this kind of speculation is a nightmare straight from PR 101. A spokesman reached Thursday at Michaels Stores, Inc. in Coppell, Texas (a Dallas exurb), quickly declined to make any comment for the record about the sniper shootings, other than acknowledging that many people, police included, were "in touch" with the company.

About three-quarters of a mile from the darkened, taped-off Sunoco where Dean Meyers was shot, a handful of customers shopped near closing time at Michaels in the Festival at Bull Run strip center in Manassas one night later. Two teachers looked for frames to put student certificates in. A teenage girl looked for glitter pens to make some car wash posters. A young couple cruised books about wedding cakes. The Muzak went off, indicating it was time to go, and all of us did that new, nervy dance of Off-Rampia, dashing for our cars in the spooky, spitty rain, weaving back and forth, feeling not quite as crafty as he is. Whoever he is.

■   ■   ■

Two weeks from this point, the sniper turns out to be two snipers, working in tandem, inspired by a laundry list of vague resentments and not terribly emphatic demands for millions of dollars in cash. Among the more curious outcomes of the arrests of John Allen Muhammad and his "adopted" teenage son/cohort, Lee Boyd Malvo, was the discovery that neither of them had spent much, if any, time exploring or deciphering the suburban retailscapes of the Washington area. They intuited all of their targets by instinct, shooting from the modified trunk of a navy blue 1990 Chevrolet Caprice that nobody on the Beltway was looking for.

(2002)

Missing Pieces

Nacogdoches, Texas

On the winding, two-lane state roads of all those heartbreaking Lucinda Williams songs, people pull over and trade tips about spaceship debris. It's like they're wanting a piece of what they cannot have; not so much the physical smithereens of the space shuttle *Columbia,* but a more elusive, emotional shard. It is, after all, the biggest thing God ever dropped on the Piney Woods of deep East Texas. "You can see a shoulder harness," a man walking a chow helpfully advises, pointing west along Highway 103 in San Augustine County on Sunday afternoon. It turns out to be a thirteen-inch piece of blackened metal, thunked hard into the ferrous dirt, bearing a tiny "Koch & Sons Co." manufacturing label, which reads: "reel, shoulder harness, inertia lock."

You can see some kind of "round doohickey" about half a mile "down the turnoff past the next church," according to the man on the all-terrain vehicle who has been cruising up and down Highway 21, and says he is headed over to the Chinquapin Missionary Baptist Church, where he heard there were pieces of humans found.

Cathy Ryan, who lives over the hill in Huntington, is out for a debris drive with her mother and daughter, and she says they just went down to a creek, a bit down the farm road a ways back, where there "was something that looked like it might have had a window on it." They took a picture of that, she says, because it looked important, but also because it was large, and people are getting picky about the size of the chunk, and whether it's worth pulling the car over to see. "You should go look at it."

Around there, over that way, down this road, in those trees a ways, left at the yard with all the trucks parked in it, no, a little past the gas station, but not past the mailbox. Not just there but: everywhere. There are pieces dotted all across, by the latest count, thirty-six Texas counties, several Louisiana parishes, and some 30,000 square miles along a trajectory that adheres to what astrophysicists know but continues to baffle the earthbound.

Here is Texas in its primordial sense—sylvan, damp, and spooky—and visually unlike the Texas of songs, presidential ranches, or movie cowboys. Here, too, are Texans themselves at their most empathetic, in a part of the state where almost anything can be interpreted as a possible message from Jesus or a visit from a UFO. Or, more often than not, it is another Piney Woods mystery that cannot be fully explained. People here have a need to come out and see the debris as naturally as they'd take a covered dish to a funeral supper—a show of grief, but also a polite nosiness. These are people who feel a special, perhaps divine, custodial role in the breaking apart and deadly end of *Columbia* on a Saturday morning in February. They are not about to go down as scavengers or gawkers. They want to help, and perhaps cry, and this is why they go out and look.

Edna Murphy stands by the shoulder of Highway 103 and waits for her husband to emerge from the thick woods. She's holding a camcorder. They live in Lufkin, about forty miles west, and are still trying to get a sense of where *Columbia*—the many thousands of pieces of it and its seven doomed astronauts—met the stretch of earth she knows best, the complicated and beguiling Piney Woods. "We got up and went to church this morning, of course," she says, "and that was pretty sad. We spent the rest of the day driving all over, just to see what we could. It's a sense of history, I guess." Dale Murphy tromps out of the brush, wearing pressed denim jeans, a starched white Western dress shirt, and a black cowboy hat, and looking like Texas incarnate: "It wasn't much," he tells his wife, pointing to the fluttering yellow tape in the trees. "A cylinder-lookin' deal, about four inches long."

"Where?" says a woman who has just gotten out of her car.

Everyone points to the trees.

Another twenty miles east, off Highway 87 in the Sabine National Forest near the tiny one-convenience-store dot called Milam, three women from Dallas get out of their Chevy Tahoe and gingerly step into what one of them says "is certainly as far in East Texas as I've ever been." They see a man in the trees up ahead, a shape they can barely make out, wearing global-positioning equipment. "What's back there?" she calls out to him.

He shakes his head.

"I guess he doesn't want us to know," she says.

We stand in the forest and listen anyway. The sun is starting to fade. For a brief second the three women take in the enormity of these woods, the way that chirping and rustling can fade to a strange silence and depth. It feels like we might have a moment of reverence here, then one of the women announces she doesn't have the shoes for this. She feels bad about what happened, but she's glad she doesn't have to go a step farther.

■ ■ ■

Some call East Texas the Pine Curtain, and not always as a term of endearment. Even people from small towns elsewhere have a sense that everything south of Interstate 20 and east of Interstate 45 is either physically or culturally impenetrable, unto its own, beyond some invisible line where iced tea is delivered to your table already sweetened. Fate could not have picked a more likely place to open a new government X-file, with local and federal agents of every conceivable stripe (even the state's tobacco-and-beverage officers are being assigned *Columbia* hunt duty) combing a haunted, lonely land. Right now it's the rainy season (forty-five inches a year on average), and the ground sticks to your boots.

In spring, foliage will bloom up over the shuttle debris, surrounding it in thorns. Chiggers and mosquitoes arrive with the dripping summer heat in the high nineties. The search area could even stretch southward, into what's called the Big Thicket, another example of mythic Texas parlance. It is a common assumption around here that there's much already hidden that's never been trod upon, including old railroad depots and early freed-slave communities that sprang up after the Civil War. Underneath all that, remains traces of a bloody history linked to French and Spanish settlements and the Mexican War of Independence. Deeper still might lurk evidence of East Texas's oldest native communities, some of which go back 6,000 years. Outdated schoolbook lore speaks of the Nacogdoche, a Caddo tribe, and a leader who sent his two sons on opposite tracks through the woods, each setting up a community: Nacogdoches in what's now Texas, and Natchitoches (pronounced "Nacka-dush," where *Steel Magnolias* was filmed) farther east, in Louisiana.

The forests were virgin and primeval for millennia, until the railroad came in the 1870s and the lumber industry boomed, creating much of modern East Texas. By the 1930s, almost all of the Piney Woods had been cut down, so much so that lumberyards fed their remaining mill houses into the saws and left. The U.S. government acquired some 2 million acres during the Great Depression, establishing three national forests; still, this accounts for only about 10 percent of the woods—the rest is privately owned, much of it maintained by the timber industry.

The ever-widening big-government search effort for *Columbia* is welcomed and aided by locals, who are willing for now to set aside the region's deep sense of private property. East Texans are now tourists in their own backyards: On the radio, residents are urged to suspend the Texas notion of finders-keepers ("Just because it's on your property doesn't mean it's yours," went one announcement Sunday). One woman complained to the Associated Press that her brother's pickup truck had been seized because he transported a piece of smoking debris that had landed on her grandfather's 350-acre farm south of Nacogdoches.

The urge to assist is overwhelming early efforts, where every person in a Federal Emergency Management Agency jacket is surrounded by a dozen onlookers. Kim Peese, a FEMA spokesperson, told the *Houston Chronicle* that there were early disputes between local and federal officers about who was in charge of the precious chunks, which are now a matter of hometown pride. "These things happen when you have people with big hearts who want to help. Sometimes you get too many cooks in the kitchen."

■   ■   ■

Driving along the area thought to be most strewn with parts of *Columbia* and its crew on the morning after the disaster, where the trees cast a stroboscopic shadow dance on the asphalt, it is easy to imagine why so many people think of these parts as a lovely, if unremarkable, place that the world forgot. Green Army helicopters roar over the still waters of the Toledo Bend Reservoir, where spikes of long-drowned pines peek through the surface.

Five years ago this month, a rare meteorological event called a "straight wind" blew monstrously across the Sabine and Angelina National Forests and toppled 4 million pine trees in an instant. The weird part was no one heard or saw 4 million trees fall over. A few trailer homes were squashed, but the only person killed suffered a heart attack. A postman traveling a dirt road near Shelbyville recalled turning around and just seeing the trees lie over in the wind. It took several hundred U.S. Forest Service employees six months to assess the damage and sell off millions of dollars in lost timber. Just another Piney Woods story that was filed under "X."

There are towns on the everyday road map (Patroon, Etoile, Aken, Milam) and some that aren't (Ragtown, Lout, Goober Hill). If you stick to the main roads, you see lumberyards, Tyson and Perdue chicken processing plants, shacky liquor and bait stores, and the occasional hair salon. As goes rural America, antique shops owned by old ladies seem to propel the economy. Some of the portable roadside signs have arranged their plastic letters into the usual grammar of undaunted America: WE PRAY FOR THE

FAMILYS says the one in front of a Mexican restaurant. (WE WILL DEAL, in front of a Nacogdoches furniture store, upon reflection, probably still refers to furniture.) Fanning out to the east, as *Columbia* did, from the fast-food-franchise towns of Lufkin (pop. 35,000) and the college town of Nacogdoches (pop. 30,000), there are modest acreages and farms with red-brick ranch homes and satellite dishes in the yard. Largely, this is the part of the world that has turned to manufactured housing. A double-wide and a single-wide on the same lot can constitute a family estate.

Had the shuttle come apart a minute or two sooner, it might have littered the flatter prairies of an altogether different Texas a couple hundred miles northeast, surrounding Dallas. If it had blown apart a half minute before that, government officials and media would now be acquainting themselves with the more sparsely populated dusty flats of West Texas and the panhandle horizon-benders near Lubbock, which is roughly 500 miles from the Piney Woods. On foot, inch by inch, Texas begins to seem more stubborn than wondrous. A Japanese camera crew has stopped to rest, momentarily, in the San Augustine Dairy Queen. They report today that they have footage of police officers, debris, and a tractor parked by a fence. They aren't sure what else to take pictures of. How many ways to zoom in on a small piece of metal sitting on a patch of grass? A local resident, Shawn Kilmer, is listening to them and decides to help, crossing the language barrier: "Y'all been to where they found part of the astronaut in Hemphill?"

What is now referred to in shorthand as "the torso spot" is fifteen miles east, on a narrow farm road in Hemphill. The torso has long since been removed, but two rescue workers hammered together a wooden cross and perched it on the spot. (The Japanese have seen that already, too.)

"I suspect," Edna Murphy says, still looking for something to get on video and send to her kids, "that they'll be finding pieces of it for years. Hunters will come across it here and there. And that's probably the pieces of it that people are going to keep to themselves."

■   ■   ■

Looping back around to Nacogdoches late on Monday, it becomes evident that the search will last a long time, but the limelight might not. Two National Guardsmen stand in front of the Ken's Minit Market on Highway 59, next to a pair of orange traffic cones. Between the cones is a scattering of a dozen pieces of Columbia. There's a round pulley-type wheel with wire spooling out from it, and wires, and small chunks of metal whitened with char. The guards are pulling twelve-hour shifts while the government gets around to claiming it. Thousands of people have stopped by. One woman says that a couple weeks ago, the roof over the Minit Market gas pumps blew down in the wind. "The paper came out and took a picture," she says, giggling. "That's what's usually big news."

Big news is leaving Nacogdoches. Downtown, where the streets are brick paved and the old movie theater has been shuttered, the doorman at the restored Fredonia Hotel snaps a group photo of another Japanese news crew and bids them a wistful good-bye. Across the street, next to the Mason Lodge, in the back parking lot next to Commercial Bank's drive-thru lanes, one of those distinctly American traditions is taking hold, the ground-zeroing, the Oklahoma Citifying of certain tragedies: People are leaving teddy bears and flowers and hand-drawn Magic-Markered messages on poster board. But there's nothing left here. The government came and took away a rectangular slab of metal that had landed here, leaving yellow tape as a gesture, and the TV satellite trucks drove away. For a day it was the locus of East Texas debris catharsis, but now it's just a bank parking lot, albeit one that gets lots of flowers.

Houston, Texas

As gorgeous as the view from space may be, the view from Johnson Space Center is more surly and bound, encompassing a solid row of motels, restaurants, apartment complexes, and big-box stores. NASA Road 1 runs the perimeter around the government's barbed-wire-and-drab-office complex on the swampy plains of southeast

Houston. It's a road where the nation's space heroes get their Chinese takeout and drop off their dry cleaning. In a strip shopping center, there is a pawn shop, an Italian restaurant, and a salon called HairTex. Next to that is Space Center Souvenirs, a cramped gift shop, which is to this astroland what a surf shop would be to a beach town. This is where you get toy space shuttles, photographs, NASA sportswear, and the much-sought-after mission patches. You can get a T-shirt decorated with cats wearing space suits, or an infant-sized onesie with the NASA logo that says "I Need My Space."

Midmorning Tuesday, three days after the *Columbia* crash, Cindy and Randy Hector are bracing for a high tide of customers to come down the road and into the souvenir shop. They'd already seen Air Force One sail overhead for a landing so that President Bush could speak at the day's memorial. The TV is on and the VCR is queued up to tape the hymns, eulogies, and somber pageantry that Cindy figures they'll watch some other day. She is now busy fretting over a missing shipment of *Columbia* patches. Someone offers to calm her with a large Dr Pepper. Her husband tends to customers, regaling them with astronaut stories to temper the sense of loss. He makes sure each of them signs his guest book.

Kalpana Chawla, one of *Columbia*'s dead astronauts, had been in here recently to buy a set of patches. Randy Hector says: "There was something on the news about them finding a *Columbia* patch in the woods, and people get all excited that it was being worn by an astronaut, but that's not the case. [Astronauts] come in here to buy patches to give to people later, so they can say the patch went to space. The thing is, you never really know if they're astronauts or not. They don't come right out and tell you."

Along this road, the space age melds with the everyday. Most astronauts long stopped looking like regulation crew-cut flyboys of yore, a worthy price of NASA's latter-day diversity. Engineers stopped wearing horn-rims and short sleeves. The future, it turned out, came to resemble Casual Friday; living among NASA is a quiet life in nerdsville. Like much of Houston, NASA Road 1 is unsuitable as a visual backdrop for grief or reflection, and doesn't offer much in the way of glamour, which, the locals say, is a point of pride. Business is simply business in this town, founded on an ethic of commerce over all else. Houston is always tearing itself up and rebuilding in the name of progress. Those who live and work in and around Johnson Space Center aren't just looking for comfort and poignancy in today's memorial service for the seven astronauts killed in Saturday's explosion; they know that to curtail the shuttle program in any way will affect them all, from executive engineers down to the people who deliver memorial bouquets from a floral shop called NASA Flowers.

"This is sort of the official headquarters for the outside world," says Richard Rogers, a longtime customer of Space Center Souvenirs. He doesn't work in aerospace, but he's one of those many self-described space nuts, able to recite the most marginal trivia of the space program. In fact, he's such a good customer that he's helping count extra inventory, cutting into surplus boxes of shuttle souvenirs the Hectors hadn't planned on selling until summertime. In fact, he's staying with the Hectors: "I live in Dallas. I work for Citibank. I spent the weekend moping and finally, last night, my wife says, 'You're going to Houston,' and called Southwest and got me a ticket."

Although some 10,000 people attend the service within the NASA compound, many more are trying to find the appropriate place to mourn on the fringes. At the Johnson Space Center's main gate, the flowers begin to pile up and perhaps overstate their intent, while an evangelical group preaches warnings of the End Times and the second coming of Christ foretold in the *Columbia* crash. At Frenchies, an Italian restaurant in a strip mall down the road where the walls are lined with autographed pictures of astronauts through the decades, owner Frankie Camera is juggling interviews with TV news crews more than serving pasta. (If they don't get what they need here, a producer says, they can always try the Outpost Tavern, where shuttle crews traditionally have a party when their spaceflight team is announced, or a Cajun restaurant called Pe-Te's, which looms large in the lore of the space cowboy.)

Back at Space Center Souvenirs, a woman with long red hair held back in a red, white, and blue scrunchy is paying for her purchases: color eight-by-ten glossies of *Columbia*'s last crew, at five dollars per print. (Prints of the doomed 1986 *Challenger* crew are three dollars.) She also asks for a space shuttle charm to put on her bracelet. Her arm has a long, red scratch, which it turns out she received in the Piney Woods. Her name is Tracey Horning and she works for the volunteer fire department in San Augustine, a small town in the middle of the debris trajectory. She'd spent the weekend looking for pieces, and says she had been part of a team that located some human remains. On her day off, she'd decided to drive to Space City, to go right up to the Johnson gate. "We worked all day long out there, since daylight, and you just get too busy for emotion," Horning says. "I didn't know what to think, and decided I needed to see the memorial, the things people had left there. I needed to see the crew's picture and put them all back together. It's not like I know them or their families. But it does feel like we did something for them."

The customers in the souvenir shop aren't paying attention when the president's eulogy ends and more hymns are sung. One woman is looking for stickers: "I just finished my September 11 memory book and here it is something else already. You can't keep up."

Rogers walks out to the parking lot to listen for the jets that will fly the "Missing Man" formation. He scans a horizon of endless power lines and telephone wires until he sees them. They curve around him and one arches up in solo salute. Cindy Hector runs out of the store with her camcorder but she is too late. The planes disappear behind the sign for the Vietnamese restaurant next door. The "Missing Man" plane pops out above the Pennzoil auto lube store sign, but by then it is just a white dot in another bright blue Texas sky, another collectible moment in the modern story of flight.

(2003)

Unassigned Lands

Oklahoma City, Oklahoma

My great-grandfather, Joseph Jacob Schneider, is fixing windmill blades on the family's western Oklahoma wheat farm on a November day in 1922 when, somehow, he loses his grip, falls, breaks his neck, and dies. This is a long way and many years from the Alfred P. Murrah Federal Building and what happened there at 9:02 a.m. on Wednesday, April 19, 1995, but it is an Oklahoma story all the same.

If there is no windmill accident, then the oldest son, my grandfather, Joseph Leo Schneider, does not quit junior college in Kansas and return home to Oklahoma to help his mother run the farm and raise the younger kids. Without the farm, my grandfather never rides his first J. I. Case Company tractor, and therefore never becomes a traveling Case salesman, and never ends up raising his own family in a three-bedroom brick house on Northwest Thirty-seventh Street, in Oklahoma City, in the 1950s. Without the windmill, he never marries Gladys Irene New in 1931 and they never stay through the Dust Bowl, the Depression, and the war years. Four children and nine grandchildren and ten great-grandchildren are not born.

But all of this did happen, in my Oklahoma.

My grandfather, J. L. Schneider, at age ninety-one, returns home from daily Mass and is carrying his laundry from his bedroom to the washing machine when he hears the explosion thirty-two blocks away. Then there are sirens and the sounds of helicopters flying over the house and south, and Grandpa knows something is going wrong downtown.

■ ■ ■

As an Oklahoman, I associate the place with luck and sorrow and a steady acceptance that life is as random as wind. Five days after the blast, I get to Oklahoma City, walk up Blue Hill, and hear a gospel choir singing. They are twenty-seven voices strong tonight from the Christian Life Missionary Baptist Church who believe themselves, as their pastor says, brought here by Jesus. They stand across Northwest Seventh Street by the perimeter fence. A green military truck full of National Guardsmen rolls by. All eyes are fixed on what remains of the Murrah Building two blocks over, shining horribly under floodlights like a gaping cadaver. The body count on the news says seventy-nine, so far.

"There, too, my heart/Singing glory to His name . . ." When their song is over, the pastor, Jayel Jacobs, gathers his flock to pray: "Lord, help the right to come out of this!"

Yes, the faithful shout. "Lord, remember those who are not with us—*Yes!*—Remember those still wanting—*Yes!*—Those still hurting, Lord!—*Yes!*—Jesus! Jesus! Jesus!

"Jesus got it goin' on in this situation!"

■ ■ ■

The small things are overwhelmed by the big thing. The appropriateness of normal life is now in question in this place, where "OK" had always been the lifestyle: Okay to dine out? Okay to go see a movie? Okay to continue with the twenty-eighth annual Festival of the Arts downtown? (Answered: Yes to dinner, but no raucous laughter. Yes to a movie, if it's a comedy. No to the popular arts festival, because they're still bringing bodies out just two blocks from the exhibition tents.)

My friend Mary Heffron Ramsey is afraid to go to Penn Square Mall to buy skin moisturizer because, she says, she doesn't feel like being in a large building with a lot of people around. "It sounds vain," she says, apologetically, "but I'm just really on edge. I don't want to go anywhere." She is sitting at her desk at work. This is how it happened, she thinks to herself: a boring hump day in front of a computer, pushing paper, talking on the phone, unwinding a paper clip.

Another close friend, because of her job, has twenty, possibly thirty funerals to attend in the coming days and weeks. That is the number of all funerals she has ever attended in her life, times seven. She doesn't own that many things black or navy to wear to all these funerals, and why would anybody? "And yet," she says, "you could go some places in this town and if you didn't know it had happened, you wouldn't know *anything* had happened." Her job, in public relations, is to keep the hordes of media away from the grieving families and funeral homes. She must keep her distance from me as well.

Another friend, Ceci Chapman, worries she didn't pray enough on the Tuesday before it happened. She worries about the spiritual undertow of it. "I tried to watch *Crossfire* last night and they were so heady . . . debating what happened. What happened here is passion, a passionate thing. It's just impossible to have that kind of head logic. There's a place for that, but that place can't be here right now."

My grandfather keeps a small, stained spiral notebook next to my grandmother's bed at St. Ann's nursing home in the northwest part of town. He was told to write down each day what my grandmother manages to eat from the spoon he holds for her, while she peers at him from the fog of pain where she now lives, defeated by strokes and collapsed bones, weighing less than one hundred pounds. Grandpa's methodical scrawl fills the pages, the handwriting I know from birthday cards and his exacting logs of car repairs, which he keeps in the glove compartment. Page after page, it's "20 percent meat loaf, 75 percent mashed potatoes, very upset today. . . ." Page after page, with little else remarked on: "Christmas Day" or "Gladys disturbed and in much pain." On April 19, Grandpa wrote: "FEDERAL BLDG. EXPLODES. . . . 20 percent lasagna, 50 percent pudding . . ."

When I was a teenager, we in the drama club stood on stage at

Bishop McGuinness, the Catholic high school, dressed as hayseeds with our cheeks rouged in pink, singing Rodgers and Hammerstein's "Oklahoma!" while our parents clapped wildly from the audience. We held hands and prayed in circles, asking God for better SAT scores and football trounces and, for others we barely knew, miraculous deliveries from car wreck comas and pancreatic cancer. We guzzled furtive beers by Lake Hefner, cheap beer, suburban brats singing songs by Prince, the Cars, and AC/DC, standing on a picnic table near Stars and Stripes Park. We were restless to the teenage core, keeping an eye out for the cop who would inevitably come down this dirt road to chase us away. There were dreams about getting out of here. You could see the water tower blinking through the trees. You could feel the wind on your face. A weathered bust of Dwight D. Eisenhower stared out over choppy Lake Hefner, a tribute to God, family, and country.

What you need to know about the urban heartland is how it can weigh upon you. What you need to know about the Bible Belt is how tightly it can cinch. What you need to know about a comfortable place is how discomforting predictability can be. Some of us did move away. Others stayed in Oklahoma, opting for a literal and emotional "Okay," something unchanging and reliable, something bland and boxed-up and there.

You either heard the blast or you didn't.

You were here for it or you weren't.

People do their best to describe it to the hundreds of reporters and photographers from all over the world who didn't hear it: Not thunder. Not a jet. Not a crash. Not a boom, but a *bum*. Framed pictures lifting up and slamming back against the wall. A noise "up there." They all thought it was on their own roof, or on the floor above, or just next door, when in fact it was blocks or miles away. No one explains it exactly, no matter how many times you ask. There is Before Murrah, and After Murrah, and small things are different now, back home.

Many people link important themes in their lives to a global sense of being Oklahoman, even to the extent of

> *making Oklahomaness the object of their "primary role*
> *identification" (Roher and Edmonson, 1964), and when*
> *taken to the extreme, this identity becomes a narrow,*
> *overly invested, constricted one that feels like a highly*
> *defended fortress.*
>
> —Howard F. Stein and Robert F. Hill, anthropologists, from
> an introduction to *The Culture of Oklahoma*, 1988

Oklahoma City sits on 623 square miles, a space larger than Chicago and New York combined. The population is 444,719, but that is misleading: About 1 million live in a tricounty area around and including the city. In 1995, 74 percent of them are white; 17 percent are African-American; 3 percent are American Indian; 6 percent are everyone else. In its worst hour of pain, my sprawling hometown was descended upon by the world's prying yet sympathetic cameras and labeled, at last, "the Heartland."

Which it never was to me. "Heart" implies a pumping, constant vitality, something Oklahoma City has not. Since farming and agriculture account for only 2 percent of the jobs, "heart" is perhaps a better analogy to the region's legendary gushers, the oil fields that brought prosperity and, ultimately, financial despair. Oklahoma City, on the map as neither "South" nor "Midwest" nor "West," is worn down by the oil bust of twelve years ago. It has been ignored by the rest of the world for decades. It has a negative self-image contrary to a dozen city government attempts (including a current $286 million downtown revitalization plan) to restore enthusiasm and bring attention to the place. Here is a city that, for a time, consumed more fast food per capita than anywhere else. Here is a self-contained world with 11 Wal-Marts, 43 McDonald's restaurants, 33 Taco Bells, 4 shopping malls, and, by one count, 522 Baptist churches. Here is a metropolis that in its wildest dreams aspired only to be more like Dallas.

It is a vast, quietly urban, politically and culturally conservative place. Its bustle is crisscrossed by fleeting moments of bucolic, weedy perfection on two-lane roads, punctuated by the kitsch of indecisive midcentury architecture—a bank that looks like a golden honeycomb dome; a twenty-foot-tall Townley's milk bottle towering above a street corner; rounded and needle-topped space-age skyscrapers that reach for a future that wasn't. I go home one or two times a year now, returning to ride in my grandfather's airplane, a 1966 single-engine Cessna he still flies; returning to watch *Days of Our Lives* with my grandmother before the strokes took her cruelly away without taking her fully; returning for the weddings of high school friends, assuring myself that nothing ever happens in Oklahoma City.

Then something happened in Oklahoma City. Driving on the familiar roads of town, I am swept into a mournful flurry of car headlights turned on in the daytime. This is everyone's way of keeping vigil. Headlights on Classen Boulevard, on Northwest Expressway, on Western, on Route 66. Headlights flickering like votive candles against the asphalt, so you can't forget, even when you try.

Six days after the blast, the TV news totals ninety one bodies recovered with perhaps one hundred still missing, with footage of rescue Labrador retrievers stressed out and howling. I come back to the perimeter line at Seventh Street and Harvey Avenue on Blue Hill, to again press my face to the fence and stare over the network TV vans at the Alfred P. Murrah Federal Building with the increasing, and quietly reverent, crowds. Funeral wreaths are being propped up on street corners. Blue and purple ribbons adorn every fence and telephone pole. Innocuous words wear new meanings: credit union, day care, HUD, Ryder truck, bureaucrat, and especially Oklahoma.

The building was another faceless slab of glass and concrete, a specialty here, a monument to red tape named after a deceased judge. Now everyone knows its twisted innards and floor plans intimately, from newspaper and magazine graphics. You hear parts of conversations in restaurants, lively discussions about how Housing and Urban Development was on sections of the fifth, sixth, seventh, and eighth floors; the Secret Service was on the ninth floor; and the snack bar was on the fourth and the General Accounting Office was on the third.

Everyone in a grocery store line is acquainted with the difference between "the pancake," where floors four through nine collapsed on top of one another, and "the Pit," where the bowels of the Murrah Building collected underground, and "the Cave," where the third floor collapsed against the second, behind the America's Kids day-care center, forming a dark tunnel along the building's south end. Everyone seems to know (or knows the nurse who knows) the doctor who amputated the trapped woman's leg in front of God and the Associated Press, a bone surgeon who heretofore was known best for his efforts to convert the city's athletic youth from football to soccer, in order to reduce sports injuries. You hear that he had to finish the job with his pocketknife. You hear that he had to borrow another doctor's shoes on the way to the Murrah.

By the end of Day Six, I count at least four deaths or injuries that are somehow connected to my world. A woman who once helped my mother sew church banners at St. Charles Borromeo, dead. A woman who graduated from Bishop McGuinness High School four years behind me, dead. A man who was in a church youth group a few years ahead of me, alive, and who was heard to have said, after he rode his desk through the air from the seventh floor to the fourth: "Sorry to drop in on you like this." His father, meanwhile, is missing, presumed dead.

■ ■ ■

My grandparents' house on Thirty-seventh Street seems at first indifferent to the mournful mood outside. My great-great-grandfather still stares with translucent eyes from his portrait above the fireplace. The clock still chimes every fifteen minutes. My mother and my aunts are still young brides in black-and-white studio shots; I am forever seventeen and shaking the archbishop of Oklahoma City's hand at graduation. While Grandpa sits in his chair and looks at more Murrah aftermath on the *Today* show (he now limits himself to some news in the morning, maybe some at lunch, and the entire newscast at ten), I take in the wallpaper and the smells of furniture polish and coffee, and reassure myself of the availability of Hershey Kisses on the kitchen buffet, my Grandma's touch. What she clipped out of newspapers—a President Day salute, a recipe, a mention of my cousin the lawyer—has yellowed on the refrigerator, in futile wait for her return from St. Ann's.

Grandpa says the windows barely shook. The house, he says, is sturdy. "I was already feeling depressed," he tells me. "There are a lot people in this town hurting right now, but you know, I have been feeling kind of down." A ninety-one-year-old man keeps his own authority on grief. He returned from ushering Sunday Mass with a free pamphlet on "The Grieving Process" and put it on the kitchen table.

Ella Hite comes on Tuesday mornings to clean my grandparents' house. She sweeps, dusts, vacuums, runs the washer and dryer, and even irons my grandfather's shirts against his polite protest. Now, she says, "I go around and catch myself staring off into space, thinking about all that has happened. I'm still saying, 'Why?'" Ella lost at least two friends from her church, Mount Carmel Baptist. More than that, her daughter had worked in the Murrah Building up until the Friday before the explosion. Ella herself worked a janitorial shift at Murrah, back in the 1970s. Her connections to it seem unending. The pastor at Mount Carmel had said the Lord promised these cruel and terrible things would happen. Ella listened and it sunk in like this: "The Lord's on his way," she says. "We got to love, hope, and look up."

Grandpa is now at the kitchen table, listening in. Murrah is where he took his Social Security paperwork. When he managed a low-income apartment house owned by my uncle, he was often in and out of HUD. "You start to think," he says, looking at a picture of one of the alleged conspirators, Timothy James McVeigh, on the front page of the Daily Oklahoman, "whether or not God has something to do with this guy being pulled over by that officer in Perry. That there's some kind of miracle in that happening so quick."

■   ■   ■

While Ella vacuums and Grandpa mows the back yard, I walk five blocks to the First Christian Church on Northwest Thirty-sixth and

Walker Avenue, another curious piece of imposing Oklahoma architecture, commonly called the Egg Church because it looks like a
giant white egg with a steeple on top. The Red Cross, with 622 vol-
unteers today, has set up a "family center" here for relatives of
those killed in the blast. The media convene in the church hall adjacent to the Egg, waiting for new shreds of grief to be empathized
with and broadcast around the world. Satellite trucks idle in the
parking lot. Newspaper reporters cram into a small performance
theater to plug in their laptops.

But the buzz among reporters hanging out at First Christian is
that there are no stories left here, no tears easily quoted because the
families are kept behind closed doors. A pool of three reporters—
one from the local AP bureau, one from the *Tulsa World*, and one
from the local ABC affiliate—is escorted into the family center by
an army major and a Red Cross official. A press conference is later
called so the pool reporters can tell the rest of us, about twenty reporters and photographers, what they saw. They describe the "total
human care" within: the trays of free food from local restaurants,
the heaps of donated toys for bereaved children to play with. They
explain what they saw in the "notification center," and the makeshift
medical examiner's office where a fax machine delivers body IDs
from downtown to an employee who, we are told, "breaks down in
most instances." (A sound bite from him, too: "I have to pause and
gather myself and I think [the families] are appreciative of that.")

We are told of the little capuchin monkey who has been brought
in to "soothe" grieving families and children. We are told of one
woman in particular, who, once informed of her husband's death,
began to cry. The monkey, we are told, touched her tears, tasted
them, and gave her a hug.

"Can you describe the notification office in more detail?" a reporter asks.

"Is there just one fax machine?" asks another.

"Are the conditions of the bodies discussed with the family
then, or does that happen at the funeral home?"

"What do the families talk about to each other? Do they talk to

each other? Do they leave once the body they're waiting for is ID'd?
Do they drive themselves home or does the Red Cross take them
home?" Later, outside the Egg Church, a woman from a West Coast
TV station smokes a cigarette. Her station, she says, is pulling out
of the "Terror in the Heartland" story as soon as half the bodies are
found and they get shots from a few funerals—one day longer, at
most. The meat of the matter, she says, has moved to Michigan
militia groups and Kansas motels. She asks me: "Did you actually
believe the monkey story?"

Walking home, I am passed by two funeral processions on
Thirty-sixth Street, heading opposite ways.

Connie Chung, the CBS coanchor, has become a sort of anti-
media rallying point in a tired, weeping city that's almost quoted out.
After the famous newswoman apparently insulted Oklahomans by
asking in the first news conference if the city would be able to "handle such a disaster," Chung rumors began to fly: Connie Chung was
handcuffed for crossing the perimeter line. Connie Chung sneaked
into a funeral dressed as a nun. Connie Chung is going to do the
newscast from the remains of the day-care center. (On Day Seven,
there is even an anti-Chung T-shirt: "Connie, Go Home.")

"That's the kind of weird thing—all this attention coming down
on Oklahoma City," says my friend Mary Heffron Ramsey, a little
miffed. "Then they'll all go home after a while. When did reporters
ever come to Oklahoma City? Even you—you'll be gone in a few
days, too, and the rest of us will still be here dealing with it."

■ ■ ■

Home is Jesus, *Jesus got it goin' on in this situation,* Jesus on bumper
stickers, Jesus in the expansive megachurches along suburban interstate exits. Oklahoma City's believers are, in descending order,
Baptist, Southern Baptist, Methodist, and then all other Protestant
religions combined, followed by a 5 percent minority of Roman
Catholics. "I used to be right up there complaining about the Bible
Belt-this, the Bible Belt-that," says my public-relations friend who
has to go to funerals all week to maintain media control; she was

raised Catholic and Catholic-schooled like me. "Now faith and church seem like the thing that's holding Oklahoma City together. I look at it completely different now."

Catholics camped together on Blue Hill the first night of the Great Land Run, the opening of what on the map was originally called "Unassigned Lands," and later became Indian Territory. On April 22, 1889, the mad dash of high hopes and patriotic lawlessness across Unassigned Lands created this place. A priest, according to church historians, likened the grassy hill, which was adorned with spring's bluest wildflowers, to the Blessed Virgin's mantle. They held Mass in a tent on Blue Hill thirteen days after the Land Run. The site seemed proper for a cathedral, which was completed in 1903 and dedicated to St. Joseph.

Much of Blue Hill was church owned. Two decades ago, the archdiocese of Oklahoma City sold the land next door to St. Joe's at Northwest Fifth Street and Harvey Avenue, land that once held a grade school and a convent, to the United States government, so that a new office federal office building could be built. That was Murrah.

Every stained glass window in old St. Joe's was blown out and smashed by the April 19 explosion. The parish priest, the Rev. Louis Lamb, was around the corner at the bank when Murrah exploded, holding a deposit receipt that, according to one story in the press, reads 9:02 a.m.; the parish secretary, not so luckily, was injured in the blast wave. The structural fate of the cathedral itself is now in question, another sorrow on a heap of sorrows, something that will have to be dealt with later.

Churches are united here now in ways unfamiliar to me. For once in Oklahoma City, it doesn't matter if you're Baptist or Buddhist. On the other side of Murrah from old St. Joe's, the First United Methodist Church also lost all its stained glass. Seven blocks from the blast, the just renovated First Baptist Church lost its stained glass, too, like a row of shiny bullets pushed over. Churches have become the primary focus of "the healing process," jetting in "grief issues" experts and holding nightly tearful huddles.

Children at my parochial grade school, St. Charles Borromeo, are coloring pictures to explain how they feel: "Confused" says one, in simple purple, blue, and yellow letters. Another is a Magic-Marker sketch of McVeigh, an arrow drawn to his face and captioned, "We care about everything—but he dosen't [sic]" and "Bomb, we don't like you."

At St. Charles—with its asphalt playground, the girls in plaid jumpers, the boys in blue slacks, the crucifixes on the walls—I feel something that is connected to the most innocent part of myself. The kids will be fine, says the school principal, Joe Sine, if a little distressed. Bureau of Alcohol, Tobacco, and Firearms officers took time out from the rescue effort to visit the cafeteria during lunch and got the hero treatment. The school held a fire drill and a tornado drill, if only to suggest that disorder and chaos have a proper response in Oklahoma. The student council sells soda pop on the school steps to raise money for disaster relief and a Murrah memorial. "But what we need now," Sine says, "is to get the bodies out, to talk about it, to move on."

At Bishop McGuinness High School, in Room 8, a freshman English class is getting ready to take a test on *A Raisin in the Sun.* The students set down their pencils at 9:02 and stand to pray. It's been exactly one week since Murrah, since the school building shook, and the kids, who were passing between second- and third-period classes, stopped and looked at one another. The day was panicky as the children of lawyers and judges and business types tried in vain at the cafeteria pay phones to reach their downtown parents. A week later, the governor, Frank Keating, whose son, Chip, happens to be in Room 8 taking the test on *A Raisin in the Sun,* has ordered the city entirely stopped, traffic and everything, for one minute. All we hear are church bells.

I sit on the principal's couch; the same faux-leather couch from ten years before, shiny and black and deep. The same principal, Steve Parsons, reminds me that at McGuinness, character is still the curriculum: "It gets back to that whole sense of people having free will," he says, and I'm taking notes and still not really hearing it: "We still teach respect, treating others with respect. It's a moral world. Lord's sake, you must have heard that enough when you were around here. That's what sees us through."

. . .

If anything, I was a strange and bored child of God in my own Unassigned Lands. I jumped off the roof wearing a Hefty bag for a parachute. I buried myself in comic books. I imagined living on other planets, in other places, with other families. The raw newness of this April in Oklahoma—the luminescent green trees and burgeoning cumulonimbus clouds—reminds me that we are in storm season. Frightening weather is a point of pride here in Tornado Alley. My mother used to love to drive out west from the city to watch for funnels and lightning; invariably our station wagon would be pelted by hail while the muddy red creeks swelled and the air turned a shade of violet. That was about the only escape Oklahoma ever provided.

Tonight, the end of Day Seven, is hampered by the wind. Murrah is increasingly unsafe for rescue workers, and at least sixty bodies are still missing.

. . .

The next morning, Grandpa looks over at me from the top of his *Daily Oklahoman* while I eat Cheerios. "One hundred and three," he says.

Businesses downtown, outside the Murrah perimeter, are slowly repairing. All the windows in the Kaiser's Ice Cream Shop and Soda Fountain building, a landmark since 1910 at Northwest Tenth and Walker, are being replaced. Kaiser's is a kind of example of the urban rebirth city leaders are hoping for, having been closed down for a time until 1993, when a cooperative of homeless people opened it as a gourmet coffee shop called the Grateful Bean. Peter Schaffer, a lawyer who helps run the Grateful Bean, says some windows blew inward, while others blew outward, no rhyme or reason to it. No one was hurt. The sheet music stand on the café's piano blew clean off.

Being in Kaiser's reminds me of bored summer vacation days, when my mother, driven to placate me, would tell me to get dressed for a trip downtown. We'd walk the streets and ride elevators and eat lunch in a restaurant. I felt utterly cosmopolitan. Beneath Oklahoma City, for reasons no one seems able to pinpoint, city leaders of the 1960s constructed an underground series of tunnels called the Metro Concourse. Despite its preponderance of outdated orange walls and creepy twists and turns, most downtown workers still use the Concourse for a quick lunch and short route between skyscrapers.

I follow the Concourse from the Liberty Tower and north several blocks, past subterranean luncheonettes and hair salons and cash machines. The hallway leading to the courthouse and the Alfred P. Murrah Federal Building grows desolate, dark, ending at glass doors where you can see nothing but endless, evil blackness.

"Don't go in there," barks an unseen intercom voice when I merely touch the door.

The public library downtown is also closed off, missing many windows, and so I head to Oklahoma City University, a private Methodist college on Northwest Twenty-third Street, to sort through the state lore I left behind in Mrs. Laverne Crumley's ninth-grade Oklahoma history class.

All ninth graders take Oklahoma history, by law. In it, you learn of the Indian relocation of the nineteenth century, *Tsa La Gi*, the Trail of Tears. You learn of the "Five Civilized Tribes" (Choctaw, Cherokee, Chickasaw, Creek, Seminole) and Sequoyah's syllabary alphabet. You take a test to name all seventy-seven counties. (Pushmataha, Pottawatomie . . .) You simulate the Land Run, dressed as pioneers, staking your claim on the school football field; half the class, according to tradition, must jump the gun and be "Sooners," winning the better land. You read Steinbeck's *The Grapes of Wrath* and watch old newsreels of Will Rogers twirling a lariat. The narratives do not come together until much later, in adulthood, if at all; usually it's the cynics who manage to form Oklahoma history into larger themes of building up and tearing down, of lawlessness in the face of government, of isolation and hard luck, of dreams deferred. While trying to come by a simple explanation of why the dirt here is so very red (it's rich in iron, for starters), I happened on a picture of Oklahoma City's Main Street snapped fifty-three years ago by the Farm Security Administration: "All the buildings in the photograph have since been demolished. . . ."

Included in the photo is the seventeen-story Biltmore Hotel in downtown Oklahoma City, which triggers a memory of my father, of sitting on his shoulders in 1977, part of the large crowd that turned out to watch the implosion of the Biltmore in a cloud of reddish orange dust.

■ ■ ■

Making my way through the crowds on Day Nine—on the news the total is up to 112 bodies recovered—to once more press my face to the perimeter fence and fathom Murrah. A wind knocks off my baseball cap, and it sails several feet before knocking into a woman's shoulder. She jumps in fear, and says, "You liked to scare me to death! I'm still so jumpy." It turns out she heard the blast in her office four blocks away. It turns out she lost two friends and knows of another six dead people.

Grandpa doesn't want to see the Murrah. Neither does my friend Ceci. She'd rather pray in her apartment, "I don't feel like I belong there," she says, with plain sorrow. Others go to the perimeter fence twice and three times a day. This is, after all, a town with not much to do but cry. Someone is having his first cigarette in ten years. Others cope in obscure ways, cleaning out their garages, polishing their tools, repapering the kitchen shelves, taking the kids to play on the rocket slide at Stars and Stripes. Funeral processions hold up traffic; headlights in daytime; Mary goes to the mall for her skin cream after all.

And I have not been the reporter I wanted to be here. I have avoided the funerals. I didn't dicker for a press badge to get closer to the mammoth, ruinous thing. When it comes down to it, I didn't hear the boom, and for that, I am hardly Oklahoman anymore, not part of this citywide group hug.

I am in my grandfather's backyard, perplexed. The apple tree is dying. We lost the big tree out front, and the bigger one out back near the garage, the one with the swing. Now the apple tree, which gave us decades of sour green apples, has parasitic borers. My grandmother would work those apples all summer, peeling and slicing them into pies and applesauce. I worked those apples with my mother as recently as two summers back. A man came out and looked at the tree and recommended it come down. "No, save my tree," Grandpa told him. "Don't cut down my tree."

So the man pruned the tree back to severe nubs. He dug a ditch around it and sprinkled an antibacterial crystal into the ground. Maybe the roots will suck that up and the tree will make it through. "Time will tell, Hank," is all Grandpa says, sounding like the grief brochure. "God doesn't give you more than you can handle. We all have a cross to bear."

An insignificant apple tree is thirty-two blocks from the Murrah Building, but it is an Oklahoma story all the same. And if I could look ahead at this point, there will come a series of unrelated moments that somehow feel connected and conclusive anyhow: Four weeks later, the 168th body recovered, the rest of the Murrah building is imploded to rubble and carted away. Three months after that, my grandmother dies at St. Ann's nursing home. Two summers after that, the apple tree is cut down and hauled off, the same year Timothy McVeigh is sentenced to die. Another four years after that, he is executed by lethal injection in Indiana. And two years after that happens, my grandfather, at ninety-nine, develops heart problems and dies on a Monday morning in April 2003.

It's another gorgeous spring day when we bury him next to my grandmother at Resurrection Cemetery. Waiting with my extended family to be driven back to church in the funeral home's sedans (so that many of us can soon enough catch flights to the places for which we left Oklahoma), I notice that Unassigned Lands are still being tamed and developed: From the cemetery I can see the roof of a new Wendy's restaurant across the expressway, where there's a ten-foot-tall inflatable sculpture of a chocolate Frosty dessert. This is Elsewhere now.

(1995, 2003)

Acknowledgments

A few of the people written about in these stories wound up wishing they'd never agreed to it, and we never spoke again; a few added my name to their Christmas card lists, and I still hear from them. Some I spent all of five minutes talking to, and some let me hang around for many months. However it happened, all of them have my gratitude, knowing that "thank you" cannot address the imperfect exchange between reporter and subject. (But one thing I know about journalism is that you never refuse enchiladas brought over to the homes of the recently deceased.)

A list I made of friends, colleagues, fellow travelers, family, and others who've helped me through the years ran long, and I started backspacing. Stet the name of my mother, Joann Schneider Stuever, who has listened to my reportage of local events, beginning when I was very young, and never ceased being a wise critic of my findings. Also my big sister, Pat Graff, wrote me postcards from her days in college before I could even read, and always treated me as if I was as smart as she is. (I do have two other big sisters—victims, again, of the ruthless economy wrought upon this paragraph.)

A fantasy: New York–based literary agent calls unexpectedly one day, introduces herself, and says your old newspaper articles should be collected in a book, which she is ready to pitch to publishers. Reader, I'm here to tell you, it happened to me. Thank you, Heather Schroder.

From there, much honorary air guitar goes in the direction of George Hodgman, at Henry Holt, who treated this project like a cereal box filled entirely with prizes, and had superb instincts for what needed to stay and what needed to go.

About the *Albuquerque Tribune* and *Austin American-Statesman,* I am proud to have done time at each, and lucky, too: I got to work in both newsrooms when they were being run with a collaborative sense of risk, fun, and hard work.

Reporters at the *Washington Post* are always acknowledging Donald Graham, the paper's chairman, in books they wind up writing, thanks chiefly to his (and publisher Boisfeuillet Jones Jr.'s) largess and long view. My thanks also to Leonard Downie Jr. and Steve Coll—for the space and time and journalistic freedom they give to their staff as a matter of policy. Eugene Robinson, who runs the Style section, sent out a memo three years ago cheerfully warning us to never write dull, and that's when I really fell for him. Deborah Heard, Style's deputy editor, is one of my favorite Wonder Women, when it comes to truth, justice, and sure decisions. Steve Reiss is a kind of superhero, too, with special powers for separating good ideas from bad ones.

I'm often writing the kinds of stories that my assignment editor, Henry Allen, already did years ago—only Henry did them with more smarts and better verbal jujitsu. This is why his careful editing of my own work seems like supreme generosity on his part; I learn something from him every day. (Thanks also to Joel Garreau, who edited me during my first year at the *Post* and got me into the paper fast and fearlessly, with wild ideas.)

Copy editors, in some predetermined injustice, never seem to get thanked, yet they work lousy hours to catch mistakes I'd be horrified to see in print. Here are some, over the years (editors, not mistakes): Bob Benz, Kelly Brewer, Barb Page, Allison Parker, Carolyn Kelly, David Hall, Scott Butterworth, Pat Myers, Laura Brown, Tom Kavanagh, Nancy Schulz, Doug Norwood, Jim Humes, among many others. Rose Jacobius, who is Style's night editor, never panics on the late-late files, and once helped me think of a dozen other nonoffensive words for breasts—besides "breasts"—between editions on a Miss America story. Also, the Style section's pre-cog, Robin Groom, gets me a press credential into events before I even know I'm going, and makes sure my articles will have pictures to go with them.

I'm going back on what I said about all those names. Here come some, for as many reasons: Janet Duckworth, Ray Schroth, Diane Porter, Anne Smith, Judy Coode, Lynn Bartels, Laura Trujillo, John Faherty, Tim Flannery, Laura "Derba" Froelich, Linda Perlstein, Elaine Beebe Lapriore, Louise Kutz, Kate Nelson, Adam Goodheart, Michael Currie Schaffer, Malcolm Ewing, Tim Gallagher, John Temple, Kevin Hellyer, Michael Arrieta-Walden, Neal Pattison, Inez Russell, Michelle Breyer, Jody Seaborn, Chris Garcia, Melissa Segrest, Patrick Beach, Linda and Marvin Resnick, Louis Schneider and John Johnson, Laura Aaron Nelson, Tom Sietsema, Paul Farhi, Mark Leibovich, Ann Gerhart, Frank Ahrens, Philip Kennicott, John Maynard, Spike Gillespie, KayLynn Deveney, Gregory Kallenberg, Stuart Eskenazi . . . and on and on.

Thanks, also, to a man whose name I love to say: Michael Wichita. (Madonna dedicated *True Blue*, her 1986 album, to Sean Penn, referring to him as "the coolest guy in the universe." In time, this turned out to be somewhat less true for her, and it forever cautions us to not think of any one guy as the coolest in the universe. But who can help it, when your boyfriend really is?)

And to correct that cruel omission above: My other two sisters are Mary C. Stuever, who bought me countless Slurpees in the mid- to late-1970s, and Ann Stuever South, who in 1977 checked me out of a dreary summer day camp for latchkey children to take me to my first screening of *Star Wars*, which she had already seen with her fiancé the night before, and knew right away that it would blow the back of my head off.

About the Author

Hank Stuever is a staff writer for the *Washington Post's* Style section. He was born and raised in Oklahoma City, has worked as a reporter at newspapers in Albuquerque and Austin, and has appeared on *Today*, MSNBC, *The View*, National Public Radio's *Day to Day*, and other programs. He lives in Washington, D.C.